BIG PAN-OUT

BIG
PAN-OUT

Kathryn Winslow

NEW YORK

W. W. NORTON & COMPANY, INC.

Copyright, 1951, by Kathryn Winslow

First Edition

971.21
W732

Printed in the United States of America

TO
Bim Schelderup

CONTENTS

ILLUSTRATIONS

PREFACE

WHEN he was seventy-four years old, Howard V. Sutherland, writer, wry raconteur, and life-long adventurer, gave up the idea of writing a book about the Klondike gold rush which he had been meaning to get at for nearly half a century. Eleven volumes of his verse and fiction had been published, and one of his plays had been produced, but his experiences as a cheechako miner were still fluttering around him on scraps of paper. At seventy-four he was too tired to collect them into a book. Resigned, he packed a huge box, putting into it these loose pages, the journal he had kept on the creeks the winter of 1898, a skimpier one kept by his friend, John Ver Mehr, a brittle bundle of correspondence, a few photographs, a musty bouquet of newspaper clippings, and several foolscap tablets scribbled over in lacy Spencerian. He shipped the box six thousand miles to me with the news that he had not abandoned the book, only the task, and that I had inherited that.

And so I began to write this book. Within a few months Sutherland was gone, but my work on the book continued. I was already engrossed in the story of "the biggest strike in the history of gold." I was collecting my own clippings, I was reading in the New York City Public Library, and I had begun correspondence from Cape Town to Nome.

A first-person account of the rush was finished in a year, with Sutherland as the narrator. The next year I wrote a novel based upon events taken from the two diaries at my disposal. I began to realize that no one could write Sutherland's book for him, that my effort would have to be the Klondike story as I had come to know it, myself. By then I had traveled twice across the country to read in libraries, and to trouble any living members of former Klondike companies whom I could find, and the retired officers of a steamship line which had long since gone out of business.

The Sutherland box was in all ways of first importance in the writing of this book. As I worked, my thoughts turned continually to my old friend, who, I often felt, was leaning over my shoulder. So let us say we got this book out together, Sutherland and I.

I am indebted to Miss Margaret Cameron, Circulation Librarian of The Harper Library of the University of Chicago, who gave me freedom of the stacks there. I am grateful also for the assistance which was so generously and promptly given me by Miss Mary Cunningham, Librarian of the Seattle *Post-Intelligencer;* by Mr. Edward L. Keithahn, Librarian and Curator of the Alaska Historical Library and Museum at Juneau, Alaska; by Mr. H. F. Schmidt, Secretary of the Southwest Historical Society in Dodge City, Kansas; and by Mr. Edgar J. Peters, Postmaster of Juneau, Wisconsin, all of whom searched the records for facts which were inaccessible to me. I also wish to thank Mrs. Alma Mecchi of Oakland, California, and Mrs. Virgi Rue Mace of Yreka, California, for the loan of personal material, and Mr. John Youell of Portland, Oregon, for directing me to sources of information.

Mrs. Bim Schelderup of Honolulu, Hawaii, was a steadying influence throughout the difficulties and disappointments which accompanied the writing of this book, and William J. Meacham nobly read through the many versions of it, which accumulated in his house, with critical attention, warmth, and uncommon tact.

IN ALL THAT WILDERNESS

In 1896, on the eve of the Klondike's big pan out, the United States was in the third year of a depression. Banks had failed, the country's agriculture, industry, and business was in upheaval, and there was unemployment from coast to coast. Heavy exports of gold had depleted the treasury, and the West was clamoring for a silver standard. Coxey's Army had marched on Washington.

Jobless men could not help sighing for the days of '49 when gold lay open as sand in the creek ruts and the hills were brittle stores of riches. And after California there had been Bendigo and Ballarat in Australia's yellow clay. Many remembered Juneau and wished for another Silver Bow. They talked of a time when nuggets were shoveled off the Rockies in Colorado, Idaho, Montana, Nevada, Utah, Arizona, and New Mexico. They had not forgotten Montana's Virginia City or Idaho's Coeur d'Alene, nor the names of a hundred Canadian creeks that once spread a fabulous grit down the gulches of the Cariboo and Cassiar. All of these had been great glittering placers, and to claim them all that a man had needed was a pick, a shovel, and a pan.

Placer gold lies near the surface of the earth, loose and free, not caught in quartz or other matrix from which it must be hewn or shattered out. Placer fields are formed by erosion which wears away the top soil, freeing the golden veins underneath and breaking them into fragments and dust. Water, wind, and glaciers distribute the golden particles. In streams the heaviest bits are quickly dropped onto the bed but dust is carried great distances until finally the lightest grain is rolled somewhere into the sand. These placers seem like a gift, like a burst sack of treasure spilled out and waiting to be picked up by anyone who passes.

The Spanish were the first prospectors in the New World. Spanish explorers, soldiers, the first conquistadores to bend over a glinting creek bed called the discovery a *placer,* a "pleasure," a "delight." They were mining in Peru, Bolivia, Chile, and Mexico three hundred years before Marshall found the nugget near Sutter's sawmill. They knew that California, too, had gold but they were too busy in other parts of New Spain to make much of a search for it. The mother lode had not been found, although early travelers to California had heard of freak discoveries and some had seen a little gold.

In the twenties, the trail blazer, Jedediah Smith, collected samples of gold ore to take back East with him to be assayed. It was good ore but it did not start a rush. David Douglas, a Scottish botanist exploring the California sierra in 1832, had a watch case made from nuggets he shook off the roots of specimen firs that he was collecting for the Royal Horticultural Society in London. Later the firs were given his name, but no distinctions came to him for his find of gold. In 1842 Francisco López washed about nineteen dollars' worth of gold from onion roots which he had pulled from a garden. The vegetables were growing in a placer field which was soon to yield over two million dollars.

From California the Spanish voyaged on up the Pacific coast, reaching Vancouver Island, Prince of Wales Island, Cross Sound, Prince William Sound, Kenai Peninsula, Kodiak

Island, and the embrace of isles called Unalaska, during a series of expeditions which took place between 1774 and 1794. At each stop formal possession was made in the name of the Spanish king, despite the fact that English navigators had preceded them in some places and that the Russians had long been settled on the land. The Spanish laid claim to the entire west coast of America. They left no colonies in Alaska, but place names of theirs remain to the present day. Among the names which were changed is that of the Copper River which the discoverers called *Rio de los Perdidos*, "river of the lost ones." A hundred years later it was still a tragic mistake to travel the Copper River into the territory of Alaska's most hostile Indians. The early history of the region is a record of massacres.

While Spain would have liked to possess the Pacific coast, her claims were vigorously disputed by England, in view of the voyages of Cook and Vancouver, and by France, because of an expedition by La Pérouse. Spain's pronouncements, and then her protests, came to an end embarrassingly, with treaties which virtually stripped her.

Russia's claim to the north Pacific went back to 1741, to the year of Vitus Bering's second voyage, during which he visited some of the islands of the Aleut Indians and mapped the first outline of the Alaska mainland. He did not live to claim honor for this for his ship, the *St. Peter*, was wrecked on the trip home and Bering, along with thirty others of his crew, all of them dying from scurvy, succumbed on the island which later received his name. Forty-six others kept themselves alive through the winter by eating the flesh of a dead, stranded whale. They buried themselves in the sand to keep from freezing to death. In summer, when the ice melted and freed the sea, the survivors built a boat out of the *St. Peter*'s wreckage and were ready to sail when, miraculously to them, hundreds of otter began to arrive on the beach. They clubbed the animals to death, ate the flesh and took a cargo of skins back to Russia. At the sight of the luxurious fur the merchants of St. Petersburg outfitted expeditions to hunt the new animal in the unknown sea. As many as thirty companies were engaged in the pursuit of otter, and soon their warehouses, ships, villages, and depots spread over the Aleutians, the Alaska Peninsula, and Kodiak Island.

It was not long before there were rumors that gold-bearing rock had been seen on the mainland and on some of the islands. This news was unwelcome to the fur merchants, who would not permit anything to interfere with the hunt for otter. Prospecting for gold was not much of an inducement when a single cargo of furs often reached half a million dollars in value. Employees were forbidden to prospect and the gold rumors were discouraged in every way.

It took twenty years to kill off the otter. Not only Russians slaughtered the animals into extinction, but there were American, British, French, East Indian and other companies rushing over the reefs with nets and spears. Rivalry made them all ruthless, and the animals were wantonly destroyed. There was nothing left in the sixties. A second fur-bearing animal which they had seen occasionally was sought after once the otter was gone, but no one could find its breeding grounds. The search for seal went on for eighteen years without a trace of success until Gerassim Pribilof acted upon a hunch.

Pribilof was one of many engaged in the search for the seal nurseries. He had been no closer to a clue than the others until he picked up the phrase "southern sea" during the recitation of a legend he heard at one of the Aleut festivals. The shaman was speaking of islands in the sea south of them. Pribilof borrowed the ship of a friend, a Captain Subov, and sailed for new waters. It took him three years to locate the seals and then it was an accident. The ship slid against a low-lying harborless isle which was invisible to Pribilof in the miasmal fog. He would not have known that he had reached his goal if he had not heard the seals barking in the distance.

It was July, 1786. He left a few men behind on the island and set his course for company headquarters.

Although he gave the island Subov's name, everyone was looking for "Pribilof's secret island" and the discoverer's name was never dropped. Four islands were eventually located in the group, all of them low, barely visible spots, nothing more than craters of submerged volcanoes. At high tide two of the islands are completely washed over.

First there was otter, then seal to hunt. What Russian had a chance to wander on land? The gold ledges had not yet been discovered, only the sight of nuggets worn on the Indians assured the Russians that there must be gold somewhere near. They did not know where to find it. In 1850 the fur company had grudgingly sent Peter Doroshin into the Kenai River basin to explore, but he had reported "no gold." In 1855 the Czar sent his engineer to take a look around Baranof Island, where the company headquarters were located. The director of the company had a castle on the hill which overlooked the town of Sitka. The whole Russian fur trade centered at this point. News of the arriving visitor came to Sitka in the way of an alarm, for the terms of the fur company's contract read that any lands bearing minerals could revert to the Czar. When the Imperial prospector arrived he was lavishly entertained for two years "pot-latching and dancing," according to the record, and he never saw Sitka's mountains nor anything that resembled gold.

The first knowledge of gold washed in Alaska by other than the Indians was the mite that the Western Union explorers, Otto von Bendeleben and W. H. Ennis panned out on Seward Peninsula. The telegraph explorers were sent to Alaska in 1865, after the first Atlantic cable failed and Percy Collins had convinced Western Union of the plausibility of a trans-Siberia telegraph to Europe. Parties were sent into British Columbia and northern Alaska. Von Bendeleben and Ennis were working in the region between Golovin Bay and

Point Clarence. They were thirty-five years ahead of the stampede to Nome, but the explorers didn't think to try sifting the sand on the beach.

About 1869 miners from the worked out Cassiars of British Columbia began to prospect their way north. Mix Sylva and his party found rich placers on Powers Creek at Sumdum Bay and on Shuck River at Windham Bay. They dug out $40,000 in two years, exhausting the fields. This was the first gold mining done in Alaska and of such importance that William Seward visited the region immediately after the expiration of his term of office as Secretary of State. Some years later lodes were discovered and the veins opened; stamp mills were put in and the region re-worked. Again it proved rich.

In 1871 an American soldier named Doyle, who was barracked at Sitka, panned gold near town. As soon as he heard of it, another soldier named Haley went into the hills to find the mother lode. Haley had mined in California and on the Comstock in Nevada before joining the army and he knew where to stake his claims. He took a number of good ledges for himself, the richest of which he called the Stewart, for his commanding officer who was lenient with leaves. After Haley began bringing the gold into town, every man in Sitka was out looking for it. Indian River was staked out in placers, and the hills behind Silver Bay, ten miles south of Sitka, got pocked and tunneled. Local residents formed two mining companies, sent out for machinery and labor, and were soon making fortunes for the stockholders. Other mining concerns were not slow in arriving, from Portland, Seattle, San Francisco, and from as far away as Madison, Wisconsin. Silver Bay became a boom town with wharves, warehouses, bunk houses, and saloons. It was the largest "city" in Alaska; the harbor was a crowd of ships. The miners were getting as high as $175 to the ton, a take that was almost unbelievable. And then all at once the gold strung out to nothing, the ledges were deserted, Silver Bay was a ghost town. Sitka was again the outpost, a rusting ruin, a remnant of the Russian occupation.

Sitka was no longer a fur-trading community. There were still about two hundred and fifty Russians living there, a number which included their half-breeds, and there were about sixty American residents. These were mostly missionaries. The army had been withdrawn. Traders, visiting marines from the revenue cutters, the customs collector, a handful of other territorial officials made up the population. Perhaps Alaska's governor might visit the hamlet capital, but for the most part that official lived elsewhere, in Washington, D. C., if he could arrange it. In Sitka they had a way of describing Alaska's government. They said, "It's seat is never warm."

Sitka was lonely, dilapidated, and excessively rainy. It was filled with croaking ravens that came out of the surrounding dark forests. The Americans complained that the Russians permitted their cows to graze in the streets, that they heard only the music of Glinka on the pianos. The ochre-painted houses of the Muscovites were falling down, the tin roofs were red with rust. With every tide the worm-eaten dock swayed precariously. The green onion-bulbed dome of the cathedral was growing dingier with each succeeding year and the brass tinkle of its Slavic bells only reminded Americans the more of Sabbath at home. Samovars, red geraniums in flower pots, potato and cabbage gardens, a newspaper which appeared on boat days, a few carriages and a macadam rim around the harbor were the most that Sitka could offer. It was not enough. The Americans had been there since the Alaska purchase in 1867, but they did not like it. Except for the interlude at Silver Bay, life in Sitka was a desolate experience.

And then all at once, in 1880, civilization leapt up the mainland of Alaska to an edge of inner coast above Taku Inlet. Two prospectors had discovered the Silver Bow. For the past two years the naturalist, John Muir, had been exploring the coast on a commission from the United States Government, which was interested in getting a report on the possible extent of the gold fields of Alaska. Muir reported that the region between Windham Bay and Sullivan's Island in Lynn Canal was "a second California." On hearing this, George E. Pils and N. A. Fuller, trading men of Sitka, grub-staked the two prospectors, Joseph Juneau and Richard Harris, to follow Muir's route.

They found gold almost everywhere they stopped. Creek after creek had colors but none was especially rich until they tried the streams near the entrance to Taku Inlet. Their boat ran aground on a bar at this point and while they were there they examined two creeks. One was full of salmon and the other was full of gold. They staked the latter and followed it into the hills to a basin which seemed to be paved with gold. They carried away a thousand pounds of ore from the area, arriving in Sitka about the end of November. There was an immediate rush for the new diggings. Thirty men went back with Juneau and Harris and other parties followed. In a few weeks the Silver Bow was taken to the last inch and, by summer, camps cluttered every hillside and gulley. A town had sprung up below. Juneau and Harris quarreled all year over the naming of it.

Neither man would give in to the other and the town was called alternately Juneau and Harrisburg. For a while the naval officers reconnoitering in the harbor called it Rockwell, for their commander. In December, 1881, a miners' meeting was held in order to come to some decision about the name. The post office had been designated Juneau since April but this was not conclusive enough for the miners. After many pros and cons the confusion ended with the motion to name the place after the elder of the two discoverers, who was Juneau. Later the mining district, which included the town of Juneau, was named for Harris.

Both men were amassing fortunes. Juneau, already fifty-two

years old, was afraid he wouldn't live long enough to spend all of his, in spite of ambitious efforts in that direction. He did. In 1888 he was living from hand to mouth, with an occasional job coming his way as a watchman on the Juneau wharf. He took the trail of '98 along with the rest of the Klondikers but he had no luck in the new mines. He went to work in a boardinghouse and died in Dawson a few months later. Friends took his body back to Juneau where he was buried beside his old partner, Harris.

Joseph Juneau and Richard Harris were not the only ones to follow Muir's route. French Pete and his wife started up the Gastineau Channel in November, 1880, a few weeks before the two prospectors returned to Sitka with their load of ore. Pete's small skiff was wrecked on Douglas Island, directly across the channel from Gold Greek. They could not go on so they put up a shelter to wait for spring. In the meantime he looked around the island. He soon found gold there but it was scattered and he cleaned up very little for the miserable work that it was. For all the rock that he was able to chip off in a week he got but a dollar's worth or less of gold. In spring the couple managed to get back to Sitka and were glad enough to see their log cabin store again, where at least they could make a living.

In a few weeks John Treadwell arrived in Sitka. He was the agent for two San Francisco men of wealth who wanted to invest in the Silver Bow, but when Treadwell got up there the best land had all been taken up and he could find nothing worthy of the investment he was prepared to make. While waiting for a steamer to take him home he got into conversation with Pete who was shaking his fist at Fate for stranding him on a barren island, only a few miles away from riches. He had not heard of Gold Creek or the Silver Bow until he returned to Sitka, and then it was too late. To top off his bad luck he had no money to pay the freight on a shipment of goods that he was expecting on the incoming steamer.

Treadwell was a mining engineer, he was familiar with mines throughout California and Nevada. He had a vast knowledge of ores. He offered to go up to Douglas Island and take a look at Pete's "Paris Mines," perhaps they might be worth something after all. If so, Treadwell offered to help Pete dispose of them. A company with capital might take them off his hands. Pete was grateful. Treadwell spent two weeks on the island and returned with samples of ore, the same low-grade stuff that Pete never wanted to lay eyes on again. He agreed at once to Treadwell's offer to take the mines off his hands for a quitclaim deed, and on September 13, 1881, the following entry was in the Book of Deeds in the office of the district recorder: *Transfer of Paris Lode from Pierre Joseph Erussard (or "French Pete") original locator to John Treadwell in consideration of the sum of five dollars ($5.00).* Treadwell also paid Pete's freight bill, which amounted to around $500.

Treadwell's employers cut him in on the mine, giving him a third of the stock. In 1882 five stamp mills were built and the Paris began to produce. Four tunnels were cut into a five-hundred-foot ledge of quartz gangue and tons of ore began to come out. Although the return was never more than $9 to the ton, and sometimes even as little as $5, the supply was endless. The only trouble the owners of the mines had was with the squatters on the beach, who claimed the right to the surface gold. They stayed on until they got several thousand dollars. Pete had never thought to wash the gravel.

The owners of the Paris now mined the adjoining property under the name of the Mexican Gold and Silver Mining Company, then proceeded south to Admiralty Island to operate the Admiralty Gold and Silver Mining Company. The last two companies were capitalized at $10,000,000 each. Only half a million had been spent developing the Paris, but when sufficient ore had been mined to warrant the expense 120 stamps were put into operation. By 1888 there were 240 stamps and in 1899 there were 880. The company was then milling 1,360,000 tons of ore a year at an operation cost of $1.25 a ton and getting an average return of $1.85 a ton. Treadwell bought out his partners and renamed the property the Alaska-Treadwell Gold Mining Company. He had the largest gold mill in the world. He was offered $16,000,000 for it but said he wouldn't sell, not for $25,000,000. It was 1917 before the mines weakened to such an extent that they began to cave in. That year all but one, the Ready Bullion, collapsed. Up to that time Pete's "worthless" ledges had produced almost $66,000,000. Ready Bullion went on producing until 1922, when it dropped into the sea.

Only a company able to invest vast sums of money in machinery could handle such mines as those on Douglas Island. The individual prospector could not work a mine for a return of only a few cents a day, which was all he would have been able to clean up after hours of toil. These were lode mines, with the gold invisibly scattered through the rock, from which it had to be washed out with hydraulic hoses or battered out and then crushed with a powerful machine called a stamp. The stamp is a pounding apparatus, heavy and huge, much like a pestle and mortar in principle. After the ore was reduced to gravel it had to be treated to separate the gold, and processed still further with other machinery. It was not an operation that could be done by hand. To make any kind of profit at all a mine of this kind had to move tremendous quantities of ore. The Treadwell operated twenty-four hours a day, every day, twelve months of the year.

Lode gold is not always so scattered and difficult to retrieve. While it may be distributed in minute films and particles which cannot be seen with the naked eye, there are also shoots or pockets of free gold in the form of flakes, spangles and grains which often gleam invitingly. The mines of Alaska's southern coast were generally of the latter type. In some areas there were both placer and lode mines. After the collapse of the Treadwell the largest mine was that of the Alaska-Juneau Gold Mining Company, located in the Gold Creek region. This was a heavy quartz gold producer. Along the coast from Windham Bay to Berner's Bay dozens of mines operated with from ten to thirty stamps each. The richest were in the Sheep Creek region where the Silver Queen was located.

In the eighties and early nineties there were mines at Funter Bay on Admiralty, on Willoughby Island in Cross Sound, on Annette Island in Lituya Bay, and on the beach at Yakutat. There was placer gold on Kenai at Anchor Point, on the Kenai River, and at Sunrise and Summit (riches which Doroshin had denied). The northern part of the Kenai Peninsula had a crust of gold.

The miners crossed Cook Inlet to the placers on Valdez Creek and the Yentna River; they found the lodes on Willow Creek; they went out to the quartz on Unga and Unalaska. In the Prince William Sound district they staked Mineral Creek and went up to the headwaters of the Chitina. They spread out over the Chistochina basin and followed the Copper to Jacksina Creek. They were at the head of Lynn Canal, a hundred miles north of Juneau, clamoring to cross the Chilkoot Pass which the Indians refused to open to them. On the beach there Captain John Healy had set up store for the prospectors. Healy had been adventurer, mercenary soldier, gold miner and Indian trader in turn, and now he cast his lot with the sourdoughs.

After the British Columbia mines gave out not all of the prospectors followed the Alaska coast to new diggings. Many went up the North-West creeks to the Yukon. Rumors of their good strikes reached the coast and brought men to the pass as early as 1880. There the powerful Chilkoots stood and refused to let the white man in. The Chilkoots enjoyed a fish oil monopoly which they relied upon for barter with the tribes of the interior, whose furs they took in exchange. The furs were re-exchanged with traders on the coast who had sugar and tea and tobacco to give.

The prospectors appealed to Captain Lester A. Beardslee of the U.S.S. *Jamestown*. Beardslee was the highest authority the people in Alaska could turn to for the territory at that time had no government. The army had been sent in at the time of purchase and stationed at Kenai, Kodiak, Tongass, Wrangell, and Sitka. A few more soldiers were on the Pribilofs, but there was no civil authority. The army could give Alaska no rule, a situation which brought on unsurmountable difficulties as time went by. Charges of idleness, lack of discipline, acceptance of bribes, other indiscretions such as the distillation and sale of liquor to the Indians, ended with the army's recall in 1870. Only one company was left at Sitka, where the customs was collected, and in 1877 the soldiers were removed from there as well. The marines took over later, but between the time of the army's recall and the installation of naval authority there was no government, nor symbol of it. The affairs of Alaska were in charge of the customs collector at Sitka and his deputy at Wrangell.

During this period five Indian fishermen employed by an American company lost their lives at sea and the chief of their village immediately demanded financial restitution from the customs collector. The demand could not be ignored because the aggrieved relatives of the deceased men began descending upon Sitka, outnumbering the whites, three to one, Russians and Americans included. An appeal for help brought no response from Washington. In desperation the people of Sitka called on the British admiral at Victoria, who sent the *Osprey* at once and finished the case of the five Indians.

Within a few months the United States Navy sent the *Alaska* to take over until Beardslee could get there in the *Jamestown*. From 1879 to 1881 Beardslee was Alaska's authority in all matters and events which concerned the territory. He was a man of strong character, wise, forbearing, and blessed with remarkable good sense. He was respected by white man and Indian alike. The latter understood a man who had a strong boat. It was the symbol of power which the army had lacked.

When the business of opening the pass came up Beardslee had no intention of forcing the issue. He chose his friend Sitka Jack, a half-breed whom he could trust, and sent him to the Chilkoots' chief with presents and his personal good wishes. Sitka Jack had unlimited time at his disposal. In a few months he returned with presents for Beardslee and the assurance that white men could use the pass any time they wanted to.

The first party to go over after the official opening was one promoted by Edward Bean, a prospector. There were twenty-five men in his group, and they went into the country as far as the Lewes River, below Lake Lebarge. The party was trailed by two men, Johnny Mackenzie and Slim Jim, who were not bound by the party's agreement with the Chilkoots not to trade in their territory. Crossing without permission, they took a barrel of hootch with them, and, in selling it to Indians whom they met, they caused so much trouble that the Chilkoots almost closed the trail again. Beardslee himself had to settle that matter.

The Chilkoots had relaxed their vigil against the prospectors for two reasons. The white men were not likely to interfere with their business of rendering oil from rancid salmon heads, and they were not after Siwash furs. Moreover, and what may have been more impressive, they would pay to have their packs carried over the pass. They would pay five silver dollars for every hundred pounds carried to the first lake. Some of the men were able to carry as much as two hundred pounds at a time, while the squaws could manage fifty pounds and the children and dogs lesser bundles.

According to the *Alaska Coast Pilot* for 1875, the Bean party was not really the first to cross. A miner by the name of George Holt had preceded them, accompanied by two Chilkoot

packers. It was known that Holt went down the river beyond
Fort Selkirk and later reached Fort Yukon in the Arctic Circle. There is no record of his return or whereabouts from that
position.

From 1881 to 1886 strikes were made repeatedly on the
streams of the upper Yukon River but the best were on Big
Salmon, Little Salmon, the Pelly, Hootalinqua, and Stewart
rivers. James Stewart, a clerk under Robert Campbell of the
Hudson's Bay Company, had discovered the river which he
named for himself in 1849, but it was not prospected until
1885. It turned out to be the richest stream of them all, paying
out as much as $100 a day to some of the luckiest. The next
year a few men were working back up on the Lewes, where
some of the sand bars were packed with gold.

Once the prospectors were over the pass the first thing they
discovered was that the Hudson's Bay Company had been
there for thirty years. The Governor and Company of Adventurers of England Trading into Hudson's Bay had come
in by way of the Mackenzie and Porcupine rivers, and later
by way of the Liard and Pelly, pressing up from British
Columbia. Their trading posts were called forts, and not without reason. In 1670 Charles II had provided the traders with
a superlative charter which endowed them with the privilege
of exercising complete executive, legislative, and judicial
powers over a territory whose boundaries were virtually the
Atlantic and Pacific oceans, the northern limits of the American colonies, which were not much above Plymouth Rock
that year, and the Arctic ice. The geographical extent of these
privileges seems to have never been without a disputant.

By the time the company forged west to the confluence of
the Porcupine and Yukon rivers to establish their first fort,
the Russians were at their elbows. Ten years later, at a point
375 miles to the south, where the Pelly meets the Yukon, a
second thrusting arm from Fort Selkirk was repelled by the
local savages. A long list of massacres and pillaged posts, in-

cluding Forts Dease, Frances, Nelson, Babine, Peace River, Pelly Banks, and Selkirk, was evidence that the Hudson's Bay Company's occupation of Indian country had not been peaceful. As to the Russians who were settled on the lower Yukon River, they had no permanent post above Nulato, which was hundreds of miles below Fort Yukon. The Hudson's Bay men, who had never gone down the river farther than Nuklakayet, believed that the Yukon emptied into the Arctic Ocean. They assumed themselves independent of the Russians until the latter visited them with an expedition which informed them that they were well within Russian America. The British did nothing about it but after the purchase of Alaska, when American concerns sought the fur trade along the river, the company was forced back to the boundary line at the 141st meridian.

Prospectors had never been shut out of the Yukon. Every Chilkoot, Siwash, and trader had seen the gold lumps in the creeks. The Hudson's Bay men who had taken the time to wash sand had found that what little panned out was hardly worth the trouble. Fox and marten were more dependable. But, if digging appealed to some men, well then let them dig. A sourdough, as any good trader would have told you, was an odd sort, a man without home ties for the most part, a wandering, foot-loose fellow, looking for a creek to make him rich. And probably just as content not to find it. Always moving along, with a shovel, pick and pan, with his optimism and a little grub. He was never without his crock of sour dough, which literally kept him alive.

There were two hundred and fifty of these sourdoughs in the Yukon in 1887. They had not all come in over the pass. A few had walked in from the east, over the Peace, Liard, Mackenzie, and Porcupine routes. They were of many nationalities: Russian, Irish, Scotch, Canadian, French, American, Norwegian. None of the Chinese had come up from the Alaska coast, where so many of them were employed by the fish canneries. In the seventies they had run out and gone up the Stikine to the mines but they had not gone into the Yukon at all. There were Swiss and German and Australian miners, Swedes and Cornishmen. Although they were of so many nationalities they were in themselves a kind of special internationality, with mutual characteristics of restlessness, independence, a trust in luck, an incurable credulity. Hope and privation were their bonds.

A prospector usually worked alone. There were few creeks with gravel rich enough to pay "wages" to more than one man. The claims were often widely separated, even miles apart if the creek was a new one. A man staked his claim, built a cabin and started digging. He had nothing but his pick and shovel to guide him to bedrock and his toil was endless. He had neither time for nor need of neighbors. If the diggings were poor there was nothing to talk about, and if the dirt was better than average he kept it to himself as long as he could. At intervals, when the wanderers met and talk was forthcoming, it centered upon the only subjects in a prospector's mind, pay dirt and low rations. The only news that traveled the creeks was the rumor of a discovery and at the first word of it every man picked up his gear and headed for the riches. A prospector would always desert his diggings, regardless of what he was getting, on the hearsay that there was more gold in the next gulch.

After the Stewart was opened some of the creeks of the Forty-Mile River, which was six hundred miles down the Yukon, were struck and proved richer than anything yet seen. Chicken Creek and Franklin Gulch started the stampede. Soon every man in the country was on the Forty-Mile. In 1892, two Russian Indians, Pitka and Sorresco, found $400 on one of the bars of Alaska's Birch Creek, farther north. At that, Forty-Mile was deserted for the Birch district which had extremely fine clean gold worth $18 an ounce, $4 more than any of the other creeks could offer. Mastodon, Molymute, Eagle, Boulder, Independence, Greenhorn, Deadwood, Mammoth, Preacher, Harrison, and Miller creeks were the richest tributaries of the Birch. A thousand men were working them. They produced $700,000 the year of 1896, the largest annual yield to date of any district in the Yukon, on either the Canadian or American side of the line.

The Birch miners built a city eight miles from the creeks, out on the Yukon River below the Great Bend. They called it Circle City because they thought they were in the Arctic Circle, but they were fifty miles below it. "City" was not American vainglory. It was mining terminology. In order to distinguish between a mining district and the camp center, the latter was called a "city." All the creeks of the Birch were in the Circle Mining District and the settlement was Circle City. All the creeks of the Forty-Mile were in the Forty-Mile Mining District and the company store, cabins, and saloons at the river's mouth were known as the city of Forty-Mile.

In 1896 the residents of Circle City were looking forward to a metropolis with wooden sidewalks, an opera house, and United States mail service. They started to build the city, but there was some trouble over lumber. The Canadians protested, accusing the Americans of poaching in their forests. There wasn't a tree in sight on the American, sub-Arctic tundra. As for mail service, Forty-Mile had offered it and Circle City could do no less. Summertime, the mail went in and out on the traders' river boats, which went out to salt water at St. Michael three or four times a season. In winter, it was a different matter. Only the dog sleds traveled in or out of the country. Mail was carried by contract, for one dollar a letter, and Jack Carr, dog puncher and freighter, had the contract. He was to make two round trips a year, for $500 a trip, following the frozen trail to Wrangell, a journey of about thirty days each way.

But in all that wilderness where the prospectors had been, from the Stikine to Chilkoot Pass, from Yakutat to Kenai, from the Cariboo to Juneau, from the Stewart to the Birch, it was Rabbit Creek in the Klondike hills that hid the real bonanza. George Washington Carmack and his Indian brothers-in-law, Skookum Jim and Tagish Charlie, found it.

Carmack had jumped ship a few years before at Dyea, at the head of Lynn Canal, and gone inland to prospect. He had married a Siwash girl named Kate and was the father of two small children. He was living as an Indian with the tribe and for this reason was known as Siwash George. Sometimes he worked for the Dominion surveyor, William Ogilvie, but most of the time he did nothing other than gather a few nets of salmon. He was about this business late in the summer of 1896. With Jim and Charlie and Kate he had taken a canoe down the river to the mouth of Deer Creek to get salmon for the winter. The men hammered down a few sticks and set their nets at the mouth of the creek. They were alone. The site had been a favorite one of the Siwash tribe but a slide had frightened most of them away and the Circle City men logging for spruce had diminished the salmon.

A day or so later a Canadian prospector, Robert Henderson, came down the creek and noticing Carmack, stopped to talk. Henderson had only been in the country two summers. He had met John Ladue, a trader, at Sixty-Mile. Ladue had told him to go up the Indian River if he wanted to find something. Henderson had not had any luck in the country and was completely discouraged. Ladue had spent a little time on the Indian River and assured Henderson that he would find more than colors there. He advanced him enough provisions to last him through the winter. Henderson worked up the Indian and crossed the Divide to a creek he called Gold Bottom. He met up with two other men and together they collected a large pile of pay dirt. In the summer they washed out $750 from it. Henderson related all this to Carmack and showed him the gold which he had in a bottle.

"Why don't you go up and try your luck?" Henderson asked Carmack. He told him just where to find his partners on Gold Bottom.

Carmack said he'd like to go up, after they got the fish in, so that he could take his in-laws with him, but Henderson objected to that. He said something about not wanting to stake the whole Siwash tribe, and he left then for Sixty-Mile to get the next winter's provisions.

After the fish were in, the three men went up Deer Creek to Gold Bottom, as Henderson had directed them, and found the claim where two Swedes, Swanson and Munson, were working. The visitors stayed awhile but didn't think the creek was worth going back for a shovel. They started for home by way of the Divide, an alternate route from the one they had used coming up. They stopped here and there to wash a little gravel but found nothing. At Rabbit Creek they turned off and at a lower fork they rested. While Carmack was in this refreshing frame of mind he noticed the rimrock in front of him. Afterwards he said that it had looked good to him.

"Jim," he said, "why don't you get a little of that there dirt and wash it in the creek?"

Jim did and at the bottom of the tomato can was a little shine. This looked so good that Carmack got up off his elbow to help. In a little while the three of them had collected a palmful of coarse grains. They put them into an empty cartridge shell that one of them was carrying and corked it with a bit of stick. Then they looked around for suitable branches to stake down four claims. It was the custom for the discoverer of a new creek to take two claims, whereas others were allowed but one.

Jim cut the stakes and put one at each corner of the five-hundred-foot claims which Carmack judged for them. Carmack wrote his own name on two stakes, with *Discovery* on one and *One Below* on the other. He wrote Jim's name and *One Above* on a third post, Charlie's name and *Two Below* on a fourth. Carmack and Charlie went on then, leaving Jim to watch things. The claims were recorded with the Mounted Police at Fort Cudahy, and then the two men crossed the river to Forty-Mile to spread the good news. By then it was the custom to announce a strike so that others could have a share in the new creek.

However, Carmack did not have a reputation for honesty and not a man in Harry Ash's saloon would believe him. "I wouldn't cross the river on his say-so," they told each other. He showed them the cartridge shell, he poured the gold out on the bar and Ash weighed it. It was worth nearly $13. Carmack's gold was neither fine nor pure, there was plenty of black iron sand in it, but it was gold. Clarence Berry, for one, slipped out of the door. Others continued to treat it as a joke. "Carmack's found gold in that old moose pasture? Tell it to the Swedes!" The Swedes were notorious for being bilked.

Rabbit Creek and other tributaries of the Deer had always been passed up by the sourdoughs. The beds were too wide, the hills were too low. It wasn't gold country; it was only fit for the moose that pastured there in summer. It was all moss and mud. Some rejected it because the water didn't taste right. Others said the willows didn't lean right. "Thirteen dollars!"

Nevertheless the dust in the shell was gold. And where could that no-account Carmack have got any gold to play a joke with? The dust was re-examined. It wasn't gold from any of the Birch creeks. It didn't come from the Forty-Mile. Every miner could identify dust by its color, fineness, the shape of the grains and its cleanness. This was not any gold they knew. "You say you got this on Rabbit Creek?"

By midnight the stampede was on. Forty-Mile was deserted in a few hours. Two hundred claims were staked before the news got up to Oscar Ashby's saloon in Circle City. Doubt delayed the men there until a letter arrived, from a man everyone knew and whom they could believe, but by the time the

Circle City men arrived, Rabbit Creek, now called Bonanza, was staked to the sixties both below and above *Discovery*. They always staked downstream first because it was believed that the chances of finding heavier deposits were better that way, in the direction of the current. When the creek ran out, at its confluence with the Deer, the claims above *Discovery* were staked.

Among those who arrived early were the constables from Fort Cudahy. Every red coat staked and by the following summer most had amassed a fortune. An entire outfit of recruits had to be sent in to replace them because in June, 1897, they went home with the rest of the Klondike millionaires.

Later, when other Canadians reached the Klondike, especially those who came the long way around from Edmonton, they found that the creeks and the tributaries, and the tributaries of the tributaries, which were called "pups," were gone.

"A man can't get a toe-hold in his own country," they complained.

Henderson, who might have found the Bonanza, never recovered from his disappointment. By October, when the creek had been staked to the eighties above, a party of prospectors wandered over the next ridge of hills and, to their surprise, found Henderson and the Swedes. Henderson asked where the visitors were from.

"Bonanza Creek."

"Where's that?"

They pointed back over the hill.

"That's Rabbit Creek. What have you got there?"

It took a little explaining before Henderson realized what had happened only a few miles away. He had not come back from Sixty-Mile by way of Rabbit, probably wishing to avoid Carmack, but had taken the Indian River to the Divide, over the trail he had cut two years before. He had no way of knowing about the strike on the new Bonanza. He told friends later that when he learned what had happened he threw down his shovel and went over and sat on the bank, so sick at heart that it was some time before he could speak.

His disappointment was partly assuaged by the Dominion Government, which claimed for him the distinction of being the "true discoverer" of the Klondike inasmuch as he had been the first to mine on one of its tributaries. He was given an honorary pension. Henderson left the Klondike in 1897, was stranded and half starved through a winter in Circle City, and reached his home in Nova Scotia, an ill man, embittered, and indifferent to the sympathy of his friends. In 1927 he renounced the pension and returned to the West, to Vancouver Island where a strike had been reported. He looked in vain for the gold, and died there.

Skookum Jim and Tagish Charlie were made honorary citizens of the Dominion of Canada for their part in the discovery of the Klondike. Carmack, an American citizen, received no attention from either government. Swanson and Munson slipped into anonymity.

2

BIG POKES

ALL DURING the winter of
1896 there was a story along the Pacific Coast about a new
strike in the Yukon. Some said an Indian had made it above
Deer Creek. Others claimed the name of the creek was
Chandik, or Throndak, or "some such name." In November
Jack Carr came out with the mail and said a white man had
made the strike and that it had occurred on one of the little
known creeks of the Indian's "big fish" river, which was called
Deer Creek by the prospectors. It was a small stream located
about six miles above old Fort Reliance. All who brought the
story down agreed that the strike was the biggest one ever
known up there. Carr added, "It'll beat California clean out
of sight" and revealed he was on his way East to get capital
with which to start a steamboat company on the river. He
said he hoped to have the company operating by summer
when the stampede started.

But strike stories had come out of the Yukon before, and
usually in the winter when there were no miners coming out
with the evidence. Juneau, Seattle, Tacoma, Portland and half
a dozen other towns had old-timers around who had been to
the mines, on one stampede or another. They had known
hundreds of creeks and they had gone on from one skim dig-

gings to the next. They had finally come home but they still liked to sit around and talk about the big strikes. The ones they had missed.

As the nuggets enlarged with each new report there was bound to be sarcasm from some sources. A saloon in Seattle displayed an enormous papier-maché nugget with a card, *Klondyke Gold,* for by spring the Indian name meaning "the river full of fish" had been twisted into a new word. The guttural Siwash syllables were almost impossible for the prospectors to pronounce, and nobody had tried to spell them out except the Canadian boundary surveyor. His try was Throndak. The miners didn't like that. They called the river Klondyke. Some used an "i" for a "y."

Now letters were coming out of the country. Astonished families read about hundred-dollar pans, of boulders turned over to pick up nuggets, of old coffee cans filled with "dust." Hometown papers published some of the letters.

Fred Fay, a miner, wrote a friend: "Circle City is deserted, everyone having gone to Klondike, where the richest strike of the kind ever known in any country was made last fall. The stories told are not exaggerated. One hundred dollars to the pan is very common. One can hardly believe it, but it is true nevertheless."

George Cole wrote his wife that he had a hundred thousand dollars in sight.

The adventuring, but nonetheless cool-headed, son of a wealthy landowner of Portland, Oregon, urged his father to start an outfitting business at once. The son wrote, "I have no doubt that 50,000 men will rush into Alaska within the next twelve months." And he added that he was on his way home to assist in the enterprise. "Meanwhile, buy at least 100,000 barrels of flour and an equal weight of meat and groceries."

The miners at Juneau and on nearby Douglas Island were getting restless. In spite of hardships remembered and many a bare creek. One said to another, "A hundred dollars to the pan! Do you believe it?" It was hard to. They all knew it was seldom that they had seen "two bits" in the pan.

In Seattle a sour voice might speak up. "You boys let me know when the millionaires get here, will you?" And the old man on the town would signal his partner, more than likely another old-timer in similar straightened circumstances, to "wake up" and move his checker piece.

In June it was time for the trading company ships, the *Excelsior* and *Portland,* to go up to St. Michael to pick up furs. When they returned they'd have proof of what happened in the Yukon that winter of 1896. You could leave that to the ships' masters, Captain Higgins of the *Excelsior* and Captain Kidson of the *Portland.* They always gave the papers a story when they got back. This was one year everybody wanted to hear the news from Alaska.

The *Excelsior* was due back first, bound for San Francisco, but if the people there had believed any part of the rumor they had forgotten it on the eve of the ship's arrival. The *Annie Maud,* a British vessel, had come into port with the bubonic plague. One person had died of the disease en route from Calcutta. The *Annie Maud* was in quarantine and amid the distress and terror of San Francisco's misfortune the first treasure ship came in unnoticed late in the afternoon of July 14.

Meanwhile a party of reporters and photographers from the Seattle *Post-Intelligencer* had been waiting two days off Cape Flattery for the *Portland.* The newspaper had chartered a tug and sent its best men out as far as the lighthouse to wait for the ship and board her while she was still off port. On Friday, July 16, she came into view. As soon as the reporters got their story the tug raced them ahead to Port Townsend and the telephones, and the *Portland* puffed on to Seattle, where she arrived the following morning. By then the Klondike story was half way around the world.

Shortly after dawn on the morning of the seventeenth the express wagons and a company of Wells Fargo guards arrived at the *Portland*'s dock. The place was already crowded with men, all the skeptics, the hopefuls, the old prospectors, the jobless. The West had drawn the unemployed from every section of the country. There they had hoped to make a fresh start with new opportunities but they were destined to disappointment. Times were as hard in one city as in another. Thousands had drifted to Seattle, hoping for a chance to go north to the gold creeks. When everything else fails, men start searching through the pockets of old mother Earth.

On the *Portland*'s dock the men who had been craning their necks over the pilings since daylight now gave a shout. "Here she comes!"

The ship came in slowly. Her whistle blew a toot or two. Finally the shouts from shore carried across the intervening water. "Show us the gold!" More than one man hoisted his sack.

The crowd surged in closer to the gangplank. A woman was seen and the men waved their hats up to her. She fluttered a handkerchief. The last thing anybody expected to see aboard the *Portland* was a woman. There turned out to be seven of them. There was Mrs. Gage, the wife of the auditor of the company that owned the ship, the North American Transportation and Trading Company. There were Mrs. Berry and Mrs. Anderson, wives of prospectors, and Mrs. Strickland, the wife of the retiring Mounted Police Inspector. There were also three prim ladies, believed to be missionaries, the Misses Sedick, Block, and Nelson. As each woman appeared on deck the crowd cheered and stamped like thunder.

The *Portland* was in. Her nose settled against the creaking wharf, the gangplank went up and the Wells Fargo guards quickly formed a line from the ship's side to the wagons. Their rifles stood in front of them like a double picket fence.

The first miner at the railing lifted a fat leather satchel to his shoulder and stepped onto the gangplank. The man behind him was hauling at a valise whose weight made him list. At that a shout went up from below. "Hurray for the Klondike!" The shout went up again and again, cracking the steady drone of voices.

The miners continued to come down, each one weighted with gold. The men were bearded, ragged, and lean. Their faces were beefy, their eyes squinted into the crowd. They had their gold in moosehide sacks, in old bits of sail, in blanket bundles. There were a few square pine boxes but these seemed to belong to the company, and there was no doubt that they contained gold dust and nuggets. Only a few passengers carried the usual travelers' luggage. Apparently there was little in the way of personal belongings. Just gold.

The sight of this unwieldy, bulging baggage was hypnotic to the penniless men who stared at it over the shoulders of the guards. It was two hours or more before all the passengers were ashore and the last wagon was gone. "He said he got his gold out in twenty-six days." . . . "I heard that old fellow say two tenderfoots kicked over a boulder and found $800 worth of nuggets." . . . "It's bigger than California!" . . .

The newsboys were soon running through Seattle's streets. Smashed all over the front page of the *Post-Intelligencer* was:

GOLD! GOLD! GOLD! GOLD!

Sixty-Eight Rich Men on the
Steamer *Portland*

Stacks of Yellow Metal

Some Have $5,000, Many Have More, and
a Few Bring Out $100,000 Each

The Steamer Carries $700,000

Special Tug Chartered by the *Post-Intelligencer*
To Get the News

And Beriah Brown's story that went with this headline gave the rewrite men of the country the phrase of the year—"a ton of gold."

In San Francisco the papers headlined the arrival of Seattle's gold ship and mentioned their own *Excelsior*. The Alaska Commercial Company's ship had brought out only twenty-five passengers, with but $189,000 in gold, aside from the company's sacks which the San Francisco mint acknowledged to be worth $250,000.

The next day, Sunday, the Chicago *Tribune*'s big story opened with the words: "Gold in Seattle today is weighed by the hundred pounds. The *Portland* is here from the Klondike and has brought in treasure weighing more than a ton."

The story was repeated in New York, Boston, Ottawa, London, Melbourne, Johannesburg. "A ton of gold from the Klondike" was the gist of them all. "Nuggets pour down from Alaska"; "The biggest strike in the history of gold"; "Inexhaustible riches in the northern El Dorado"; "A stream of gold"—with these phrases the story was relayed around the world.

Each prospector was interviewed and his story flashed out over the wires. From then on papers throughout the country ran columns of information and advice about Alaska. From the lips of the returning miners, readers learned of experiences which from any other source would have been too fabulous for belief.

The most popular interview was that with Clarence J. Berry and his wife, "the bride of the Klondike." Berry had gone up to the Yukon in 1894 where he prospected the deserted claims around Forty-Mile, but got nothing. He returned from the North the next fall to marry Ethel Bush, the girl who was waiting for him. The two determined to try the creeks again, together, and three months after their March wedding they were furnishing a cabin in Forty-Mile.

Saloonkeeper Ash gave Berry a bartender's job for the winter, which was how Berry happened to be one of the first to hear Carmack's story. He had to borrow grub and equipment to go, but he got to the diggings in time to stake *Forty Above*. He was forty claims above *Discovery*, not a very good prospect. Later he bought on Eldorado, where he struck his first pay dirt. His top gravel there washed an average two dollars to the pan. Most of the pans on bedrock paid him $50. It was to *Five Eldorado* that Berry referred in his interviews with the newspapers, when he said, "I took out my gold in box-lengths twelve by fifteen and in one I found the sum of $10,000." Nobody knew exactly what he meant but it sounded lucky. A "box-length" was a segment of a sloping string of boxes, each one being fifteen feet long, a foot high and a foot wide, in which the gold was caught by cross cleats and washed out with a whisk broom.

Eventually Berry became the owner of *Four, Five*, and *Six* Eldorado, but the first year he had bought only half of *Five*. It paid him $130,000. The owner of the other half of the mine got out only $35,000. *Five* gave Berry the month's $300 champion pan for March, 1897, as well as one of the largest Klondike nuggets ever found. It weighed nearly a pound and was worth $231. After he had bought *Six*, another large nugget was found lying on top of the ground there.

But the reporters liked to ask Mrs. Berry about nuggets. She said that one of her pastimes in the Yukon had been to wander over her husband's claims searching for them. She picked up nuggets big and small, and had collected over $10,000 worth to take home for souvenirs.

Most of the miners on the *Portland* were young men. William Stanley was the only one with gray hair. He and his partner, Gage Worden, came out with $112,000 between them. Stanley's son, Samuel, and Gage's brother, Charles, were remaining in the Klondike to look after the twelve claims which the four men had acquired between them. The Stanleys and Wordens had met the year before, going up on the boat, and had become partners. Worden said they had barely started to work their holdings. Stanley judged their claims were worth $2,000,000, and stated, "The Klondike is no doubt the best place to make money that there is in the world."

Before going to the Yukon, Stanley had owned a small bookshop in Seattle. "No business" forced him to give it up and seek a livelihood elsewhere. He told reporters he had never held a pick in his hands before he went to the Klondike. The Worden boys, formerly from Kansas, had come West to look for jobs. The only work they could get was milking cows. They took a chance on the Yukon.

Mr. Stanley was asked, "Sir, do you think that any other creeks in the Klondike will prove to be as rich as the Eldorado?"

"Yes, I do," he said. "Bear Gulch is another Eldorado already. There is double bedrock in Bear Gulch although very few know it. The bedrocks are three feet apart. The lower beds are as black as a black cat and the top bedrock is as bright a gold as any you ever saw." Most of the Klondike gold was found in black iron sand.

John Wilkerson had $50,000 with him. "It was a lucky turn of the wheel of fortune for us," he said. "Without practically a stroke me and my partner are coming out with $25,000 apiece." Wilkerson had his gold in a leather sack secured by three broad belts, the main one of which snapped just as he was about to carry his treasure ashore. Wilkerson's partner was William Sloan.

Dick McNulty had $20,000. Frank Keller had $35,000. C. A. Brannan, an eighteen-year-old lad, had $3,000. McNulty's opinion was that the placers in the Yukon were tenfold richer than any ever found in California.

Frank Phiscator came out with $96,000. F. W. Cobb, his partner, stayed behind to continue working their several claims. "We've got millions," Phiscator said, meaning dollars.

Many of the men coming out in 1897 were going back in

a year to give the partners who had stayed on the claims a chance to come out and enjoy their share of the riches. No claims were left idle. Berry had sent for his brother, Frank, to come in and look after his interests throughout the coming year. Some let out their claims on what were called "lays," or mining leases on a share-the-gold basis.

J. S. Clement had $50,000, exclusive of nuggets.

"Sir, are you going back up?"

"Yes, but not to work. I'm through. When we took out the last of it I threw down my shovel and said, 'Goodbye, old boy, I'll never pick you up again.' Nor will I. I have been very poor at times in my life, and I was when I went up to Alaska, and I assure you it is a very comfortable feeling to know you have a competence for life."

It was rumored that Inspector Strickland had brought out as much gold as Berry but he would give no statement. But many were glad to see themselves quoted in the newspapers: "I do not believe it would be possible to exaggerate the wealth to be found up there and the future will add to rather than detract from the marvelous stories already brought from there." "Well, it was providence that did it. My claim will average $16 and $17 to the pan and in addition to what I have already got out there is at least $100,000 in sight." "In those seams I found a clay exceedingly rich. There was a stratum of pay gravel four feet thick which was lined with pure gold. Bedrock was about sixteen feet from the surface, and I cleaned up $45,000 off it."

The express companies refused to disclose the amounts of their gold shipments, but Judge Bond of Seattle told a friend that he had been privately informed by an officer of one of the companies that his company had weighed out between 2,300 and 2,800 pounds of gold in each of their four shipments from that city. The Judge pointed out that if other concerns did anything like that amount of business the *Portland* must have delivered nearer $2,000,000 than $800,000.

He was right. The mints and assay offices verified the value of deposits which brought the figure to over $1,000,000 more than the sum which Captain Kidson had received in the *Portland*'s safe. There had been a freight charge on the gold that each man carried, the total of which appeared as the ship's cargo. Monday's headline in Seattle was: GOLD SMUGGLED IN BY KLONDIKERS. It seemed that every man aboard had smuggled a poke of nuggets into his bunk. Berry, for one, had brought in $84,000 worth of them, not a cent of which the *Portland* had any record.

People were telling each other that Klondike nuggets were as big as peas.

When the home-coming miners reached their native cities they were followed by throngs who were not only eager to meet the celebrities but who also wanted advice about getting to the Yukon, and where to find the mines, and what to take, and when to go. The unmarried miners were getting married. In Tacoma Jacob Wiseman could get no peace. He changed his name and fled to Los Angeles to get away from people.

The Klondike story was humming everywhere. Three tons of gold washed up out of a creek! The thought was staggering. The latest news was that they were digging chunks of gold out of the hilltops. Prospectors as far away as Kalgoorlie, Australia, had heard that the nuggets were the size of a guinea hen's egg.

The governor of the North-West Territory of Canada made a statement to the press. He said he believed that the real mass of golden wealth was still untouched, for only a few miles of the dozens of creeks in the Yukon district had been worked. He electrified everyone with the message that there were fully nine thousand miles of golden waterways waiting to be explored and prospected in the Territory.

A Canadian, one Douglas MacArthur, who had come down on the *Excelsior* and was on his way home to Grenelge, Montreal, said, "Take plenty of grub."

In the San Francisco *Call* people read: "The nuggets are reported as big as potatoes. A boy picked up one that weighed twenty-one pounds. It was worth $5,700." And H. Dore, back home in Montana with a $17,000 bag of nuggets, told the editor of the village paper, "The people of the Pacific Coast will be astonished at the amount of gold that will come out of the Klondike. No, I can't give figures. I'm not much on figures. Well, then I'll say millions—and I mean more than two. To make a long story short, I think Eldorado Creek is the greatest placer proposition in the world. There has never been anything discovered on the face of the globe like it."

3

"A GRUBSTAKE FOR GOD'S SAKE!"

At ONCE passage on the *Portland* jumped from $200 to $1,000 and instead of waiting until August to return to Alaska the ship was scheduled to sail in five days. The *Al-Ki* beat her to it, with eighty men bound for the pass at Lynn Canal. When the *Portland*'s $1,000 fares were sold out the latecomers paid an extra $500 to anyone willing to part with his berth. Seattle was seething with commotion.

The newspapers were filling their editions with interviews, with firsthand accounts of life in the far north, with estimates of the Klondike's likely yield for the next five years. There were pen-and-ink reproductions of the miner in proper Yukon dress, of miners digging, of miners washing, with the garnered gold heaped up like porridge, of miners weighing their pokes in at the express company. There were sketches of nuggets drawn exactly to size, of Mr. Berry's gold sacks drawn exactly to size, of husky dogs much smaller. The papers printed maps and published tables of the comparative average mean temperature of places in cold climates.

Biographies continued to appear along the pleasant theme,

"from poverty to riches." Old-timers were called upon to describe the Yukon's terrain and geography. They told about the earlier strikes and explained the various kinds of gold which the region produced. The steamship companies' lists of ships that would sail north within the next two weeks were published on the front pages of the papers.

The *Portland*'s master announced they would be a day late in getting away. The hurried sailing, the problem of so much passenger freight going up, the lack of accommodations, and the possibility that the crew of the vessel would disappear at St. Michael and go up the river with the rest of the gold hunters had given the company more than enough to think about. Not only the captain, but the office manager and clerks were having to dodge would-be passengers on the street. "I'm going up on that boat of yours if I have to ride the smokestack," became more of a threat each succeeding day.

Every available ship on the Pacific Coast was being pushed into service. Not only the ocean-going vessels of companies that were not on the Alaska run, not only freighters and tankers, but old craft that had been rusting in the graveyards of every port were resurrected and pulled to the docks to be hastily made ready for a voyage to Alaska. Whalers, pleasure yachts, sailing schooners, every sloop, cutter, and ketch was sailing north. In two weeks the established shipping lines had received over two thousand reservations which they were unable to fill. Eighteen Atlantic liners steamed for the Horn to accommodate them.

Shipping companies mushroomed by the dozens. Wherever a brig or a coal barge or even a fishing smack was idle, it was incentive enough to start someone in the passenger and freight business to Alaska. In San Francisco the *Call* reported that two gasoline launches had been chartered and were leaving with the speed of a man who wakes up ten minutes before his train starts.

The crews for many of these makeshift vessels were re-

cruited anew with each sailing. There was no trouble getting
a crew together because every able-bodied man seemed to be
on his way to Alaska and many of them were only too glad
to work their passage. Since it was seldom the skippers had
made an ocean voyage, nor seen Alaska, this was no time to
quibble over a seaman's papers. The trip north was known
to be a smooth one. Just like a lake voyage, didn't the excursion folders say? Vacationists had been going up to see the
glaciers for the past fifteen years on what was, in the words
of the Pacific Mail Company, "a blithesome voyage, without
a blemish." The boats took the placid inland passage, thread-
ing their way between the 50,000 islands of southeastern
Alaska. One travel writer described the trip as "a protracted
marine picnic on the waveless arms of the ocean."

In a month's time the wreckage was strewn up the coast
like a trail and flotsam and jetsam were floating all the way
from Bering Sea. Even ships with veteran masters sank. They
struck the rocks or ran aground, tangled in seaweed, or they
were beached by the unfamiliar tides. But gold seekers were
descending on the coast like locusts. They fought each other
for space on any kind of vessel at all that was headed in the
direction of Alaska.

The Seattle hotels were happily bursting with business.
Their registers proclaimed that the guests were from almost
every state in the union. The papers reported, "The vanguard
from the East is here." It was almost the end of July.

The *Portland* had sailed on the twenty-third with 125 passengers and 1,100 tons of freight. The *Queen* sailed the same
day with 250 passengers. The *Cleveland* arrived from Juneau
with a cargo of $180,000 and the miners who had brought it
out over the pass. The *City of Mexico* sailed. The *City of
Topeka* sailed. The *Umatilla*, another summer excursion
boat from Alaska, arrived with an unexpected load of miners
bringing out gold. She came into San Francisco on the twenty-
second and left the next day with 400 aboard. The *Victoria*

sailed, with more horses than passengers. The *City of Seattle* was being remodeled to carry three times her normal number. A hurry-up job was started on the huge collier *Willamette*, to put a thousand bunks into her hold. On the twenty-ninth the *Excelsior* was ready to leave San Francisco.

Ten thousand persons jammed the *Excelsior*'s dock to see her go. It was reported that San Francisco had seldom seen such a crowd. A police squad arrived and it was every newspaper reporter for himself. The pencils were flying. Among the passengers were men of wealth bent on investment as well as "broken-down miners," or to put it another way, "men of culture, name and character were jostled by every range of mankind that could rustle a stake." All were wormed aboard by police escorts.

A number of women were going north. At the rail they clutched their *bon voyage* bouquets, gilded horseshoes, and paper novels. Fluttering, last-minute notes were passed along from hand to hand through the crowd. The women began to dab their eyes. Somewhere on deck a concertina played airs from "The Bohemian Girl," and more than one man had his arms around a comforting demijohn. "They were leaving behind them homes and loved ones, while the future, albeit with rosy fingers, beckoned no man knew where."

At the gangplank Louis Sloss, president of the Alaska Commercial Company, was still turning away passengers. He had been saying the same thing for a week, ever since the last berth was gone. He said it again: "Our next steamer for the Yukon will not leave until next year, in June 1898. We can't take your money, as much as we'd like to, ladies and gentlemen, not because we can't get you to St. Michael, but because we can't get you up the river to Dawson City." He told them, "Thousands of you have begged us for passage but I assure you there is not a berth to be had. Yes, we can carry 200 passengers instead of 100 but we have limited ourselves to 100 because we can't get you up the river. Ladies and gentlemen, we will not send more people to St. Michael than we can get up the river!"

At that the *Excelsior* had to make room for twelve more.

A number of men had tried to pass themselves off as coalers, oilers, firemen, and deckhands but all were returned to the wharf. Also a stowaway named Birdie. She was turned over to the good ladies of the Methodist Mission. "Of a titian type," she was reported to be, and from Denver.

At 2:40 P.M. the *Excelsior* backed into the bay and sailed "amid the waving of thousands of silken American flags."

From mining camps all over the country the prospectors were on their way. Those who had hung over the scant and deserted diggings of Tombstone, Creede, Cripple Creek, and Hangtown made their way to the coast. Even the grizzly prospectors on the dusty ridges of the Panamints had got word of the new strike and were on their way "to Klondike." They had picked the hills for silver and gold and found so little. And now heard that a Captain John G. McGregor from Minnesota had washed a pan worth $3,000. And on a little finger of a creek in Alaska.

On July 31 the *Rosalie* sailed and the *Al-Ki* was back and ready to go again on August 2. The *State of California* sailed, and the *Noyo* and the *Walla Walla.* The *Willamette* was gone with her thousand bunks all filled. The *Cleveland* sailed. The *Eliza Anderson* was ready to cast away. There wasn't room to squeeze a cat on any one of them.

In California the mines at Sonora and Angel's Camp had closed down for want of men. The gold mills on Douglas Island were operating with a skeleton crew. A minor boom in Washington's Cascade Mountains was temporarily eclipsed. But in large round numbers the miners could not compare with the thousands who rushed for the creeks without so much as ever having seen a placer layout. In fact, many were not planning to dig, at least not very deep. They imagined that the gold was lying in a long shining ribbon at the bottom of certain creeks and that all that was necessary was to wash out any gravel which might have accumulated, and then to fill up the sacks and come home. They were in great haste to get there before all the gold creeks had been claimed.

Cowhands came from Texas and lawyers left New York City. The canneries in Alaska were closing. The whalers deserted and left the fleet locked in the ice at Herschel, which was conveniently not far from the mouth of the Mackenzie River. In California's Sacramento Valley the fruit picking stopped. Not for lack of hands, for women and children picked, too, but because the river boats were being towed up to St. Michael and there was no way to get the fruit to the wholesalers in San Francisco. The boats were bringing a price three times that of their original cost.

Bookkeepers, drygoods salesmen, bank clerks, school teachers and druggists, tailors, streetcar conductors were ready to go. Each person had to haul to the wilderness with him all he would eat, use or wear for a year because he would find nothing there and he would not be able to leave the country once winter set in. Waiting for ships, the tenderfoot checked over his outfit.

Men knew what to take with them. About two thousand pounds made up the weight of each man's outfit. Every newspaper, store, and travel office posted a basic list. It was somewhat as follows:

Flour	500 pounds
Bacon	200 pounds
Sugar	100 pounds
Beans	100 pounds
Dried fruits	100 pounds
Evaporated potatoes	100 pounds
Corn meal	50 pounds
Rolled oats	50 pounds
Rice	50 pounds

Corned beef	48 two-pound tins
Lard	30 pounds
Yeast	36 cakes
Coffee	25 pounds
Tea	5 pounds
Cocoa	5 pounds
Condensed cream	48 large cans
Salt	25 pounds
Pepper	1 pound

This list did not include food for the dogs, which usually required each an extra two hundred pounds of corn meal and about the same amount of fat bacon.

Fancier outfits included two-pound tins of butter, rounds of cheese, vinegar, tins of cookies and cake, pickles and some of the sweet spices. Holiday fare such as boned turkey and mince meat were added to the really de luxe outfits. These were the kits with a wash basin and a dozen bars of castile soap, with a fur robe, a pillow and an eiderdown. All sorts of people went to the Klondike. Some went up in silk-striped shirts and others wore homespun. Some took hand-painted glass lamp shades and hand-painted cuspidors. There already was a cat or two in Dawson. Most men planned to bake their bread on the steel of their long-handled shovels and to put their gold pans to several uses.

As important as food was the hardware a miner needed. This was the list that was recommended:

Gold pans (2)	Whipsaw
Long-handled shovel	Bull saw (five-foot length)
Spade	Bull saw files
Pick	Drawknife
Granite buckets (3)	Brace and bits
Whetstone	Ax
Hammer	Hatchet
Nails (20 pounds)	Chisels (3)
Handsaw	Calking iron

Jack plane	Lash rope (200 feet of assorted
Square	sizes)
Pitch (15 pounds)	Pocket rule
Oakum (10 pounds)	Duplicate handles for all tools

These were the tools needed to build a boat and a cabin, to sink timbers in a mine, to erect a windlass, to build a rocker and sluice boxes, a dam and other structures.

In addition to food and tools each man would need matches, cooking utensils, such as a coffee pot, a frying pan and a kettle, a tin cup and plate, a knife, fork and two spoons. He would be carrying bedding, a tent, a special Yukon stove, and two outfits of clothing suitable for a hot summer and a very cold winter. He could also use a sled, laundry soap, candles, a six-inch magnet, hunting knives, fishing tackle, a rifle and ammunition. He would need an oar and a sail. Waterproof sheeting in which to wrap the freight was worth considering. He might want a sleeping bag, or a lantern (and kerosene for it), an alcohol thermometer, a can opener or a compass, and other small luxuries. Most men brought tobacco with them. A few had books.

If a medicine chest was being carried it might have been assembled after reading a paragraph similar to the following, which appeared in newspapers around the country:

"One should be careful to take a few compound cathartic pills, liniment for sprains and colds on the chest, tincture of iron to enrich the blood, extract of Jamaica ginger for the stomach, laudanum, vaseline, carbolic ointment, salts, bandages, surgeons' lint, a surgeons' sponge, belladonna plasters, mustard and adhesive plasters, cough tablets, liver pills, powder for bleeding, Monsell's salts for hemorrhages in accordance with each person's liability to attacks of the trouble, iodoform, chloroform, witch hazel, absorbent cotton, quinine capsules, iodine and toothache drops."

In general, it was well to remember that "weak hearts and weak lungs cannot face the northern blasts. Weak eyes will

be sorely tried in the snow-clad land. Those who are subject
to troubles of the heart, throat or lungs, should stay religiously
away from the Klondike. The medicine chest will be a futile
resort for them, and some volunteer sexton will likely do for
them the last earthly office before the Alaskan spring blooms
again in May."

There were over five hundred miles of rough water between the passes and the creeks. The part of the trail which
led down the river and through the lakes had been sketched
in papers and illustrated weeklies. "On a Raft" was a familiar
subject. The prospectors would have to build their own boats.
But how many had felled a tree or whipsawed it into planks,
cut these into boards and fitted them into a watertight boat?
Who had built any kind of boat, a raft even?

Policemen, livery stable boys, milk cart drivers, factory
hands, cobblers. . . . Did they realize what the Arctic winter
was like? That with the dark, a loneliness and melancholia
would settle upon them, a mood which they might not easily
throw off? Not in a cabin whose floor was the bare dirt, whose
walls had no windows, whose only light was a can of flickering
grease. They might not have as much as an ounce of gold
dust to cheer them up. They stuffed tobacco and Sloan's
liniment into their bundles. They made sure there were
enough blankets and socks.

College boys left their classes. In August a poll of the
graduates of California medical colleges incidentally revealed
that half of them had left for the gold fields. In Oakland, a
news item announced that Captain Haskell, of the University
of California's football team, and Theodore Barnes, the
University's crack sprinter, were on their way to Alaska.

Butchers, teamsters, and barbers, men everywhere were
leaving their jobs and getting ready to spend the whole winter,
if need be, on the creeks. Families were separated and wed-
dings postponed while men sought each other for partners
in the great adventure of making a fortune. Now, for the first

time, a prospector had a partner. Was it because they thought two could dig faster than one?

Something else a Klondiker thought he should have was a dog. When he was not accumulating provisions he was out looking for a suitable animal to take with him. Sometimes men were seen running through the streets with dogs tied to children's sleds in the hope of breaking perhaps a shepherd or a setter to the work. However, it is a rare dog that will pull anything, being an animal that follows or runs with a man, and not ahead of him pulling a burden. But if the dog didn't adapt himself to the idea at once, well, there was no time to bother with that then. Just put a rope around his neck and get him aboard the first boat that came along.

City after city reported that the gold fever had struck it. They made it sound like an epidemic. "The Klondike fever has struck Alameda. Conductor William Parke of the electric road has engaged passage and is prepared to undergo any hardships that may fall to his lot."

Many sold out their business to get ready cash for the trip. In San Francisco the columns of the "People's Popular Wants" were soon doubled.

> FOR SALE. Fine saloon in lively neighborhood. Magnificently fitted up. Large place. Is doing an excellent paying trade. Place worth fully $1,500 but offered cheap as owner will leave this city soon.

> FOR SALE. $400 buys sewing machine store. Leaving city. Good chance for smart party.

> FOR SALE. Good paying restaurant. Busy corner. I need cash.

> FOR SALE. Fine meat market. Owner away. Wife must sell.

> FOR SALE. Will deed my ranch for a stake in Alaska. Make me an offer.

And in adjoining columns:

> KLONDIKERS. Two Great Dane dogs. Cheap.
> WANTED. An Ark. Must be in A-1 condition and cheap for
> cash. Give price, size and where Ark can be seen.

The "Argonauts," as they were called now, were mortgaging their homes to buy gold pans and long-handled shovels, picks and woolen union suits. They needed tents and sleds and rations. And the fare to Alaska. If a man did not have any ready cash, nor the wherewithal to raise it, he asked someone to grubstake him to the mines. He offered to go north for one or more persons, with whom he would divide what gold he might locate and bring out. This arrangement was always on an equal share basis. If a man's wife and family were anchors to his ambition the grubstakers were often willing to take over their support during the prospector's absence. The "People's Popular Wants" were beginning to run over into the news.

An advertisement in *The New York Times* asked for five or six men with $1,000 each who were willing to grubstake a small party to the mines. Thirty-two answers were received. In Berkeley, California, this appeared:

> STUDENT has scheme to take party of ten to Klondike.
> Many local business men are behind the project. $500
> required.

It was not so expensive to go to the Yukon from the Pacific Coast since there was no railroad fare to pay for a cross-country trip. This plea appeared in Seattle:

> WANTED. Twenty ladies to organize a company to send
> eight men to Alaska. $200 required.

A man in Chicago placed this advertisement in the paper:

> WANTED. A victim of the cigaret habit would like some
> philanthropist to grubstake him in the Klondike. Has had
> considerable experience digging wells and other work
> suiting him for mining.

In Kentucky the Richmond *Register* got together $1,200 to send a fellow reporter to the mines and in Lexington the *Herald* collected $1,000 for the same purpose. Twenty members of the Seattle and International Order of Railway Workers put up $600 each to grubstake a party from their membership. In Tacoma the streetcar conductors sent nine men to the Klondike and in Chicago the clairvoyants banded together and sent a medium (male) to carry out the messages received from the spirit world as to the best place to dig.

If a man had a friend or a relative from whom he could borrow, he quickly enough asked for a stake. The telegraph offices in Seattle were crowded twenty-four hours a day with people sending frenzied requests for money to get them to Alaska. The Western Union manager of that city told a reporter that his company was shocked at the number who were planning to leave their jobs. He said the messages were just about all alike: "Send me $500. News not exaggerated."

Men were being grubstaked in Portland, Tacoma, Astoria, and Seattle to an extent undreamed of before. The fever was apparently hottest the nearer it got to the trail. Some local houses who were losing long-time employees forwarded them enough funds to see them through a winter on the creeks. Many businessmen were willing to risk $5,000 for $50,000.

Secretary Gage of the Treasury made a statement to the press: "A pleasant feature of the Alaska situation is that it is a poor man's diggings. A man with a brave heart, sound body, nerve, and courage may find a field for his enterprise without the intervention of capital as an employer." His daughter-in-law was the Mrs. Eli Gage among the *Portland*'s passengers on that great day, July 17, 1897. She was shortly returning to the Klondike to be with her husband. A party of six was going along with her in a yacht which was being built in Toronto especially for the trip.

A Boston news release disclosed: "Fourteen Hebrew working men of this city out of employment are determined to walk to Alaska or lose their lives in the attempt. They are led by Charles L. Wise of 287 Hanover Street. In 1891 Wise ran for mayor of Hartford on the Socialistic ticket and came within 300 votes of winning. The party will start tomorrow."

The ships were coming back, with more miners, more gold sacks, more nuggets. News artists were busy sketching miners' portraits, mastodon jaws, and totem poles. The totem poles were at Wrangell, not Dawson. At the mines the bones of prehistoric elephants had been unearthed, rousing the scientific curiosity of the Smithsonian Institution which planned to send a party to see them. More to the point, the mining laws of the Klondike were published and the method of mining in frozen ground was explained.

There had been a new discovery on the American side of the river, on a creek called Monument. The gold was panning out "fine" dust worth $18 an ounce. Klondike gold was "coarse" and worth no more than $16 an ounce—"but they're washing $10,000 a day there on one creek after another. They've got the gold in every pot and fry pan and no way to get it down out of the hills. A man can't carry his gold, he has to wait for the pack train." Also, a new Klondike creek had been discovered, one called Victoria. The pans were averaging $22 on the surface and bedrock had not yet been reached.

The telegrams began, "A grubstake for God's sake."

Railroads all over the country were losing men in large numbers. This put a strain on the service inasmuch as the roads were running on an extra heavy schedule, rattling across the country with up to ten additional coaches every day. A hundred thousand one-way tickets to the coast had been sold before the middle of August. The Chicago *Tribune* described the situation as an "exodus."

In the eastern cities the railroads had taken special cars around, with Klondike exhibits and a barker to spiel the latest information as to the richest claims, the heaviest nuggets, and the fastest way to get to the creeks. The cars displayed facsimiles of world famous gold chunks, such as Australia's "Welcome" which weighed almost two hundred pounds, and her "Welcome Stranger," which weighed even more. California's largest single chunk of gold was a Carson Hill nugget that weighed 195 pounds troy. Its likeness was also a part of the display.

There were bottles of "dust" to show the variation in texture, color and purity of the placers in different countries, as well as among the creeks of a certain region. And there were photographs of the tent cities at the mouth of the Klondike River, of the miners sluicing on the big pay creeks, and of other tempting subjects. Local merchants of the cities which were passed en route often displayed their version of the ideal miner's outfit, perhaps with a collapsible stove or a balloon tent. Or maybe they were showing the Klondike Bicycle, or some of the new compressed food tabules, or one of the folding boats that had just been invented.

In Ottawa the papers quoted the Dominion's surveyor in the Klondike, who said that in his opinion the six hundred claims which had been staked would produce $70,000,000. But the highly favorable possibility of new discoveries on other gulches, and the future development of claims already found but not yet worked, soon made that figure obsolete. Free lance estimates were always news.

On August 8, 1897, Director Preston of the United States Mint issued a statement in which he pointed out that the total gold production of the world was $205,000,000 for the year just ending and added that he believed the 1897 yield would soar to $240,000,000 and that in the last year of the century it would very likely exceed $300,000,000.

The fortune hunters naturally knew where to look for these extra millions. They painted KLONDIKE OR BUST on their bundles. And newspapers gave away colored maps with each new subscription.

Joaquin Miller, the poet of the Sierras and California's beloved old man of "The Hights," booked passage on the *City of Mexico* as a correspondent for the Hearst papers. He said, "I am going up to get the information for the poor men who mean to go to the mines next summer. If I find the mines limited either in area or thickness, my first duty will be to let the world know." He took a forty-pound knapsack of bacon, hardtack and tea with him, and a flute, besides his notebook and a couple of pencils.

"I will not need the usual provisions," explained the poet, "because, having got right down to the bedrock of the cold frozen facts, I shall take the next steamer leaving Dawson and return straight to San Francisco."

On August 28, the *Portland* returned with a disappointing cargo of only $100,000. She had missed the *Portus B. Weare* at St. Michael. "But we're going back," Captain Kidson said, "and the next time we come out we'll bring home three or four million dollars."

The small cargo was particularly embarrassing because a rumor had risen that the ship would be waylaid by pirates on her way back from St. Michael—"Mongolians, believed to have been recruited from San Francisco." This alarm had reached such proportions that Mr. Weare, President of the North American Transportation and Trading Company, had wired Mr. Gage to see if he couldn't send a revenue cutter to convoy the *Portland* home. Mr. Gage sent the *Bear* but there were no pirates. While the *Portland* was en route home, the president of the Alaska Commercial Company in San Francisco was asked if he was worried over the safety of the *Excelsior,* also coming home. Mr. Sloss replied crisply that his company was not likely to ask any favors of the government. In San Francisco the cartoonists made the most of the subject by drawing pig-tailed pirates and Chinese junks in the Bering Sea, and Mandarins bringing the *Portland* to San Francisco, and so on. San Francisco was having another siege of fierce tong wars just then, with wholesale killings and other unsavory events in its Chinese quarter, but it was extremely improbable that these gangs gave a thought to the Bering Sea.

The *Portland* was making another trip to St. Michael. Her passenger list was as tight as ever. An editor in San Francisco clucked, "This Yukon delirium, this auriferous swoop on the frigid zones . . ." But James McMahon, until three years before a longshoreman on the Tacoma wharves, was showing off his $65,000 in virgin gold. "All you need is a pan and plenty of water," said he.

Captain A. J. Balliett, one-time star of Yale's football team and one of her crew's star oarsmen, left his law practice to sail with the *Portland*. Ex-Governor John H. McGraw of Washington also bought one of the $1,000 tickets. McGraw hoped to recover his personal fortune, which he had forfeited when a deficit was tardily found in certain accounts of his previous administration as sheriff of King County. Ex-Brigadier General E. M. Carr, of the State Militia, was going with him as his partner.

Nearly three weeks had gone by since the coal boat, *Willamette*, had started out, but she was still in Puget Sound. As a matter of fact she was listing and lagging just out of Seattle, having gone from port to port in the Sound to pick up freight until the thousand passengers aboard her had threatened mayhem. And then, as she finally headed for the north, she had improvidently broken down. Her passengers and all her horses, dogs, sheep, and cargo, were on the banks beside her. The men were in a bitter frame of mind. None could get back his fare-money. The *Willamette*'s owners were making repairs as best they could.

The cartoons began to appear. The most vulnerable topics were the crowded boats, the spilled rafts on the river, the creeks which the tenderfoot could not find in the Yukon's wilderness. There were jokes about the big black bears, and the bigger mosquitoes which men were afraid of, and finally the bones which the miners were finding instead of nuggets. The Klondike adventure seemed to be quite jovial after all. And although not too much was ever said about the ladies up north, a cartoon appeared once in a while showing a boatload of picture brides.

It was getting late for travel in the Arctic. The Yukon River would soon turn into a trough of ice and the passes would choke with blizzards. But still the trainloads poured into San Francisco and Seattle. In desperation Secretary of the Interior Bliss issued a public warning. He called attention to the fact that thousands of people and their freight were still at the passes, waiting to move into the Yukon and it was very unlikely that they would be able to do so before the winter set in. He begged those who were attempting to get to Alaska to postpone their trip until the next year. He said, in plain words, which every paper printed, "I am moved to draw public attention to these conditions by the gravity of the possible consequences to people detained in the mountainous wilderness during five or six months of the Alaska winter, where no relief can reach them, however great the need."

The Canadian Minister of the Interior warned that his government would in no way be responsible for getting provisions into the Yukon during the coming winter. An editor in Juneau wrote an editor in Portland, "It is time to stop the mad rush. Thousands are bound to die on the beach." The people of Skagway drew up a petition and sent it to the Seattle Chamber of Commerce imploring them to "stop the rush in the name of humanity."

Newspapers came out at once with headlines: BLOCKADE AT DYEA. . . . THOUSANDS MUST RETURN FROM DYEA. . . . JAMMED ON THE BEACH. . . . The editors did their best. Nevertheless twenty-one steamships, two sailing vessels and two scows cleared Pacific ports that very week. Shoe clerks, cable car gripmen, hack drivers, grocers. . . . If no passenger ship was available there was still a chance to board a tramp on which the premium was but $100 above the posted ticket price.

Coming down from Dyea the *City of Mexico* struck West Devil's Rock in the fog off Sitka and sunk.

"Last chance" advertisements were still running in the East for booking on the *Humboldt,* a new steamer with an experienced captain. He had made seven trips to the Yukon. The *Humboldt* was going to St. Michael and the fare on her was but $300 from Seattle, with 150 pounds of baggage carried free, and another 1,000 excess pounds permitted to each passenger, and carried at ten cents a pound. The company which sent the *Humboldt* guaranteed arrival by September 15, whereas the *Portland* on her last trip north promised arrival at the creeks by June, 1898. The late boats that year increased the population of St. Michael.

United States Inspector of Hulls, Captain W. J. Bryant, warned that all steamers would be inspected for overcrowding. The *Utopia* was forced to tear out a large number of bunks in her hold to permit the circulation of air.

Indignation over water-front conditions in San Francisco was expressed at the weekly meeting of the Labor Council of that city. A delegate brought up the question of a five-dollar-a-month raise in pay for all seamen. They had refused to ship out without it. At that the general scarcity of seamen was discussed. This led to a formal protest, for the record at least, concerning the circumstances under which the *North Fork* had sailed on August 14.

This aged schooner had set out for St. Michael with a ferry boat in tow. Experienced seamen had refused to go with her. The men on the water front who knew the schooner, the difficulty of towing, and the weather to be encountered, did not expect the ferry or the schooner to make St. Michael and they had said they would rather walk all the way than take such a risk. The *North Fork,* moreover, carried no lifeboats.

The pay increase was not settled but Captain Bryant repeated that all vessels would be inspected and licensed. "There is not going to be another miscellaneous mixup of men and women with the live stock," he said.

Next, the overloaded *Willamette* received an order to have eight hundred of her bunks torn out before she could proceed to Dyea.

Moran's shipyard in Seattle accepted orders for fourteen sternwheelers and six barges and put 2,100 men to work.

The fortune hunters were now on their way from across the world. Three hundred Scots were on the Atlantic, bound for Montreal, with plans of crossing Canada in the spring and entering the Yukon by way of the Mackenzie River. And though a shipload of titled Englishmen were dissuaded at the minute from leaving Southampton, ninety hardier Norwegians left Christiania to sail around the Horn. They expected to be in Skagway when the trail over White Pass opened in June.

Reports told of miners coming from Australia, New Zealand, South Africa, and of would-be miners sailing from Samoa, the Sandwich Islands and Cairo. Three hundred and fifty women sailed from New York on the *City of Columbia* to make the 16,700-mile trip by way of the Horn. Some of these said they would take out a miner's certificate and scoop up nuggets for themselves. Others had business projects in mind. "There are other ways of making money in a mining country," they reminded, "than by digging it out of the ground."

It was known that a few women had brought out fortunes. Miss Nettie Fancher had mined $25,000. Mrs. Mary Thompson had washed $18,000 in six weeks. A Mrs. Bill Dill had helped her husband work his claim and together they had cleaned up $90,000 before the summer ended. A number of women were said to be making money with restaurants, boardinghouses and bakeries. Hanna Gould, "a capital physician," said the Chicago *Record,* was in the *City of Columbia*'s party, taking up a portable hospital which she planned to install in Dawson City and operate along with other ventures, among which were a clubhouse for miners and a brokerage business.

Mrs. Keuhne Beveridge, a sculptress of New York City, said she would brave the stormy sea voyage, the freezing ride on the sledges, and even the weary walk over the icy pinnacles, provided there was gold at the end of the trail. Mrs. A. W. Little was described by reporters as a slender, delicate, little Kentuckian going for the experience rather than for the gold. "She has money and her trip is one of sightseeing only," said the paper.

It cost each lady $800 to sail on the *City of Columbia* and receive a year's rations for Alaska. Five hundred applications were received before December when the ship cast off with the lucky ones.

4

KLONDIKE! ALASKA! YUKON!

WHILE TENS of thousands set out for the gold fields there were many left behind who wanted to go but for whom the trip was not possible, for one good reason or another. But the stay-at-homes were every bit as eager to get in on the bonanza as were those who took the trail. The thought of so much wealth lying about on the ground, free for the taking, was maddening when they knew they were not going up themselves to get it. The next best thing to do was to grubstake somebody, a total stranger if necessary, who promised to fill a sack or two for the staker. But if one didn't have the money for that there were mining company stocks that sold for as little as a dollar and there were development companies, steamship companies, all kinds of sure-money ideas that advertised for stockholders and backers. People felt that a Klondike investment was literally as good as gold. Everybody coming out had a fortune with them to prove it.

There were people who had no intention of going to the Klondike but who planned to make the most of the golden opportunities which it offered. They lost no time in getting started. Printed announcements of the greatest investments of the age were soon flapping in public places. Broadsides and billboards explained all details and letters inspired quick action.

ALASKA HO!

Who has not heard of Captain Jack Crawford! Poet, Author, Scout, loved and honored by Army Men for his uprightness and integrity, high in the regard and trust of the newspaper profession! Captain Jack counts among his friends most of the prominent men in the country, beginning with President McKinley! Experienced, vigorous and shrewd, he will lead and direct under this Corporation an expedition of practical and expert miners in the new Alaska Gold Fields. Mother Lode Claims will be taken up for this Company to be sold at enormous profits, often without expending much capital in their development. There are no promoters' shares and no concealed profits. Every share guaranteed. Write for prospectus.

No sum of money was too small to interest a Klondike, Alaska, or Yukon syndicate and no project was too large to embark upon. At the end of the 1897 summer a country-wide check of the capitalization of Klondike-Alaska-Yukon syndicates astonished some people with a total of over $164,500,000. The ceiling was unlimited and the scope had no perimeter. There was a company for everything, to build steamships, railroads, wagon roads, water ditches, wharves, electric light plants, to start farms and cattle ranches, to install the telegraph and telephone, to operate aerial tramways, to haul freight, to thaw the frozen ground. Several intended to explore all of Alaska in view of other mining possibilities. Some corporations planned cities and others proposed to dredge out harbors on the coast. It cost very little, only one dollar, or at the most ten dollars, to hold a crisp new certificate in any one of these projects, an investment which might well "make a fortune" for the holder.

Toward the end of that summer, the Chicago *Tribune* reported that a great corporation was being organized in that city for the purpose of developing the interior of Alaska. One hundred million dollars was the stake and while the names of the promoters were temporarily withheld, a few hints as to their plans were made known. The corporation would build and operate not only coastwise steamers to St. Michael but would also put a fleet of sternwheelers on the Yukon lakes beyond the passes, to carry the miners to Dawson in safety and comfort. A number of trading posts would also be opened and the corporation's mines ("among the richest claims in the Klondike") would be worked with the most modern mining equipment yet to be introduced into the region. "It is no secret," the *Tribune* admitted, "that this great enterprise is easily the most extensive one ever to be attempted on this continent."

With an aerial cable tramway over Chilkoot Pass, the Dyea Transportation Company was going to make the Klondike trail as enjoyable as a Sunday outing. The tramway was designed to rise from the floor of the Dyea canyon and cross the Chilkoot summit. The prospectus declared this engineering feat was the greatest ever to be attempted anywhere. However, it was not being built to haul passengers, but only freight. The company frankly said that it did not want to run the risk of losing lives. Yet, by not having to carry and relay forward his two thousand pounds of personal freight, the miner could speed on into the Yukon, while his outfit came on behind him "by air" and river barge. Juneau, Seattle, and San Francisco capital were behind the undertaking.

To catapult Alaska into Utopia it was necessary to develop the mines exhaustively. Gold must be kept coming out of the ground in ever greater sums, attracting more and more capital, bringing in thousands more of people every year until this last frontier disappeared and the Arctic cities created enterprises to meet the flow of wealth. Men felt they had discovered the mother lode of the Americas. They looked on the map and saw the mountains which puckered the western coasts of the two continents and decided they must have a common geophysical source. While gold had been taken from the North American Rockies, the Cascades, the Sierra Nevadas, the Mexican Sierra Madres, and all down the cordillera of the Andes, the richest finds had now been at the top in the newly struck Klondike, indicating that the source must be in the near-Arctic regions. Miners and "experts" alike agreed that it was "extremely likely" that all the alluvial deposits had been erupted, washed, and moved by ice from some fabulous single reservoir accumulated before the age of man.

The naturalist and traveler, von Humboldt, thirty years before said he thought such a mother lode might turn up in Alaska and others lost no time in pointing out his prediction when at the end of the century gold was getting thicker and grittier. Such a field of nuggets as Eldorado Creek had tumbled along could only mean that the source was near, for the characteristic of the placer mine is that coarse gold and chunks of gold lie near the source, while fine dust, being lighter, is carried farther away. In all the digging, the Klondike had pointed to no mother lode. Mining experts turned to the Yukon creeks of Alaska for the matrix, the source from which fragments had been torn loose and ground to dust, to be carried away by water or other agents and left at random in receptive gravels.

Parties went to prospect the Koyukuk, the Innoko, the Kuskokwim. Explorers followed the Tanana up from its mouth on the Yukon. Others pushed farther into the Copper River area. If the coast diggings at Juneau and island placers found on Alaska's submerged shelf could yield such quantities of gold as had been discovered within the previous twenty years, then who knew what might be found in the seemingly endless ranges to the north of the Gulf of Alaska? What might the great peaks be concealing under their glacial scabs?

Capital for such major undertakings came readily. Many

people found they had belated but great faith in "Seward's Icebox" after all. Before the close of the summer of 1897, representatives from Wall Street houses and other moneyed interests from the East, including the firm of M. Guggenheim and Sons, were numbered among the passengers on the big ships *Portland* and *Humboldt*. Daniel Guggenheim said, "For some time my firm has had expert mining engineers at work in Alaska, and their reports leave no doubt that the Yukon gold fields will prove the richest in the world. My opinion is that as soon as the country has been opened up and shipping facilities furnished, the output of gold will be simply enormous."

Aside from those who had vast sums to spend there were poorer men who hoped to make sudden money by hanging onto the coattails of the former.

Men worked ten-hour days for $2 or $3 in 1897 and thought the wages all right. When they heard that men on the creeks refused a wage of $15 a day just to shovel gravel off the deeper deposits, they found it hard to believe. But labor was not to be had when every man wanted to dig his own gold. Whatever the wages, laborers were not for hire, except on lays or guaranteed shares of the cleanup. In the States men told themselves there was no chance to lose on an investment in a country like that.

Poor men found themselves talking about sums of money they would never have dreamed of discussing before they heard about the Klondike. But they couldn't pick up a paper without getting into five- and six-figure news.

YOUR FORTUNE! Will you sit idle and see such a chance pass you by, and will you be one of the people that said, "I had the opportunity but I missed it?" Better say, "The opportunity was presented to me and I grasped it." We need an additional million dollars within the next sixty days to develop and carry out our gigantic plans. Only $5 per share is the price of the public subscription. No pro-

moters' shares. See **Mr. Gannett** today in Room 9, Flat
Iron Building.

The people were publicly warned by the government, by
experienced investors and bankers, by friends, to beware of
swindlers, and that all was not gold that glittered in the
Klondike. The get-rich-quick fever was far too hot to be chilled
by sermons. There was too much big money in the Klondike.
The little man said, "Those big boys know what they're
doing." The paper said that California's aged bonanza king,
"Lucky Baldwin," was going up in the spring. . . . That five
wealthy citizens of Los Angeles, Denver and San Francisco
were putting money into a $5,000,000 corporation. . . . That
Seattle capitalists were planning to take a huge centrifugal
pump to the creeks to get the gold out with more speed and
less waste. . . . That Jack Carr, the former Circle City mail
carrier, was one of the members of a new company which
would begin ferrying passengers to the mines in June. . . .
That Moran Brothers in Seattle were constructing three
new steamers and a number of tugs and barges for the North
American Transportation and Trading Company. . . . That
a senator was aboard the *Humboldt*. . . . That the new
Cudahy-Healy Yukon Mining Company was capitalized at
$25,000,000. . . .

"Those boys don't throw their money down holes—not unless the holes are right down to bedrock!"

The Pullman Palace Car Company had completed a model
of an electric sleigh for the Great Northern Mining and Transportation Company, which proposed to carry winter passengers to and from the creeks. The vehicle was to be heated
by steam and lit by electricity. The berths would be elegantly
upholstered and the journey undertaken at the breathtaking
speed of sixty miles an hour.

The Klondike Combined Sledge and Boat Company offered

a sectional steel sledge-and-barge which it would put on the market before the second summer of the rush. The invention would be fitted out with sails as well as oars and there would be air chambers for buoyancy, burglar-proof compartments for gold. The best performance was likely to be when the contraption was in the water because then it would float, whereas on land it would have to be dragged over the rocks and through the mud like any other sled, only this one would be clumsier to handle.

Central heating had been thought of, with coal for fuel and a system of pipes which would distribute warmth to every miner's cabin. Other heating schemes, including one to force steam into the frozen gravel of the creeks, were waiting for sufficient capital to enable them to be developed.

But none of the heating inventions could compete with the old standby, the so-called Yukon stove. None of them could match it for practicality. It was light and easy to take on the trail. An open fire was useless in the winter unless one had a few cords of wood to burn at every camp site. As soon as the tent was up the stove was opened, and the long collapsible pipe withdrawn, pushed through an opening in the top of the tent, and the thing was ready to go. Kindling was always carried in the firebox from one stop to the next. The stove was merely half of a sheet-iron barrel divided into two compartments. The fire burned in the front section and the oven was behind it.

Inventions in food appeared. In New York a chemist had prepared a thirty-day supply of food which could be carried in a pocketbook. It consisted of capsules, buttons, and pills. It could be worn as a "dinner belt" if one chose, and it weighed ten pounds. The inventor claimed that one of his sausage-like cylinders would turn out a dozen plates of soup, that a quart of his beef stew was hidden in a capsule, that a loaf of his bread took no more space than a soda wafer. All one needed was water to produce food from these marvels. Each button of coffee made a cupful, each potato lozenge produced a heaping plateful.

Other suggestions for the Klondiker, though not so miraculous, were still novel at the time, and appealed to the traveler as weight-savers. Saccharin was the most popular concentrate, being three hundred times as sweet as sugar, and taking up practically no space at all. A number of common foods were desiccated, or dried, "to one-tenth the weight of the fresh product." Besides raisins and currants, there were dried apples, peaches, pears and figs, potatoes, onions and turnips. Stoned, dried olives were said to be very nutritious and were brought forward as "a recent Californian arrangement." Peanut meal, strawberry tablets, malted nuts, cakes of chocolate-kola, malted milk tablets and even poi were called to the Klondikers' attention.

While much of the investment offered was legitimate and had behind it established and dependable houses, there were also a number of companies selling stock whose only recommendation was the use of one of the magic words, "Klondike," "Alaska," or "Yukon" in their titles. Doubtless some of these unknown companies were as highly principled and reliable as their competitors who had a reputation to defend. However, it was also true that some companies were more imaginative than others, if they were actually not a cut above intrigue, and while overenthusiasm and even misjudgment can be finally forgiven, cunning forever smarted those who had been stung. Some invested in Arctic gophers trained to claw holes in gravel—especially hard, ice-stuck gravel—to relieve the weary miners of toil. Gopher farms were promoted and stocks in them seriously purchased.

Some of the ideas were not dishonest but just impractical. A gray-haired, bearded and wise-looking old gentleman named Thomas Arnold sought capital for his Alaska Carrier-Pigeon Mail Service Company, which intended to photograph messages at the creeks ("reducing them to an area about that of a needle point," said the old gentleman), and deliver them to Juneau within twenty-four hours. There the messages would be speedily enlarged, enclosed in envelopes and mailed in the usual manner. The unconvincing detail which squashed this early airmail was the delay in returning the homing birds to the creeks in time to make the next twenty-four-hour schedule.

Some of the ideas were an inspired kind of lunacy. Like felt-lined cabins that were to be collapsed and shipped, then stood up again upon arrival. Like mosquito-killing germs which, when released at the proper season, would exterminate these pests whose attack was horrible to man and animals alike. In 1898 the city bacteriologist of St. Louis, Dr. Armand Ravol, had collected a particularly lethal set of these germs to dispatch to the Klondike before the next summer's larvae hatched.

Nicolo Tesla had been credited with the invention of the first gold-detecting apparatus to exploit the newly discovered X-ray. To use the machine, two shafts were to be sunk, separated by the thinnest wall of earth, it being, of course, logical to sink the holes in an area where one at least suspected the presence of gold. "With these instruments, the accidental element in mining will be largely eliminated," said Tesla, showing off his invention to reporters. It was necessary to have a man in each shaft, one moving the X-ray machine, and the other the screen, working in unison on opposite sides of the test wall. The man with the screen would readily detect the gold deposits. "In most cases," the inventor disclosed at the end of the demonstration, "the best results will be obtained from small beds of sand or gravel which have been thrown up by the shovel for washing." In other words, after the scientific miner had dug up his ground, and accumulated his gold dump, he could then test it by X-ray instead of by washing it in an old-fashioned pan.

There was nothing in the world like a Klondike bicycle. The one which was conceived by "General" Jacob S. Coxey promised to carry five hundred pounds of freight and one passenger, but not at the same time. Coxey was the leader of the march from Ohio to Washington in 1894, a mass demonstration which intended to take a stand on the steps of the National Capitol and there to propose a new theory of government. The movement became a laughing stock. As for Coxey's bike, it was a folding, rawhide-bound, sectional-collapsing and wheel-flying sort of thing, with devices for carrying extra pounds when necessary, attached to the handle bars and rear forks. The inventor himself explained in the advertisement:

> The plan is to load it with a part
> of the miner's equipment, drag the
> vehicle on four wheels for ten
> miles or so. Then the rider will
> fold up the side wheels and ride it
> back as a bicycle, to bring on the
> rest of the load.

The prospectus seemed to lack a period in the last sentence. It should be placed after the word "up."

Barbers, midwives, clairvoyants and many others sought financial assistance to go up and get into business at the creeks. A city had grown at the mouth of the Klondike River, and it would have need of many services. Book dealers, embalmers, jewelers who specialized in creating nugget stickpins, etc., dressmakers, "lady typewriters," and dentists appealed to sources of assistance for a chance to go north. The barbers' syndicate seemed to have the best chance of success. It was known that the cold-country miners stayed carefully shaven all winter long because a thick, warm, and moist beard would become an ice mask in a few sharp minutes out of doors. A mustache, even, could catch a man's warm breath and snap his lips together, provided the temperature was low enough.

Charlatans made the most of the heyday. They had only to pose as a returned miner and discretely disclose a three-finger brassy poke, or a knuckle of fool's gold, to sell an interest in a nonexistent mine. This hoax was repeated with the greatest success both among the easily deceived and those who considered themselves too canny to speculate in mining stocks. Some of these duped men appeared in the Klondike to record and work their paper claims.

The wags said some southern Californians were promising to start fruit farms in the shade of Mt. McKinley. A detective agency tried to arouse interest in sending one of their men north to hunt criminals known to be at large and who might have gone to the Yukon's turbulent scene to escape the law. Only those criminals with a sizable reward posted for their return would be searched for, and those who had invested in the project would collect their share of the reward.

Business houses looked for agents and drummers.

> WANTED. Go-getter to take line of ear muffs to the Klondike.

> WANTED. One of this city's oldest mercantile firms will choose two qualified young men to open a branch business in Dawson City. Miners need not apply. Only men of high character will be considered regardless of experience.

The government was called upon to make investments in the territory which it had neglected for so long. It was learned that Senator Wilson of Illinois pledged Portus B. Weare of the North American Transportation and Trading Company that he would work for the immediate establishment of an experimental farm in the Yukon Valley. Wilson said he thought Congress would appropriate not less than $15,000 for this purpose.

Meanwhile, Swan Frederickson, a hardy Norseman who had been years in the service of the Hudson's Bay Company, sought $100,000 to start up the Alaska Settlement Company. His scheme was to encourage Norwegian immigration to the southern Yukon region with a view to having the colony become a permanent settlement engaged exclusively in farming, thus providing fresh vegetables, grain, milk, butter, and fresh meat for the busy miners to the north of them.

About this time Congressmen discovered an old bill passed in 1867 to provide funds for the settlement and development of Alaska, and to open an overland route between the United States, Asiatic Russia and Japan. In discussing this bill it was seen that such a road could pass conveniently near the Klondike gold fields. The rumor was that Chicago capital was especially interested in this phase of developing Alaska.

Many colonizing projects were started in various parts of the United States, one of the most ambitious being a plan which began among members of the Beecher Memorial Church of Brooklyn, New York, and which was soon being agitated among a chosen list. The leader of the group explained that, "in getting together a party of colonists we have been careful to enlist only those of good moral character, who, if possible, have a church standing, although the latter is not a necessary requirement. In the establishment of a church, denominational lines will be obliterated, and it will be known as a people's church. If we cannot get a minister to come along with us, one of the party will conduct the services."

According to the printed plans of the group, it would cost each member $1,000 to join, the sum to be used in buying outfits and provisions. Wives were permitted to come along at the same price. "We will also take along horses and mules and guns and ammunition and everything that is likely to be needed." This included portable houses, "which we can erect as soon as we arrive." The colony planned to settle on the United States side of the line at a place not too far from Circle City where it was known there were no forests from which to build houses. But there was something better—"a mountain of gold which was said to be the expected fountain head of the gold fields."

This was not to be a collective group, for each man was to stake his own claim and "reap all the gold nuggets that may be his lot to find."

While some of the colonists were for calling the settlement Greater New York, it was decided to call the second United States city in the Yukon valley, Brooklyn City. Streets would be laid out, and a general store established with New York prices, plus a freight charge, for colonists. Klondike prices would prevail for all others. Besides the church, there would be a school, a newspaper, a post office, the telegraph and a telephone system.

"We feel very confident," said the leader, "that our colony will increase rapidly after we are once started for it will be a great inducement to people, particularly the people of Brooklyn, to go to the gold fields when they know there is a colony to welcome them and that they will not be among strangers." Aside from preparing this place in the wilderness, the announced intention of the group was "to advance Christianity as well as civilization, and at the same time to make money."

In Chicago Miss Lillian Lemmon had got The Woman's Klondike Club going, in preparation for the trip to the mines in the spring of 1898. Her club required only $10,000 capital, which would be supplied by the participating women. The group was almost complete. Said Miss Lemmon, "Miss Florence King is a lawyer. Mademoiselle Napier is planning to buy mines. Miss Mattie Hunter is a shrewd business woman who will find an ample field for her talents in a commercial way. As for myself, I intend to take along a hectograph and get out a small daily paper. Then I will conduct a sort of mining exchange where transfers of claims may be negotiated. We are now looking for a capable woman physician to join us."

A *Tribune* reporter asked Miss Lemmon, "Aren't you going

to look for husbands among the miners who have made the lucky finds?"

"Sir!" she answered, "we are business women, not adventuresses."

Women were welcome in the Klondike. The first thing John J. McKay, returned miner, said upon reaching Seattle was, "Any woman, innocent or full of guile, can become a bride, with a wedding present of thousands of dollars from the happy groom, within thirty minutes after she lands at the creeks. There is but one lady in town who is not married and she has refused every single man in Dawson City. And they have knelt before her with uplifted hands full of gold. She wears short skirts, carries an umbrella, and wants to vote."

In September, 1897, there were less than a hundred women in Dawson City, the metropolis of the creeks, while the men numbered four or five thousand. A public-spirited woman offered to send four thousand spinsters from New England. She was sociologist Charlotte Smith, and she pointed out the great mutual benefits to be received through her plan. She appealed to John Cudahy to help her get the women up to Dawson City. She wrote him, "While these women will offer the comforts and affections of home to lonely miners, it will also be a god-send for them. They are living under such wretched conditions in the mill towns." Cudahy thanked her for the letter and declined the opportunity and the free use of one of his boats.

Matrimonial agencies sent word to the miners. A note was seen on one of Dawson City's posts which called attention to "The Best Matrimonial Paper in the United States," and gave its address in Detroit, the use of which would bring a list of eligible partners among the absent sex. Advertising of this kind was common from coast to coast in the States. The same agency perennially hawked "rich husbands for poor girls" and promised to send, upon receipt of one dime, a long list of the names of wealthy gentlemen, young and old, who were looking for honest young women to marry. People were still sentimentally attached to Cinderella.

While romance had great appeal, the occult impressed many people. The adventures of Jules Verne were no less enthralling than spectral events which took place before one's very eyes. In the West especially, people believed in mediums and sooth-sayers and mountebanks of many kinds. They bought charms, bet on elusive peas under shells, and faithfully consumed the "Indian herb" remedies that were bought in tent shows.

The human mind was certainly a great thing. What wouldn't people think of next? New inventions were coming out all the time. Moving pictures had been made of the Passion Play, and some people had seen the much-talked-about horseless carriage. On July 11, 1897, Professor Salomon Andrée and two companions had soared away in an attempt to cross the North Pole by balloon.

Passenger balloons for a speedy trip to the Klondike suggested themselves to inventors. Frank Corey in Kalamazoo started to build an airship and had requests for more passengers than he could carry north in a year. He said he would take only two men with him on the maiden voyage, but after he had located one or more claims for himself, and got things in running order, he would return and inaugurate a fortnightly schedule of Yukon flights.

Don Carlos Stevens, another balloonist, was backed with $150,000 by the Jacobs Transportation Company of Seattle. He planned to take his ship, when he built it, to Tisklo Bay by rail, and to make the ascension from there. Tisklo Bay was near Juneau and but an estimated two days' journey over the clouds to Dawson City. Said Stevens, "When I get to Tisklo I'll hang out my sign, *All Aboard for Klondike,* and when I've got my passengers I'll cut the rope and away we'll go." He did not say how many passengers he would take up. It was a disappointment to many that no airships ever left the ground.

5

UNEASY LIES THE HEAD

IN WASHINGTON President McKinley met with the Cabinet to discuss sending troops to the Klondike, to some point near Circle City. Before the end of July Secretary of War Alger was making preparations for the military expedition which was to number fifty picked men under the command of Captain P. H. Ray. Those who questioned the President's authority to order such an expedition without the sanction of Congress were informed that the Executive branch of the government had such power in a case of emergency and that the immediate protection of American citizens in the Klondike was considered to be most critical.

There were many who questioned the wisdom of the expedition, pointing out the embarrassment that was likely to follow with the certain desertion of any number of the men when they reached the Klondike. The comment was that the soldiers would all be digging gold the morning after they arrived. Pondering on this the President advised Alger to make an exceptionally careful selection of the men. It was finally decided to send Captain Ray and Lieutenant Wilds P. Richardson to the Klondike to look things over before the fifty arrived. Ray and Richardson were to play a crucial role in mitigating the hardships of the starvation winter.

In Ottawa the ministers of the Dominion Government were becoming uneasy. Millions of dollars' worth of Canadian gold was being shoveled out of the country and emptied into the coffers of the United States mint, while the Minister of Finance was not putting by a penny for the Crown. And, as if the Klondike strike was not dilemma enough, reports were being circulated that the entire coastwise strip of southeastern Alaska was auriferous—with the boundary line between Alaska and Canada yet to be settled. Her Majesty's government was urged to press the United States for an immediate settlement of the line before another Klondike opened up. With the coast swarming with gold hunters, and both Great Britain and the United States contesting the rights of each other to govern the region, the Canadians pointed out that cool-headed negotiations would then be all but impossible.

As things developed, it was 1903 before President Roosevelt pushed a boundary agreement through a so-called impartial tribunal of peers. Upon hearing the names of two of the three United States members of the commission, the Canadians refused to co-operate, saying that these members were openly in favor of their country's claims and were unqualified as arbitrators pledged to heed both sides of the question. Their objections did not stop the meeting which went through on schedule, closing the subject with four votes in favor of the boundary as put forward by the United States. The Canadians could never forgive Lord Alverstone for siding with the Americans.

At the time of the rush the boundary question had not come within sight of agreement. Ever since the purchase of Alaska in 1867 the obstacles blocking the settlement had remained precisely the same. In the first place, the meaning of "coast" was different for each country. The Canadians interpreted the coast as following the general direction of the shore, while to the Americans coast was coast, wherever it rimmed the edge of Alaska, no matter how far inland it followed the bays, inlets and channels. This variance in interpretation provoked an especially argumentative point as to Lynn Canal, which had a hundred-mile reach into the interior and three so-called ports. A second attack was directed at Portland Channel. Did the channel run north or south of four islands that lay some ten or fifteen miles northwest of British Columbia's Port Simpson? Where did the channel actually begin?

In the third place, according to an Anglo-Russian treaty of 1825, the boundary was defined at the crests of the mountains which lay parallel to the coast, at no point removed from the coast more than ten marine leagues, or about thirty-five miles. Canadians contended that no such parallel mountain chains existed in this region. With that the Americans wanted to close the subject with a thirty-five-mile coastal rim, pushing the Alaska boundary back that many miles from the actual shore. In order to strengthen this claim the United States prepared to establish a boundary post at Lake Bennett, thirty-five miles inland from the head of Lynn Canal.

However, Clifford Sifton, the Canadian Minister of the Interior, was privately informed of the plan and immediately sent Major Perry and Colonel Steele with forty Mounted Police constables to take possession of the top of Chilkoot Pass. The pass was at the first summit of the first mountain encountered inland from the head of the canal. The arrival of Perry and his party, with sufficient provisions to last them through the winter, and another year if need be, was a stratagem which Sifton said later saved the Dominion twenty years of negotiations. He said he believed it would have taken that long to oust the Americans once they had gained a foot-hold at Bennett. In this case possession was ten points of the law. A year passed before the Americans reluctantly conceded the boundary point at the top of Chilkoot.

Aside from these issues, other problems added to the thirty-six-year stalemate over the boundary. Congress would not vote the money to pay for the ten-year surveying project outlined by the Army Engineer Corps, the agency which would have to do the work. The Army estimated that it would require nine years in the field and one more in the office to complete the survey and that it would cost $1,500,000. Later, a $500,000 bill to pay for a joint survey lasting only four years was also shuffled out of the way. In the perpetual summer daylight no surveying could be done. However, during the winter, when the stars were visible, it was long enough and clear enough, but the temperatures were too extreme to permit the engineers to work long out of doors. There were, then, out of the whole year, but a few weeks of surveying weather. The Dominion surveyor, William Ogilvie, had been at the job for years.

From time to time meetings were called, surveys were discussed and projected, even the personnel for these was selected, but nothing came of all this. A three-cornered correspondence went on interminably between London, Ottawa, and Washington. Occasionally some incident occurred to stir up the dispute which otherwise might have disappeared out of periodic indifference.

In the pursuit of the possession of what is now southeastern Alaska, both countries remained adamant in their positions and thoroughly uncompromising. In 1887, at the conclusion of Lieutenant Frederick Schwatka's Yukon reconnaissance voyage by raft, which was the first exploration of the river from its source to its mouth, the Canadians protested to Washington, taking exception to Schwatka's implication that Chilkoot Pass, or Perrier Pass as he called it, was within United States territory. Moreover, they called attention to the fact that he had not observed the courtesy of applying for permission to enter Canadian territory, although, as they rather petulantly added, it was unlikely that a scientific expedition such as his would have been rejected.

In 1888 the complaint was lodged in Washington which accused the United States of attempting to exercise jurisdiction over White Pass. This was the year the British and Americans met to discuss the Alaskan seals and the United States was on the carpet for having captured a large number of British sealers and their cargoes. During the arguments over what was and what was not legal pelagic sealing, the British once more officially announced their claim to the territory at the head of Lynn Canal. The claim was not disputed. Perhaps it was merely disregarded for the time being. The United States Customs Regulations continued to prohibit the landing of British vessels anywhere along the Canal and the British did not try to get in. Juneau was designated as the legal port of entry for foreign vessels in the vicinity.

Before the Klondike rush, Juneau was as good a port as any but after 1897 it was a hundred miles south of the passes. Even then the Canadians obeyed the regulations. As Minister of the Interior Sifton said, they hoped to gain more by maintaining friendly relations with their neighbor than by having what he called "a serious collision" from which retreat might be disastrous, as far as getting the boundary settled. Premier Sir Wilfrid Laurier was not so patient. He said outright that the Canadians had a grasping neighbor and implied they had better watch out for their interests.

At the first signs of the rush in 1897 the United States claimed the ports of Dyea and Skagway. Great Britain rejected the Skagway claim on the grounds of her own previously made assertions, and also that of Dyea because both towns were merely points of access to the Klondike gold fields. She refused to consider them independently from the Klondike, which was unquestionably within the North-West Territory of Canada. However, there were far more Americans in Dyea and Skagway than there were Canadians and the communities became "American" in spite of the Crown's opinion to the contrary. The Mounted Police held onto the mountain tops behind the beaches.

On July 22, 1897, five days after the arrival in Seattle of the *Portland*'s "ton of gold," the Commissioner of Customs in Ottawa wired the Treasury Department of the United States as follows:

MAY GOODS PASS FROM JUNEAU, ALASKA, TO YUKON FRONTIER WITHOUT PAYMENT CUSTOMS IF PARTIES PAY FOR UNITED STATES OFFICERS ACCOMPANYING GOODS? PLEASE WIRE REPLY AND INSTRUCT YOUR OFFICES AT JUNEAU.

The telegram was answered the same day:

ARRANGEMENT SUGGESTED IN YOUR TELEGRAM UNDER CONSIDERATION, WILL ADVISE YOU TOMORROW. WOULD IT FACILITATE MATTERS TO MAKE DYEA A SUB-PORT OF ENTRY?

The Canadians replied:

IT WOULD FACILITATE MATTERS TO MAKE DYEA A SUB-PORT OF ENTRY PENDING SETTLEMENT OF BOUNDARY QUESTION. IF AGREED TO, PLEASE WIRE INSTRUCTIONS TO ALLOW BRITISH STEAMERS FROM CANADIAN PORTS TO LAND AND RECEIVE PASSENGERS AND GOODS AT DYEA.

On the twenty-third the Canadians were advised that Dyea had been made a sub-port of entry. In Seattle and San Francisco the local merchants preparing for a landslide business in outfits to the miners howled in the trap. The coast newspapers came out with headlines, and editors blamed the Alaska Commercial Company, the seals and weak government officials for delivering them to their enemies, the merchants of Victoria and Vancouver, B. C.

The San Francisco *Call* said: "THERE IS RIGHTEOUS INDIGNATION IN THIS COUNTRY TODAY OVER THE DISCLOSURE THAT DYEA HAS BEEN MADE A SUB-PORT OF ENTRY FOR CANADIAN VESSELS. THE ACTION WAS HASTILY COMPLETED AT THE REQUEST OF CANADA, MADE ONLY A FEW DAYS AGO. NO EXCUSE CAN BE MADE THAT WILL JUSTIFY THIS ACTION ON THE PART OF OUR GOVERNMENT. . . ."

Outraged mercantile and grocery firms set up a hullabaloo that was heard in Washington. Pacific Coast businessmen demanded their "rights as American citizens," which they identified with the privilege of monopolizing the sale of beans and gumboots. It so happened that the hucksters of Chicago, Kansas City, and elsewhere were not involved in the competition so that it could be directed against foreign tradesmen exclusively and the newspapers could blubber that "John Bull was grappling for the Yukon trade but that the merchants of Seattle would war for their own."

Petitions were signed in San Francisco to demand that the United States close the port of Dyea to all foreign ships. Now and then a voice was heard to close the port of Juneau as well.

In Washington Senator Perkins called in the reporters. He told them, "You can blame the seals. The British are willing to meet with us again to negotiate further concerning certain unsettled aspects of the sealing question." It was plain that Dyea had been exchanged for good will. It was no secret that the country still hoped to keep the British out of the Bering Sea fisheries, that the subject of seals was a major one in Washington, and that of outfitting the Klondike miners was not. Senator Perkins and others were not aware of the excessive slaughter which had occurred and that the collapse of the sealing industry was at hand. New London, Connecticut, was still manufacturing thousands of the six-foot clubs which were used to beat the animals to death.

Seattle called a mass meeting of its merchants in order to plan a concentrated program of defense against Canadian greengrocers and saddlers.

The Canadians urged their government to exclude the Americans from the Klondike and be done with it. The Alien Labour Law was re-examined, but no reasonable application of it could be made. The law provided only for the exclusion of undesirables, and the Ministers knew that it would be going too far to label the prospectors as such. They decided instead to appoint a commissioner for the new Klondike and to send with him a carefully selected group to serve as judges, registrar, mine inspectors and so on. With them would go a detachment of eighty Mounted Police.

A per diem royalty was considered. In the United States the newspapers got wind of this and printed stories about a $50 daily royalty to be collected from every American in the Klondike with a pick in his hand. The talk of keeping the gold in Canada for the Canadians had made the ink sputter out on the copy desks. A news story in San Francisco with an Ottawa date line said that protests had been pouring in from the United States denouncing the royalty but had been disregarded pending a report by the Dominion's gold commissioner as to the practicality of such a levy.

The matter of a daily royalty was eventually dismissed and in its stead a registration fee was required in the guise of a Free Miner's Certificate costing $15 and which was renewable at $100 a year. Also, a general tax was levied upon aliens owning claims in the Yukon, in the amount of 10 per cent on yields up to $500 a month, and 20 per cent on mines producing sums over that figure. And this was not street-corner talk. The Canadian Government published its intentions where all could read them. The Americans were stunned.

In Victoria, British Columbia's capital, where it was learned that the Americans must go for their certificates, the Board of Trade posted the following placard:

NOTICE TO ALL KLONDIKERS

The Yukon fields are in Canada.
Goods purchased elsewhere than in
Canada are subject to a customs
duty upon entering the Yukon. A
strong force of Customs Officers
and Mounted Police is stationed
at the passes. Customs certificates of purchases made in Canada
will prevent a delay by either

Canadian or United States officials. Victoria, B. C., is the
best place to outfit and sail
from. All steamers will call
at Victoria.

With the placard was posted the list of goods on which the
new customs duty would be leveled. It was a long list and
the duty imposed was approximately an over-all average of
25 per cent on nearly everything the miners were bringing
into the country. It was levied upon all of their provisions,
wearing apparel, hardware, tools, and mining equipment, as
well as upon their dogs and horses.

Examples were: Sugar taxed at $1 a pound; baking powder
at 6 cents a pound; butter at 4 cents; lard at 2 cents. Bacon
and all tinned meats drew 25 per cent. Hardware was taxed
at from 30 to 35 per cent per item. Ammunition took a 30
per cent toll and firearms 20 per cent. Maps and charts were
taxed 20 per cent. Wool blankets were subject not only to
a 25 per cent tax but to a charge of 5 cents a pound weight
as well. Candles were taxed at 28 per cent; edge tools at 35
per cent; rubber boots and footwear of all kinds at 25 per
cent. Socks called for 25 per cent, plus 10 cents a dozen pairs.
Union suits, sweaters, and all knit goods required a payment
of 35 per cent. All grains, flours or meals cost 20 per cent.
Tobacco was listed at 12½ per cent, plus 42 cents a pound
weight, while pipes took 35 per cent, and cigars and cigarettes
26 per cent, plus two dollars a pound weight. Dogs and horses
cost their owners 20 per cent. The very bags and canvas sacks
in which the gear was wrapped were subject to a 20 per cent
tax. All of these percentages were levied upon the new-goods
cost of the items.

Under such headlines as CANADA TIGHTENS THE CINCH, San
Franciscans read about the tax in reports filled with the words
"knavery," "extortion," "envy," "injustice," and "our covet-
ous neighbors." The newspapers called attention to possible

reprisals. "Retaliation is now in order, following the recent exactions put upon Americans in the Klondike," cried some. "What are the means by which the Canadians can be called down off their high horse?" asked others. It was said that Secretary of the Treasury Gage favored a policy that would cause the Dominion to regret its hasty demands. The Chicago *Tribune* said, "If Congress were in session there is little doubt that legislation proposing various forms of reprisals on Canada and the Canadians for the Klondike exactions would be introduced at once in both the Senate and the House."

Two reprisals suggested were that the United States revoke the privilege extended to Canadian railroads to transport goods in bond across the States, and that British subjects owning property in the United States be penalized in some way under the Alien Land Act. People were told that Canadians were permitted to dig without cost on the American side of the boundary. They answered, "The U.S.A'll soon put a stop to that!" Actually, United States mining laws required citizenship of locators but in the far north, if this was known, nobody paid any attention to it.

At the time a thousand chests of tea were discovered to be crossing the United States bound for the Canadian border, and some citizens proposed stopping the train and demanding duty to the last leaf.

Upon second thought some prospectors heading for the Klondike decided that the tax was too preposterous to be true. "They're just trying to scare us out of the country, that's all," they said, and went on packing slabs of bacon and sacks of flour into what was to be a future tent.

In Ottawa they amended the mining laws so that the length of the Klondike creek claims were cut from 500 feet to 100 feet, and every alternate claim was reserved for the Crown. This also was too unreasonable a move for most Americans to take seriously. They were glad to see the Free Miner's Certificate reduced to $10, with a $15 annual renewal instead of the $100 which the Canadians first said they wanted. The Americans guessed the Canadians would come down off their high horse by themselves.

The Treasury Department received another telegram from the Customs Department at Ottawa. The message was:

FREIGHT AND PASSENGERS FOR YUKON ARE GOING IN BY WHITE PASS AND THE LANDING IS AT SKAGWAY BAY THREE MILES SOUTH OF DYEA. AMERICAN VESSELS DEPOSIT FREIGHT AND PASSENGERS AT THE BAY BUT PRIVILEGE REFUSED TO CANADIAN VESSELS. CUSTOMS OFFICER CAN AS CONVENIENTLY PASS ENTRIES AT SKAGWAY AS AT DYEA. WILL YOU PLEASE INSTRUCT OFFICIALS BY WIRE TO EXTEND PRIVILEGE OF LANDING AT SKAGWAY BAY TO CANADIAN VESSELS AS CONCEDED TO AMERICAN VESSELS?

On the following day a reply was received to the effect that Canadian privileges at the port of Dyea had been extended to include Skagway, and that the deputy collector in charge there had been instructed accordingly. The Canadians were still obliged to pay for the services of a customs officer to escort their goods from the canal to the Yukon boundary posts on the mountain tops, as had been agreed upon in the telegrams exchanged the previous month. The fee for this service was $6 a day.

By March, after extensive negotiations, the escort fee was removed and Canadian goods were thereafter permitted to cross United States territory without fee or duty of any kind.

6

KLONDIKE OR BUST!

THE EARLIEST known routes to the Yukon were those cut out of the wilderness by the Hudson's Bay men coming West from the Mackenzie River, reaching in on the Liard and the Porcupine. The first Yukon post was Fort Macpherson on the Peel River in the Arctic, near the Peel's confluence with the Mackenzie. From Macpherson the traders crossed the mountains in 1846 to La Pierre's House on the Rat River, a tributary of the Porcupine, and followed the latter river to its mouth at the Great Bend, where Fort Yukon was built in 1847.

Meanwhile, the Dease, Frances, and Pelly rivers were discovered by other company men coming in on the Liard. Posts were established on these rivers, the last being Fort Selkirk at the Pelly's mouth, built in 1848. It was two years before the traders received supplies or communications from headquarters. In 1852 the post was abandoned after an Indian attack. Until the seventies, then, the only route to the Yukon was the Mackenzie–Fort Macpherson–Fort Yukon trail. In the early eighties the prospectors were coming in from Lynn Canal and already the Alaskan traders were on the lower Yukon, following it in from the sea.

It was not until the Forty-Mile strike in 1886 that the two

trading companies, the Alaska Commercial and the North American Transportation and Trading Company, found it profitable to operate four sternwheelers between them. These were 300-ton burden vessels. After Circle City was founded in 1893 five vessels paddled the river all summer long. In 1897, when the sudden swarm of boats bound for the Klondike came scurrying up the river, they frightened the tribes of Innuits and Malemuts into their huts. The next summer there were thirty-four steamers on regular runs between St. Michael and Dawson City, and nobody knows how many privately owned small craft, how many homemade barges, how many "wildcats."

By 1898 the United States Government had begun to exert some authority over the fly-by-night outfits which were carrying people into the country wholly unprovisioned. The first gold hunters, who were ignorant of the conditions awaiting them in the Klondike, believed that they could buy from the trading companies all the food necessary once they reached pay dirt and panned out a day's gold. In order to carry as many passengers as they could, it was an advantage to the boatowners to omit the enormous amount of freight which should have accompanied each person traveling to the gold fields.

The "starvation winter" of 1897 had taught the United States a lesson. Between the strain it had been under in trying to keep five thousand Americans from perishing at Dawson City, and the failure of the expedition which it organized for their relief, the Army felt no compunctions in issuing a stern warning to all shipmasters engaged in the North Alaska trade. St. Michael's Island, and the territory and seas surrounding it for one hundred miles in every direction, became a military reservation, under the command of Lieutenant W. P. Richardson, and the War Department announced that all persons would be prevented from landing anywhere on it unless they were able to give "abundant and satisfactory" proof of their ability to provide for themselves for a year. As the Major General put it: "The United States Government has been the chief financial sufferer through the actions of the companies in carrying prospective miners to Alaskan ports who were not fitted out for a stay in the country. The government has had to care for them when misfortune overtook them and they became dependent on public bounty for existence. A determination has been reached to put an instant stop to this."

That summer of 1898 over 50,000 people were carried up the river. Passage to Dawson City was included in the fare from Seattle or San Francisco. Ocean liners brought the passengers the first 2,750 or 3,575 respective miles of the voyage between these cities and St. Michael, and there they were met by the river boats and taken the 1,500 remaining miles to Dawson. The fare had always been $150 but now the fast boats sold their tickets for $1,000 and even this sum could be often jacked up by scalpers who resold the fares for premiums.

The high cost of the river trip kept many from enjoying it, while others who could pay the price were in too great a hurry to spend six weeks getting in to the creeks. They looked for a shorter, if harder route, taking one of the prospectors' trails from Lynn Canal. Government and company men whose heels were not burning them, women with children and most of the theatrical troupes went in by way of the Yukon River. A passenger list would be likely to include the representatives of banks and syndicates going up to buy mining claims, various United States and Canadian officials entering a term of duty, nuns, card dealers, saloonmen, newsmen, a school teacher, a minister's wife, dance hall girls, a few actresses. The boat trip was for those unable to cope with the hardships of the trail and was advertised as "elegant."

The John Ladue Gold Mining and Development Company announced in its brochure: "Our vessels are lighted by electricity, have elegant tables and accommodations, ladies' boudoirs, porcelain bathtubs, and steam heat." The North American Transportation and Trading Company put on a new boat, the *Cleveland,* and urged all comers to take either it or the *Portland.* Their advertisement began: "Avoid the pass! It is fraught with dangers!"

Nevertheless it was "over the pass to Klondike" for many. Too many men had sold all they owned in order to make the trip, if they had not borrowed or begged a grubstake. They had no money for fancies, not even for a cut-rate voyage on one of the less reliable ships that offered to get them there for $195 plus only five cents a pound for freight. The minimum fare to the head of Lynn Canal was $75, and that was about all most men could spend in addition to the cost of their outfit. It was nearly 600 miles to the creeks from either Dyea or Skagway, and although every man knew that these were difficult miles, they cost him nothing from his purse and they could be covered in perhaps a month if one were traveling light, and lucky.

There were other trails besides the two from Lynn Canal. At least 7,000 persons took the Stikine River in from Wrangell. They went 140 miles up the river to a point called Telegraph City, so named because the telegraph company had planned to cross the Stikine there on its way to Russian America. The camp had been abandoned since the sixties, but from its site a portage went over the mountain humps to the head of Lake Teslin, and from there it was a final 700 miles by raft to Dawson. Leaving the lake, which was 100 miles long, one continued on the Hootalinqua River to the Lewes River, one of the early names for an arm of the upper Yukon River, and after many perils approached the mouth of the Klondike and Dawson City. There was likelihood here of passing Dawson because of the turbulent eddy caused by the incoming river. Many a raft went on by to be laboriously poled back up the river, if they were not left behind on some quieter bank while the men walked back with the gear.

Another trail started at Juneau, where the Taku River took one back to the Nahkeenah, 70 miles to the latter's source, and then across country another 70 miles to Lake Teslin, and so down to Dawson. On the Taku, as on the Stikine, a flat-bottomed boat could be used, if the travelers had one, while on the Nahkeenah a canoe was necessary. Lieutenant Schwatka's widow was an enthusiastic plugger for the Taku Pass, which she revealed her husband had recommended ten years before as a pack train line to the interior. An Eastern syndicate began a survey for a railroad from Taku River to Lake Teslin.

Jack Dalton's trail, used to march animals down to Selkirk, was known to be an easy one. It started behind Pyramid Harbor, followed the Chilcat River a circuitous 40 miles or so to a 3,000-foot divide. After crossing this, another watershed was climbed 20 miles farther on, and then the country rolled gently down through grassy valleys all the way to the banks of the Lewes River. A raft could be built below Five Finger Rapids, which left all the hazards of the river behind, and from there it was scarcely a two days' trip on the swift current to Dawson. While the Dalton trail was tempting, it was relatively unused because, as the men said, "There's too much walking." Three hundred and fifty miles of it.

There was still another route from the coast, a route which started at Valdez glacier, one which few would take although on the map it looked like a direct trail to Dawson. On the shores of the Gulf of Alaska, where the Copper River comes down and around Prince William Sound, there had been mining camps since the early nineties, but the country had not been penetrated any distance beyond the camps because of the unfriendliness of the natives. A story told about nine Russians who had insisted upon going inland in the year 1831. Evidence gained later, although conflicting in detail and related by other Indians, still left no doubt that the men had been massacred on the second day of their journey. W. H. Dall, who from 1866 to 1868 directed the telegraph company's Yukon explorations on the lower river, was well informed about the savages of the interior and the remarks entered in his journal were not encouraging to travelers.

However, by the time the miners had camps up the Copper River as far as the Chitina basin it looked like Klondike prospectors could get across the mountains to White River and be practically in Dawson. Some tried it. The venturers were not only open to constant attack but they had to make their own trail over the glaciers and through the bleak canyons. A few men made it, arriving in Dawson at the point of death from hunger and hardship.

Whether the trails were desperate or easy, long or short, none but the trails from Lynn Canal were popular. If it wasn't the Indians, or the lack of a flat-bottomed boat or canoe, it was a justifiable hesitation on the part of tenderfeet to start over unknown country alone. The gold hunters wanted company, they wanted to make the great adventure together, both for protection and because there is something about the gregariousness of a stampede which is irresistible. They crowded onto Chilkoot Pass and White Pass, following each other in single file, horse to horse, sled to sled, raft to raft. From the beaches into the mountains and down the lakes and rivers, they stuck together in a 575-mile chain of hope, misery, and death.

Inasmuch as the Hudson's Bay Company had long since left the Yukon valley, all the trails which led to the Klondike now started from United States territory. The Dominion Government was anxious to find an all-Canadian route for Canadians, one which would encourage countrymen to buy their goods at home and to proceed to the mines without the embarrassment of paying a tax or fee to the United States Government and without having to step foot on foreign soil.

Several routes were suggested to Minister of the Interior Sifton, whose job it was to plan the all-Canadian route. An attempt was made to relocate some of the old Hudson's Bay Company trails. Sifton sent a party of Mounted Police into British Columbia to search for a trail leading to Telegraph City, where a wagon road could be built over the portage to Lake Teslin. Later a railroad could replace the wagon road, and steamers would meet the passengers at Lake Teslin and take them speedily to Dawson.

The proposed railroad turned into a major political battle. The government offered the company building the road 25,000 acres of land for each mile of road constructed. It was this that set off the opposition. Who was giving this wealth away to contractors? Who was parceling out the natural resources of the country to certain individuals? Was there a sinister explanation for such favoritism? The anti-railroaders looked everywhere for one while the pro-railroaders shouted in Parliament and press that not more than 35,000 acres in the whole grant could possibly be gold-bearing. But in 1897 and 1898 Canadians were certain the whole Yukon was a bed of gold. One member of the clique which was fighting Sifton said, "It is impossible to estimate the value of this tremendous area. One single gulch might bring in millions of dollars."

The issue and the oratory stirred the Dominion for a year. Sifton himself made a four-hour speech to the House. But the railroad was never built. The Canadians were saved from "the recklessness of an ignorant administration" and the region remained a wilderness with its natural resources intact —and quite barren of gold, as time eventually proved.

While the government was fighting over the railroad to Teslin, another combine of companies was planning a rail and boat route west all the way from Hudson Bay, that would terminate at long last in Dawson, getting around by way of the Mackenzie River. The engineer and general manager of this project stated that next to the founding of the Canadian

Pacific Railway in 1881 this overland and river route was the most important pioneering proposition ever called to the attention of the people of Canada. This route was not established either.

However, a trail to the Klondike by way of the Mackenzie River was being suggested from all sides as the most feasible and direct route. A railroad surveyor named Higgins urged Canadians to adopt the "backdoor route," as it was soon called, and in support of its practicality he spoke out at length.

"The jumping-off place," said he, "is Edmonton, Alberta, which is 1,772 miles from Chicago by rail. A stage line runs from there to Athabasca Landing on the river of that name, and from there you can take a canoe and go down with the current to Athabasca Lake. Then on into Great Slave Lake, through which the Mackenzie River runs and by which you reach the Arctic Ocean. When the mouth of the Mackenzie is reached the Peel River can be taken south to the Rocky Mountains, which are crossed by trail. When across the range, the Stewart River opens the way to the nearby Klondike regions."

This swift-sounding description of the trail was both misleading and geographically unrealistic. One did not cover 3,500 miles so easily. It was 96 miles to the Landing, over a "road" which none could boast of. It was 550 miles on the river to the first lake, and 400 more to the second, after which it was 1,450 miles on the Mackenzie River. On his voyage of discovery Mackenzie made as many as 100 miles a day during part of the time, with the canoemen working 24 hours a day, resting only every two hours for five or ten minutes, just time enough to refill their pipes. Morning and night each man was given a dram of spirits, "high wines" as Mackenzie called them. The Indians had grumbled and lagged on this schedule although the hardened voyageurs had gone through with it, getting the explorer back to Great Slave Lake from the Arctic in a roundtrip record of 102 days.

The city man on his first journey to the Arctic Ocean would probably jog along at a pace considerably slackened from this. From the mouth of the Peel River one did not cover the Rocky Mountains very quickly, especially since the old Hudson's Bay portage trail had disappeared from sight. If one did cross the mountains in the right direction it was not the Stewart one encountered but the Porcupine. It was a good ten days' trip on this river when the company men made their regular trips to Fort Yukon. From Fort Yukon it was 300 miles to Dawson on the Yukon River, which at the bend was seven miles wide, a thrashing and powerful course. A canoe was not likely to make it, for coming from Fort Yukon this last stretch was against the current.

Nevertheless the Mackenzie route was publicized far and near, across Dominion and Empire. People were informed: "The gold seeker who takes the backdoor route to Klondike will travel through a country which has been placed in song and story by those who sang and wrote of the deeds done by trappers, voyageurs and other adventurers." One traveled this route in the wake of Alexander Mackenzie himself, re-enacted history, so to speak, as he journeyed down the great river which was so wide at certain places that Mackenzie for a time thought he was on the Pacific Ocean.

Remembering that this had been the route of the fur traders, some said that enough hides and furs might be taken en route to pay all the expenses of the excursion. One of the advantages of the Mackenzie trip was its economy. A pamphlet informed prospectors that canoes could be picked up cheaply from the Indians and that a party of three could provide itself with provisions for the entire trip for the sum of $35 for all. "Pork, tea, flour, and baking powder will suffice." On the other hand, pemmican was ideal for the trip. Pemmican was made from game meat and sugar, with maybe a few raisins thrown in, mixed with lard and stuffed into a hide bag, with the hair side in. Batches of 10 pounds each were recommended. The stuff would keep for months in a cold climate. To use it, as much was dug out as needed, and fried in its own fat.

Higgins discouraged pemmican. On a map, he had read the names of several Hudson's Bay Company forts, almost all of which were obsolete however, and mistakingly concluded that there were trading ports located conveniently all the way up the Mackenzie River. In that case, he pointed out, prospectors could travel light for they would have to carry only enough food to last them from one post to the next. He didn't mention the stock of provisions, clothing, boatbuilding materials, and mining equipment which a prospector in the Yukon might find handy. He never mentioned gold pans, or a pick and shovel.

Another spokesman for the backdoor route said that the distance from Edmonton to Fort Macpherson could be covered in sixty days or less, but added that if the Peel River should be frozen, dog sleds would be necessary to take the men on from there to Dawson. "Indians" would furnish the dogs and the sleds. "Guides are unnecessary; the route is so clearly defined."

So little was known about the regions near the Arctic Circle that no one refuted these statements. Monsignor Isidore Clut, O.M.I., the bishop of the territories of Athabasca and Mackenzie, was asked for a statement. He was known for a lifetime of work among the Athabascan Indians but he had never been to Dawson, although in 1872 he had gone by boat from San Francisco to Fort Yukon, quite a journey for the time. Travelers sought his word on the subject. "In my opinion," said he, "this route is by far the safest and most practical way to Klondike. It may take longer, but the difficulties which the prospector faces in going in by way of Fort Macpherson will be certainly very much less than those he will meet over the passes on the Coast."

When it came to eating, a Mr. Curran of Chicago saw no

reason why miners could not live on the same rations which were provided the Mounted Police. Upon Mr. Curran's authority, it was learned that each policeman was given a pound of flour and a pound of bacon a day, which, he said, "sustains the life of those in the Government service and often sends them back living pictures of health to the friends who saw them leave their Eastern homes frail and delicate." Mr. Curran had no use at all for food in tins. "Tinned goods are out of place in the traveler's outfit," he said, "for the reason that they take up room and are not valuable as food." He listed the fish and wild fowl which he intended should hook his line and fall to his rifle when he made the trip himself in the coming spring.

It was true that the Hudson's Bay posts had shipped everything from walrus tusks to swanskins and goose quills, along with pelts of endless variety, but it was not likely that wild turkey and ptarmigan would be roaming the Arctic banks of the Mackenzie River. Nor herds of caribou. "The friendly Indians" were nomadic. However, as many as 30,000 of them had been tributary to a trading post at times when there was trading to be done. Therefore it was unlikely that Klondikers would be able to find an Indian to buy a canoe. Even if they had, it would have been wise to take the Indian along since a birch-bark canoe is not the steadiest craft in the world. Not even with just a little kit of bacon and flour to steady between one's knees.

The Mackenzie was a dreary desolate river, with scarcely a habitation on it, Indian or otherwise, and its shores, which even in midsummer were crusted with ice, had nothing to offer in the way of subsistence, not even wild duck eggs such as were found by thousands in the reeds of the lower Yukon.

The artist, A. H. H. Heming of Montreal, a popular figure of the time and known as an outdoorsman, offered his opinion of the route. "All one needs is a good constitution, and some experience in boating and camping, and $150." Heming knew the river but he had not crossed the country to the Yukon.

An alternative all-Canadian route was sometimes mentioned. This one also began at Edmonton and went north as far as Lake Athabasca, where the Peace River comes in. The Peace was followed to its source, where the trail broke into "a ramification of routes," one of which was the Liard River. If and when the Liard was found, it was up the Liard and down the Dease to Telegraph City, the portage to Lake Teslin, the raft to Dawson. If going from the lake to Dawson was easy, the difficulties of getting to the lake were tremendous, and not many had the courage for it. The circulars advertising the Mackenzie were more enticing. "Down grade all the way, your canoe carried by the current, or your sails blown along by the favorable winds, only two big portages to cross, an abundance of fish and wild fowl along the way. . . ." The people who got off at Edmonton were unrealistic too.

Punishing as this route was, and certainly it was enough to try the patriotism of the most loyal subject of the Crown, 2,000 persons were known to have started out upon it. But the flesh was weaker than the spirit and many turned back. Hundreds more lost their lives. At the end of the summer of 1898 not more than five men could be found in Dawson who had come in by the Mackenzie River, and these had lost their outfits and arrived starving and at the point of collapse. At the end of the next summer the names of 30 persons were on a report which credited them with having taken this all-Canadian route from Edmonton to Dawson. Some of the 30 had started out in 1897.

7

SKAGWAY AND DYEA

WHILE THE easiest route to the creeks was by way of St. Michael and the Yukon River, it was much quicker to get there by way of the Lynn Canal and the overland trail. The beach at the beginning of the Chilkoot trail was first known as Ty-ah or Dy-ah. (The gold miners always spelled it "Dyea.") Four miles down the beach, at a place where a retired sea captain had homesteaded, and which the Indians still called Skag-wah, "place of the winds," there was another beach. This second camp grew faster. In August there were 15,000 people in it and they called the place Skagway.

The mining season was short. For only four months of the year, from June through September, when the creeks were running and the sun was beating down twenty hours a day, did the ground soften up enough to dig into and readily allow the miner to extract the pay dirt and wash it for gold. On the other hand, during the winter the only work done on the claims was the setting of long-burning bonfires which thawed the gravel a few inches at a time and made it possible to pick out the dirt in crumbs and set it aside for the summer cleanup. Cleanup referred to the various washing operations which were done with water. There was, of course, no water during the winter except that which was melted from icicles.

In order to reach the creeks before June it was necessary to start into the country not later than March. In winter it took thirty days by dog sled to go from Dyea to Dawson, but no freight could be carried on such a trip and none but a thoroughly experienced driver would attempt it. The Klondiker was in a hurry and was temperamentally a man to take his chances against great odds, but he was no Peary and he knew it. Yet he wanted to get over the passes while the trail was still crisp with the dry light snow which covers the ground in regions of intense cold and over which he could make good time with a sled. In summer the melting snow floods the creeks and softens the banks. It did not take long for boots and hooves to churn the trail into glue. But in spring, the lakes, and the rivers which link them, are frozen over, offering slick surfaces which can be crossed as quickly as a dog can run. With a chance to use his sleds for the first two weeks, a man could get as far as the third lake before the ice weakened.

Naturally every Klondiker wanted to get to the creeks during the summer, work out his claim and get back with the gold before the hardships of winter set in. Every moment which delayed him was of utmost concern. He lost no time in crossing the country, if it was his misfortune to start a thousand or more miles behind Klondikers from the coast cities. He fought them for space aboard the first Alaska-bound vessel leaving port, and once in Skagway or Dyea he pushed his way into the line for the passes. In the rush it was every man for himself, or every set of partners for themselves. No sooner had they been landed and their freight been thrown upon the beach than they began to dash and scurry about.

A contest and struggle took place at once. At Dyea, which had no wharf, the passengers and most of the freight reached the shore by scow or canoe. The vessels were forced to drop anchor in the open roadstead of the canal, to disgorge cargo and passengers as rapidly as possible and to get out when the tide turned. Bales of hay, drums of kerosene, lumber, barrels of whiskey, all such items as would float were thrown overboard on the in-going tide. Horses, sheep, dogs, whatever livestock the vessel carried also hit the icy water, and were forced to swim for the shore.

It was not long before a wall began to rise at the muddy rim of the canal. It was a toppling wall of mixed-up outfits, of bags and sacks and boxes, a stack of abused property which angry owners would have to identify as best they could. Some of it was watersoaked, much of it was burst open, everything was in chaos. While one man rooted out what was his another's sank from sight, where one slipped another was caught, what one retrieved another challenged, and while all were cursing and diving at the pile, like gulls over swill, they forgot about the tide. But inevitably that gray lip came closer to suck the mess back into the water.

When, at last, a man had his property together, or what was left of it, he had to look around for a place to pitch his tent. There was scarcely any beach and camping space had to be gained quickly if he was to be anywhere near the trail. It was an advantage to be near the river so that the outfit could be moved into line with the least difficulty, getting the bags and boxes ahead in five-mile relays, until all of it was on the way. Whether a man used horses in summer, sleds in winter, his own or an Indian's back, all the gear had to move forward this way in relays.

When the camp site was his, the next thing a man had to find was fuel for his stove and a few spruce boughs to sleep on. The boughs made what was called an "Alaska feather bed." If supplies had to be bought from the stores in Dyea, or a horse had to be shoed, or a man was looking for an Indian to pack for him, he secured these in competition with a hundred other men who were just as eager and hurried as himself.

Partners were really beginning to appreciate each other.

They could divide the work between them and perhaps to-gether manage to get what they wanted. While one looked for the gear, the other could set up the tent; while one cooked and fed the dogs, the other could load the sled or pack the horse. There was no time to lose. An hour lost in Dyea meant one less pan of gold washed in Eldorado.

Although two thousand persons returned from Dyea and Skagway in September, 1897, when they were convinced of the impossibility of crossing the passes and going on down the Yukon to Dawson before the winter cut them off, hun-dreds stayed on, determined to get through the next six months in some fashion. They had a winter's supply of food with them, there was timber for cabins, and Skagway was already somewhat of a town. It had a permanent population of five thousand men and fifty women. Many died during the winter. One diarist noted, on the authority of a saloonkeeper, that meningitis had killed forty-six people in Skagway and about twenty in Dyea.

Digging gold was not to everyone's taste. There were those who saw business opportunities in these coast towns. Out-fitters, hardware merchants, blacksmiths, hotelkeepers, men with pack trains, carpenters and others saw the chance of a lifetime. Also, eating houses, sawmills, express companies, places of entertainment were needed. To provide these things a great variety of people descended upon Skagway and Dyea at the beginning of the rush. It seemed inevitable that pros-perous cities would grow up at these gateways to the Klondike. In 1897 and 1898 many people seemed to think there was no end to the golden gravel. Each week reports came out of still another creek which had been discovered with banks of glittering dust.

Railroads were planned to leap over the passes and take the passengers down into the Yukon where steamers would meet them for a comfortable ride to Dawson. Compared to the 50,000 or more persons who were known to have passed through Skagway and Dyea during 1897, the number to arrive in the future was anybody's guess. If men were willing to come in such great numbers to walk to the Klondike, how many more might make the trip when all inconveniences had been removed? With a harbor one of these cities might become a metropolis.

Unfortunately, a harbor turned out to be impossible at either place, however much they dredged and scoured the canal. Skagway compromised with wharves, long thin arms which reached out to the ships and gathered in their cargoes. After that few ships bothered to go another four miles to Dyea. They landed passengers and freight at the wharves and headed home. Those who planned to go over Chilkoot had to hire barges to take them and their outfits on to Dyea.

There was no stopping thousands of men who arrived in one or more boatloads a day, moving in tons of goods, hundreds of dogs and horses. Shacks and shanties went up as fast as men could raise the scantlings. Men staked their camp sites like they would a claim on the gold creeks themselves, so precious was every foot of land. The gold hunters had to camp for a week or two until they could find a packer who was free to move their goods over the pass. Some of these men met misfortunes of one kind or another in Skagway and were forced to give up the Klondike trip. Others decided to make the most of the opportunities at hand. The population of Skagway grew.

From a tent town spread out over a mud flat Skagway became a "roaring" city in a matter of months. By the end of the summer of 1897 there were 1,200 tents and nearly 100 frame buildings scattered along the beach where the Skagway River sought the sea. The beach was all mud and clotted sour weeds. A half mile of it belonged to Captain William Moore, who had been squabbling with Americans since the

Cassiar boom in the seventies. Moore tried to run the squatters off his land, but succeeded only in driving some of them up into the canyon, a mile of which was also his land.

The eventual suit which followed took the remainder of the Captain's lifetime. Moore accused the United States Government of shoving him out of his property, in an act perpetrated by thousands of its gold-mad citizens trespassing on British soil. He charged the Americans with incorporating the city of Skagway upon his legally purchased property and of subdividing his land into town lots, one of which he was offered since his cabin was built upon it. When he refused to accept the lot from the hands of the new possessors they tore down his cabin and destroyed his goods. He raged to the United States courts and spent himself fighting for redress. At the very last he was awarded 25 per cent of the assessed value of the lots, which amounted to a trivial sum and only increased his bitterness and hastened his death.

It was not long before the squatters were pushed off by a group of men who took over the town, had it incorporated as the city of Skagway and divided into 3,600 town lots. In 1898 the city limits were four miles up the canyon and the population, including the transient hordes, was a fluctuating 15,000 to 20,000.

In Dyea, the Chilkoots stared at the tumult which had come over their village. What had been a bleak, but placid, strand of bog, with a few cedar-slab shacks, had overnight begun to churn with invasion. This was no doing of their cousin Chilcats, Auks, or Takus. It was an invasion of white men who passed them by in great haste. Men climbed onto the beach by the thousands, bringing with them every kind of bundle and sack. The Indians saw animals and barrels, boats and boards, astonishing things wash ashore to be snatched up and hurried over the mountain. They could think of nothing to compare with such a scene except, perhaps, the thick streams of salmon which turned up the rivers in the summertime.

At first the Indian men went out to the ships in their dugout canoes and helped bring in the freight. They met the barges and carried the men in on their backs, to save them wading in the icy water. Chief Isaac, who had traveled among Christians and accepted a name from them, collected a two-bit piece of silver for every man who carried a burden for the visitors. But, whereas before only an occasional boat arrived with a party of prospectors, now the stream of men was unending. The canal teetered with vessels as far as Chief Isaac could see, and he learned that thousands of men were getting off at the river below and that the trail over the mountain there was as crowded as the pass in back of his own village.

It was true, though incomprehensible, that men in such throngs had come after nothing but the yellow pebbles which were sometimes seen in the faraway creeks. The Chilkoots knew the place well, where the white men were going. They often camped at the mouth of that particular river when they were in the country trading with their Siwash neighbors. They had caught a few fish at the place but they had not been interested in the river's gravel.

The Indian village at Dyea was about a mile from the beach, spread alongside the Dyea River which ran out of a steep gorge and into the sea. The flatland between the Indian huts and the canal was soon a crowd of coffee tents and hotels, makeshift saloons, forges, corrals, and temporary camps set up by the men passing through. Before the end of the first summer Dyea's main street had half a mile of shacks, the false-front kind typical of the nineties. Yukon Trading Company, Lodgings, Supplies, Dance Hall, New York Kitchen were some of the names spread across the fronts of these raw unpainted buildings. When Skagway had town lots and names on her streets, Dyea was still a rough camp. Although both places were full of saloons, gambling houses, brothels, and thick with riff-raff of all kinds, Dyea's quota was smaller and her gamblers and criminals second-rate. But only because the pickings were leaner on "poor man's pass."

Dyea's street was ankle-deep with slime. In some places the mud came to the wagon-wheel hubs. The lumps in the mire were dead horses that had fallen there from exhaustion and hunger. No fodder was available for the animals, and at $200 a ton hay was too expensive. The horses were commonly worked on a diet of packing straw, and often on nothing at all. A month's work was all a man expected from an animal and then it was turned loose, bleeding and raw to the bone from pack sores, skinny as a snake, shoeless and completely broken down. If there had been another trip left in the creature, it would not have been turned loose. These dying beasts wandered through the camp until they collapsed. In Skagway it was even worse because there were three times as many horses working on that pass. Most Klondike diaries mentioned the dead horses. "There was a carcass every fifty feet." Or, "A word here about the cruelty to animals, which pen can scarcely describe." From another: "There is nothing more revolting than stepping through a bloated wormy hide." Many had to because the trails were blocked with dead animals, while in camp the streets were so full of filth that it was worth taking a chance of avoiding it by crossing on any convenient body.

Liquor flowed freely from the barrel and the Chilkoot had a seal purse full of silver with which to buy all he wanted. As a consequence the supply of Indian packers began to drop off. Five cents a pound had always been the packing rate but when the gold rushers began competing with each other for the Indian's services, the price jumped. First to ten, then to seventeen, twenty, thirty, and finally to forty cents a pound. Even on the pass an Indian could be stopped, offered a higher price than he was being paid for whatever he was carrying, and be immediately secured. The Indian would throw down his pack and return with his new employer to pick up another backload at five or ten cents a pound more.

Moreover, when an Indian had a purse full of money he was not likely to be pushed onto the pass at all. He preferred to make the most of Dyea's attractions. And when he had a mind to he went down to Skagway for a real blowout. To get an Indian to work was a job in itself, and his price developed into more or less of a bribe.

On the other hand, when an Indian worked he took his family with him, each strapped with a suitable burden. He himself could carry from one hundred to one hundred and fifty pounds, his wife took seventy-five, and each child from twenty-five to sixty, depending upon his size. Even the dog had to work. He carried about fifteen pounds in a saddle-bag arrangement. When the party came to a stream the dog was carried over, pack and all. In addition to the pack, each carried his own food and a blanket. The food, carried in a seal-skin pouch, was dried salmon and a few pinches of tea. A tomato can or something of the kind was taken along to boil the tea.

Not many Klondikers could pay forty cents a pound to have two thousand pounds of freight moved over the pass. Few could pay half as much for the use of a horse. And even if they had the price, the chances of getting an Indian or a horse were never immediate. Those who could afford to brought horses with them and the others simply moved the stuff over on their own backs, seventy-five to a hundred pounds at a time. In winter they could sled four hundred pounds over in one load. Some sleds were pulled by dogs, if the Klondiker had the right kind of dog. One man had a team of goats, another two oxen. But the majority were pulled by man power. A broad band around the body, high up under the armpits, was the harness. It was not hard work over a slick trail, but it was extremely slow.

In Dyea there were many second looks at the freight a man

had with him. Back home it had been easy enough to throw in this and that, an extra sweater, beeswax, a padlock, a pocket mirror, scissors. Now everything was checked and re-checked. Perhaps something important had been omitted. Coming up to Dyea on the boat the men had had a chance to compare outfits and to learn a few "pointers" from old-timers who might be returning to the fields. A man with Yukon experience was well worth heeding when life itself depended upon the freight which each one was taking in.

Was the outfit rock-bottom? Tent, sled, air-tight stove, four blankets, plenty of beans? Or was his the "ideal" outfit with all the little extras he thought so important in New York or Pittsburgh, or wherever he was from? A fur-lined sleeping bag, a sewing kit, collapsible cups, celery tablets. Did he have mosquito netting? If he had overlooked it, he scurried around now trying to buy five yards of it. Back home who would have believed that mosquitoes could kill a dog? They attacked even bears, on the eyes, nose, and ears, blinding and enraging the animal until in its helpless wanderings it became lost and mired in some marsh where it died, not from wounds, but from thirst and hunger. In the summertime one could not see the hide or fur of an animal, it was so thickly covered with these insects, which would hang on until crushed. In Dyea mosquito netting cost $5 a yard.

Here three other purchases were necessary. These were two pairs of moccasins, a pair of caribou mittens and a Yukon sled. The Yukon sled was seven feet long and slightly less than eighteen inches in width. The frame was light, made of four long pine slats that rested on four crosspieces of ash. The runners were also of ash and had a two-inch brass shoe. Iron was not used because of the danger of splitting in low temperatures. The trading companies sold the sleds for $10. The other items had to be bought from the local squaws, whose prices were usually $15 for two pairs of moccasins and $5 for the mittens.

Had the miner brought black glasses? He would need these in the snow. Citric acid to ward off scurvy? Liniment? Plenty of candles? What could he leave behind? Did he need two frying pans? Soap? He could hold onto the package of rivets and get rid of the can of maple syrup. He mustn't forget the quicksilver.

It was easy to see that the most "rock-bottom" outfit weighed very near two thousand pounds. If a man had a partner many things would serve them both and lighten the load considerably. But every ounce was counted. Not an extra spoon, photograph or yard of rope went over the pass but that the bearer was aware of it and willing.

Aside from the weight, there was that unpleasant business of Canadian duty to be considered. Thirty per cent on ammunition, 35 per cent on edge tools, 20 per cent on flour. . . . They said to each other, "There'll be broken bones at the customs."

8

SOAPY SMITH

NOT ALL of the year-round residents of Skagway were engaged in the kinds of business which offer a service to the public. A small but tightly-knit group served but one master and that one was the famous knave known as "Soapy" Smith. Jefferson Randolph Smith, whom his biographer called "the Robin Hood of the frontier," had many adventures, all of them closely watched by the police. Although he will not be forgotten in Denver or Creede, his greatest triumphs came to him in Skagway.

Born in Georgia, Smith left home in his early teens to ride the Texas range. He left this occupation in order to follow a circus, but not as a member of it. During a visit to his first circus he lost a month's hard-earned wages outside one of the tents, trying to locate a pea under a walnut shell. He had lost, but to one of the game's greatest of all time manipulators. He had paid for an exceptional lesson in the art. Later, comparing the ease with which he had been separated from his money to the hard work of riding herd, Smith made up his mind to leave the longhorns and get himself a walnut shell.

With a little practice he was able to master the sleight-of-hand, discovering he had quite a talent for this sort of thing. Thereafter he followed a circus, waylaid the crowds on their way in, and very easily extracted their money. Smith was no ordinary street-corner bunco. He had a gentleman's appearance and soft, Southern speech—and a "gift of gab" that won him an audience anywhere.

The circus wended its way to Leadville which was then a booming, gold rush town thronged with rich and restless men who were looking for novel entertainment. Although Smith, the "thimble-rigger," was doing all right by himself he was not above studying the game of a worthy competitor. There was another bunco at Leadville whose performance was merely that of seeming to wrap, but not to wrap, a ten-, twenty- or fifty-dollar bill around a cake of soap which any man in the audience could buy for a dollar. From time to time a lucky customer, usually a young boy, would unwrap a bill and give fresh impetus to the game. Smith, not yet twenty, got himself hired to the job of lucky customer.

Some time after, the two left town and while the originator of the soap game was never seen or heard from again, the helper turned up in Denver with a thick black beard and a suitcase full of soap. He was an immediate success. And not only with soap, although this "trade" gave him an undying sobriquet. He had a whole bag of tricks plus a nimble imagination which kept him constantly thinking of more. In addition to his own performances he engineered the work of a band carefully chosen by him for their professional assets. With these henchmen Smith rose to fame as the boss of Denver's underworld.

When news reached him of the great silver strike at Creede, he and his pick of "con" men rushed there at once to take over the camp, and when Creede was finally abandoned he returned to Denver to resume dictatorship there. This time he did not last long. When he left, ousted by a seasonal reform movement, he was completely broke. A brief trip to Mexico failed to catch the cunning Díaz in a military plan thought up by the now "Colonel" Jefferson Smith. Once more he returned to Denver's Seventeenth Street with a supply of soap. But a rival gang had taken over and Smith was in for trouble. In the midst of embarrassing admonitions the news reached Denver that gold had been discovered in the Klondike. Someone has said that the news reached Smith's ears like a clarion call to opportunity.

He and the five men he took with him had a slight skirmish in Seattle, where they tried to raise a stake in their own way. Not the law but Seattle's own cheats and thugs, fearful of competition, hastened the departure of the interlopers. They reached Skagway just before winter closed that port in 1897. It was a setting made to order for them.

An unorganized lot of hoodlums had already drifted into Skagway and Dyea. They had been assaulting and robbing men on the trail all summer. There were no police. The only law which the Americans had heard of was the one forbidding the sale of liquor in the territory. But nobody paid any attention to that. The saloon was the best "legitimate" business that either Dyea or Skagway had. The summer of 1897 waned with twenty-five saloons going full-blast in Skagway, and the next year there were seventy of them there. Game rooms and dance halls were run in connection with these establishments.

Into this community hundreds of delayed Klondikers were forced to settle down for the winter. While the merchants of Skagway hoped to supply them with extra foodstuffs, and find beds perhaps for those who failed to build a cabin, there were others who planned to comfort and entertain them. Smith and his gang merely looked forward to getting their money away from them. A man had a chance to lose "fair and square" at the gambling table. If not, he might lose it with a bludgeoning.

All the winter of 1897 and on into the next summer an enormous amount of money poured into Smith's headquarters. He named his saloon Jeff's Place, but Jeff Smith would always be "Soapy," even in Skagway where he had never sold a single cake of the stuff. Although Smith was a crook and a crook's leader, he was a cut above the ordinary criminal, and the plug-uglies and strong-arm men whom circumstances forced him to associate with were personally distasteful to him. Moreover, he berated them for their outrages and more heinous deeds, which apparently he was unable to stop. But he protected them, as he felt he ought, and was never known to have betrayed one of them, despicable and cowardly though the crime might have been. Smith stood by his men.

The wealth that came to Smith disappeared almost as quickly as it was gained. He simply gave it away. He was known for an easy touch, providing the hard-luck story had a sincere, if familiar, ring to it. He gave shelter to any number of penniless Klondikers and kept them from starving to death that first winter in Skagway. That he might be responsible for their pitiable condition was beside the point.

He fed stray dogs. Hundreds of them had been dumped on the town after a mass canine kidnapping along the Pacific Coast, which came to nothing. Reports that dogs were selling in Dyea and Skagway at $100 apiece encouraged their prompt arrival. Good sled dogs did bring a high price, but mongrels picked off the streets of San Francisco and Seattle were useless in a harness. When the mistake was discovered the animals were abandoned by their disappointed keepers, and these miserable, hungry, roaming curs would have died at the first signs of winter had not Smith come to their rescue. He started an Adopt-a-Dog movement and managed to find homes for them. He kept six himself and fed any strays that had been overlooked in the drive.

This puzzling, sentimental, and even foppish man, for all his moral callouses, was not without a following of friends and admirers, men and women outside of his criminal ring. There were two Smiths, doing good deeds and bad. His tremendous conceit would not permit him to be less than dictatorial. He lived for homage. In return, if there was a church to be built or a fire hose to be purchased, Smith would do it. He supported widows and their children, especially those who were left destitute by sudden acts of violence. He always sent out twenty-dollar bills at Christmas, an idea which struck him in Denver and which he continued self-righteously throughout his short life. He was happy to administer justice at all times whether it was over run-away-girl trouble or a waterfront strike. His decision closed the altercation.

Bunco Chief Smith had organized the Law and Order Committee of Three Hundred and Three in answer to the citizens' Vigilance Committee of One Hundred and One which was organized twenty-four hours after his arrival in Skagway. The Vigilantes at that time posted a warning to "all confidence sharks, bunco men, sure-thing men, and all other objectionable characters" to get out of town, or else. "Or else" was mostly a disapproving glare because there was no way to enforce the warning. The marines in Dyea, numbering exactly six, were empowered to act in either town only in case of riot. They had no other responsibility to the citizens.

When news arrived in May, 1898, that the battleship *Maine* had been blown up in Havana harbor three months before, Smith got together a company of infantry to avenge her. He called this collection, largely recruited from among his assorted assistants, the Skagway Guards, and when Secretary of War Alger declined their services it was a hard blow to the "Captain."

But the Fourth of July was coming and Smith did not intend to let the opportunity pass. The United States and Spain had been at war two months and a display of patriotism was in order. He would impress the world, and Secretary Alger, with Skagway's love of country in this moment of crisis. He went ahead with elaborate details. Every child would have a supply of firecrackers and his fill of free peanuts and candy.

He blazed the streets with flags and miles of Seattle bunting. He invited Governor Brady of Alaska to make a speech at the patriotic exercises. And Brady did.

The day began with a send-off of dynamite sticks exploded from the near-by mountainside. A fleet of buggies set out after all the ladies so that they would not have to walk the muddy streets into town. Badges and ribbons were pinned on committee members and honored guests. Throughout the city there was deafening assurance that the people were having a good time. The gunpowder was puffing small bitter clouds and the torn firecracker paper was a red confetti. And then the parade started. It was led by Grand Marshal Smith on a prancing pony. He was wearing a brand-new white twenty-gallon hat which had reached him all the way from Texas. He swept the air with it as he smilingly passed along the cheering line of march. Behind him stepped his Skagway Guards in their new uniforms, while a lusty band played "Yankee Doodle Dandy." Schoolchildren, local civic and fraternal organizations, appropriate floats passed by. After the parade came the program and speeches. Finally rockets seared the evening sky which, too bad, was not dark enough for splendor at that time of the year.

Four days later Soapy Smith was dead.

Literally hundreds of men had been fleeced, hijacked and robbed by the Smith gang. It might have gone on indefinitely had not some minor cog slipped into place that July 8 and turned the wheel of Soapy's fortune another way. A man arrived in town unnoticed, returning from Dawson with a quite insignificant poke of $2,700. Like so many others he stepped into Jeff's Place and in time found himself coming-to in an alley. And, of course, minus his poke. He went to the newly arrived United States marshal, whom he asked to get his money back for him. The marshal seemed unable to do anything about it. The man told his loss to people along the street. And suddenly the citizens of Skagway had had enough of thuggery. Someone rang the town's fire bell and when the crowd came it was decided to put an end to the reign of gamblers and rogues. A committee was chosen to call upon Smith at once to demand the return of the man's poke.

Smith refused to take the loser's part. He said he did not know anything about the affair and pointed out that the man had obviously entered his establishment of his own free will, had tried his luck, lost, and now was squealing. Smith's attitude did not please the Vigilantes, who cleaned their guns for the expected show-down. Smith's men, already well-armed, hung around headquarters. The streets filled with angry, shouting people. The United States District Judge came over from Dyea and himself asked Smith to see that the money was returned. He gave him until four o'clock that afternoon to do it.

When four o'clock came Smith stepped out of his saloon, rifle in hand. He warned the crowd that there were five hundred armed men behind him and that the matter of the poke had best be settled quietly. In other words, he thought the matter should be forgotten. No one answered him. He stared into a silent crowd. At last he turned and stepped into the nearest saloon for a drink.

All the rest of the afternoon and evening he walked the streets carrying his rifle. He went in and out of familiar places, always to drink alone. Nobody approached him. The Vigilantes, meanwhile, were in Sylvester Hall deciding upon a course of action. When too many faces in the crowd looked suspiciously like informers it seemed wise to adjourn and go to the end of Juneau Wharf, and there they continued the discussion. They did not know it, but Smith's band of thugs and gamblers had deserted him, almost to the man. They were not the kind to face fire. Three or four of the original group stood by but Smith, ever confident, assured them that he could settle things single-handed.

Late in the day, as near night as Skagway could get in July,

Smith was impatient for an immediate show-down and headed for the wharf. Frank Reid, on guard, stopped him as he stepped onto the pilings. Smith refused to halt or drop his weapon. With Smith's shooting reputation in mind, Reid had leveled his six-shooter with his command to halt.

"For God's sake," Smith cried, "don't shoot!" But his hand still balanced his own rifle at his side. He came on.

The trigger of Reid's gun snapped. The gun failed to go off. Desperately Reid cocked again but it was too late, Smith had fired. Reid returned the shot as he fell. And shot again. The second bullet was unnecessary for the first was already in Soapy Smith's heart.

Leaving Smith's body where it lay, the Vigilantes fell upon the town, raiding one place after the other, slugging, shooting, wounding and killing. Forty prisoners were taken to an improvised jail but a mob stormed that shack and was about to conduct a mass lynching when the marines arrived from Dyea. Martial law had to be threatened before the prisoners could be put safely back in jail. They were shipped out on the first vessel returning to the States and warned never to set foot again on Skagway's beach. The rest of the town's underworld had fled on their own, just ahead of the Vigilantes' cleanup.

Reid died of his wound twelve days after the shooting. By then Skagway was a law-abiding community.

Not so in March, 1898. Then it was still a camp full of toughs. Years after, when the prospector, John Ver Mehr, talked about the trail of '98, he liked to include a story about the stopover he and his two partners had made in Skagway, en route to Dyea. They had left the ship to give the town the once-over, as his story goes. "We made a beeline for Soapy Smith's saloon. We knew it was the first thing they'd ask us about back home. 'Did you go to Soapy's place? Did you see him?' Well, we never saw him but we were in the headquarters of the famous Three Hundred and Three. And it was a big disappointment, let me tell you. It looked just like any ordinary saloon. We didn't see anybody that even looked crooked in the place. We called for our drinks and paid. Then, just as we were about to throw the liquor down, a volley of shots let loose that raised us off our heels. Wasn't anything. Just one of the men in there that had shot off his revolver to scare us greenhorns. He called us 'cheechakos.' That's the name they had up there for the new arrivals. Well, they all had the laugh on us. They saw they scared us bug-eyed. We beat it and went on back to the boat. We were just boys, the three of us. We never in our lives had been 'shot at' before. But we were no different from the rest. The Klondike was full of boys like us. Greenhorns."

9

POOR MAN'S PASS

THE TRAIL to the Chilkoot Glacier followed the Dyea River for the first ten miles. In summer it was possible to freight the outfit forward in canoes, but this was an Indian's job for it required no small skill to push a canoe up the shallow spiral of water with the slim craft grazing the rocky bed beneath. The bank of the river was the trail and it crossed from side to side about every two hundred yards. The tortuous stream was scarcely fifty yards wide. Of course, the trail was always wet and slippery in the summer. In some places saplings had been thrown down to make a corduroy road and a toll was collected at these points by the road builders. Logs were set across the stream at other places but the men who contributed these were perhaps in too great a hurry to stop for pittances.

The walls of the gorge were dark with cottonwood, poplars, birch and spruce. There was every kind of berry in the under-brush—strawberries, raspberries, cranberries, blueberries. The Chilkoot Indians gathered them up in skins for eating with salmon oil. This delicacy, which was the Chilkoots' standard of barter, was made by the canoeful. The bodies of the fish were split and impaled on sticks to dry but the heads were buried, and after a certain time excavated and put into canoes with hot stones. This rendered out the oil. Sometimes candlefish were used instead of salmon but the result was equally high in flavor.

There were berries everywhere in the Yukon, all the way down to the Siwash villages, but berries without oil were a pretty poor dish. As long as the Chilkoots came over the mountain with their product they could barter black fox off every Indian they saw.

All along the river there were flowers from May to September. When the poet and correspondent, Joaquin Miller, arrived at Dyea late in the summer of 1897, he was enthusiastic over the scenery. It was Miller who offered to make a quick reconnaissance of the gold rush in order to bring the "true facts" to the people. In his first dispatch he wrote:

"I feel that the quest, so far as a poor man's getting here goes, has been settled for me in the affirmative. Truly, if this had been my own woods on 'The Hights' the scene could not have been more pretty. The tall cottonwood trees moaned and groaned . . . water came tumbling down out of the wooded valley walls, down out of the clouds, great nameless cataracts. . . . Well, I trudged along over the slippery rocks and sand and saw fishes leaping in the air, and then a bank of mammoth English primroses! My boots became yellow from the blossoms, reaching almost to my knees. Think of blossoms like that in Alaska! A kingfisher flew by. A prettier walk than I found there on the bank of that swift stream could not be found in the United States. It reminded me of Los Gatos, California, only on the hillsides there were great gardens of snow instead of gardens of grapes and prunes."

The poet played his flute as he tramped along through the woods. He had only a light pack swinging from his shoulders. Apparently he did not notice the men tramping with him for he never mentioned them. His letters, which were syndicated and widely read, described the scenery with great care but he gave no account of the unpleasant aspects of the trip. He

said nothing about dead horses and blowflies, about mosquitoes or sump holes, he avoided the subject of the river's pol-
lution, although, like everyone else, he must have dipped up
his drinking water from it.

Twelve miles up the river a cleft in the canyon opened
into Sheep Camp, erroneously so-called from the mountain
goats that once were plentiful there, and from this flat meadow
there was but one exit, the pass. The woods had vanished and
sheer glaciers hemmed the valley in. A lip of one curled into
the valley from the north, reaching down from a two-thousand-
foot ledge, a wall of blue ice that was three hundred feet
wide at the valley floor. The blue glacier, like the others,
came forward invisibly, never resting, grinding its way, a peb-
ble or a boulder at a time. There were momentary splatters,
short crashes, roars as the mountains cracked open. In the
stillness of night the men who were camped in the valley
could hear the least push of the glaciers. All night long they
could hear the snapping and turning of the ice.

From Sheep Camp the trail twined off into tracks that
struggled upward over shelves of ice in winter and over
slippery shale and granite boulders during summer. Two
such boulders were called Stone Houses "because they were
each as big as a house." First one and then the other rolled
down into the Dyea River during the spring floods so that
by 1899 the Stone Houses had disappeared.

Four miles from Sheep Camp a formidable glacier blocked
the way. It was this mass that was called The Chilkoot. There
were actually two passes over it, one to the left and up and
the other straight ahead through a prominent center defile.
From June to September The Chilkoot was a cliff of sliding
rock. The rest of the year it was ice, into which steps had
to be hacked for the men to ascend. The grade was 30 per
cent; 35 per cent the last half mile. There was nothing to
hang onto to keep from being blown off the face of the pass
during the storms which almost continually raged around

it summer and winter, battering that impregnable jaw. Fog and driving sleet tossed over it or hung on it like the hair of a monster. Men talked of The Chilkoot as if it were a malevolent thing capable of wrath and punishment. They pointed out the lines of its face in the stones and ice.

At the sight of The Chilkoot, Miller wrote home: "A stately peak, communing with heaven. This wonderful white scenery! . . . One constantly thinks of the Transfiguration all along this land of whiteness and blue. Heavens! Had I but years to live here and lay my hand upon the color! This fearful and wonderful garment of the Most High God!"

Even when there was no snow on the lower part of The Chilkoot, when the climb was made over a cascade of bare crags, it was still a difficult ascent. From the bottom of The Chilkoot the packs were carried on each man's back for no horse or dog could take a burden over the top. It was almost impossible to get an animal to go up the face of the glacier, even with its master. Horses had to be blindfolded. Dogs were often carried. Before 1897 there were hand-operated cables to hoist the outfits over but these were only temporarily installed for special parties. That year several cables were strung and worked from small engines, and the service rate was from eight to thirty cents a pound, depending upon the kind of freight.

The pass was easier, and also safer, to cross in winter. A fall in the snow merely sent a man into slush to his armpits. In summer there was no avoiding the rocks. The men kept in line as they climbed from one fingerhold to the next, and there were steps hacked out of the last seven hundred feet of ice, and guy ropes. At every twentieth step there was a resting place for four men at a time. At the very top the men helped each other over with drop ropes. It took from three to six hours to make the climb from the bottom of the pass. In case of a blizzard most men preferred to wait below in their tents, but if a storm came up after they had started there was nothing to do but hang on. Storms were frequent and they occurred all through the year, winter and summer alike.

The two partners who first cut the steps in the ice made so much toll money that they never did go on to Dawson. Finally they sold out the "concession" but the new managers failed to keep the steps in good condition, too often feeling the urge to go back out to Dyea for a little recreation. In 1898 the Mounted Police took over the job, continuing to collect the fee, and in addition installed a rescue station. The fee was charged only for the first trip of the day and a man could cross free thereafter until midnight. However most men could make only one trip a day.

Returning for the next seventy-five pounds, or whatever he could carry, a man used one of the troughs to the side of the trails. These were chutes in the snow, worn shoulder-deep by thousands of men using them day after day. It was a swift ride and a hot one but a canvas pad underneath helped some. In summer this sort of descent was impossible.

The uncontrollably bad thing about the winter trip was the weather. The temperature in March was not much below zero but it was windy. The howling gales rasped steadily, tearing at fur and leather, penetrating it as if it were muslin. No matter how a man bundled up, the wind reached in somewhere. Muscles were constantly cramped from the cold. There was no time on the trail when a man felt comfortably warm, not even when he was inside his tent with the faithful stove going like a forge. If he stepped back a foot he was in an icy draft. He could never take off his coat, relax, drop his shoulders. After a miserable day he was still hunched over, trying to coax warmth from one part of his body to another. In bed he had to curl in his blankets, folded like a jackknife. If he had a dog he slept with him for warmth. The cold never let him go.

There was constant danger from freezing to death. If he perspired and his body was cold, the moisture soon turned to ice. If this occurred during sleep he would not awaken. When he was working, hauling, pushing, keeping the sled on the road, it was easy to perspire. If he didn't dry off immediately and change into dry clothing his wet skin would freeze. If his moccasins got wet, or even slightly damp, he could lose a toe unless he discovered the danger in time. Even when he did save his skin from freezing, the effects of frostbite are much like those of a burn. The skin would sluff off from a minor frostbite but a serious condition would bring on painful blisters and deep sores. Under such conditions it was an ordeal to be chafed by clothing and to continue on the trail, sledding, making camp, cutting firewood.

Freezing could be avoided, it was practically unknown among the Indians. It was necessary to work slowly and not to become overheated at any time. Few Klondikers knew how to dress properly for the climate. A fur coat was a mistake although several men brought them. The best over-all outer garment was a parka made of drill cloth, which came below the knees and had but one opening, a hood. The hood was usually lined with fur which extended about the face for protection against the wind. The blue-striped drill cloth resembled mattress ticking, but was heavier.

The trail was so defined that there was no getting out of line, every man had to follow one behind the other, and the pace was set by the slowest. If a sled turned over, or a dog refused to go on, if one was suddenly sick or another must stop to adjust his freight, then the whole line stopped. Every mile was a series of delays. The halting march was a nightmare to men stampeding after gold. The line kept moving by day whatever the weather, as long as one could see the man ahead. At night the line stopped.

There was very little daylight as early as March, and that was more of a twilight than anything else. The snow fields made it seem light and there was no difficulty in following the trail, nor any possibility of getting lost since all kept to-

The *Excelsior* and a few who couldn't get on her

On the beach at Dvea

Two hundred pounds of flour, fifty pounds of sugar . . .

Shooting Miles Canyon (*Historical Pictures Service*)

Dawson and Klondike City, September, 1898

Dawson, June, 1900

Dog-team express, Dawson

First tourist excursion, Pacific and Arctic Railway

Diggings in Skookum Gulch

Summer diggings on *Twenty-nine* Eldorado

gether, but the ghostly gloom was depressing and it got on everybody's nerves.

In the meantime men's intestines were balking at the half-raw beans and uncooked dough cakes which were the general bill of fare. There never seemed to be time enough to cook the beans through. They were brown beans but the prevalent pink color of rawness soon gave them the name of "Alaska strawberries." The flapjacks were made by throwing a handful of snow into a sack of flour, adding salt and baking powder, stirring the mess into a ball and dropping it into a skillet of bacon fat to fry.

Here again was a time when a partner made a big difference. One could take the sled while the other cut wood and kept up the fire so that hot coffee and beans would be ready at the end of the day. When a man was alone he was too weary to care what he ate. He was ravenous for food but the supper he dished out for himself gave him no appetite. He was chilled to the marrow, he longed for a good night's rest. Instead, he puttered over a fire, prepared his miserable meal, divided it with his dog, and after he had eaten went hunting for firewood. He would have to split this into ready kindling because he couldn't take a chance on being without immediate fire. If he should come in from the trail wet every moment counted against him. He certainly could not take the time then to chop wood. And after the fire seemed to be set for the night, he would lie down on the snow and try to go to sleep.

The jostling of too many human beings, thrown together with their weariness, illness, dirt and discontent, wore on nerves of iron. Every man on the trail was drugged with fatigue; almost everyone was suffering from dysentery. Limbs ached, eyes were red from the constant blasts of wind. There had been no washing to speak of, and bodies and clothing were strong evidence of the fact.

As the weeks went by many dropped out of line with just

enough food to see them back to Dyea and the first boat home. For them the vision of gold had tarnished. Those who went on felt the strain more and more each day. Tempers were short. The dogs were cursed and beaten unmercifully. Men fought with each other over nothing at all. Partners broke up, split outfits, and went on alone. There was bloodshed. And still the line kept moving—a hundred and fifty pounds, two hundred, four hundred, relay after relay, five miles forward and five miles back.

The three partners, Ver Mehr, Hawley and Ray, went on. Ver Mehr's notes of March 11 read: "A week moving 4,500 lbs. 5 miles. River is frozen and the dogs are wonderful but we feel it. Damned hard work. H. and R. working #1 load ahead from here. I'm cook this camp and H. next. R. will take all care of the dogs from here on. 17 below but don't seem that cold. Very clear."

The entry for March 17 was: "9 round trips to Sheep Camp, our second stop. Four blizzards. I'm working with Ray this week. Face all raw again in spite of bacon grease and ashes. What would I give to have a hot bath. ?? Hah."

Ashes and grease were used as a protection against wind and snow burn. Everybody plastered themselves with this old-timer's "salve." Nine round trips in less than a week was good going. But Ver Mehr and his partners had two dogs broken to harness and Ray had the knack of handling a sled. All three boys were tough youngsters, physically speaking, and they were determined to get to Dawson and make a fortune apiece.

There were three camps between Dyea and the pass. The first was about five miles up the river, the second was Sheep Camp, and the third was at the foot of the pass. It took the three boys twenty-one days to bring all of their freight up to The Chilkoot. Meanwhile, on March 23, Ver Mehr wrote: "Nobody speaking on the trail. We move forward like dead men. Not even a howl out of the dogs. The Chilkoot is in front of us. The dogs are only decent uncomplaining members of this party. R. pulled his knife on me yesterday. Maybe I deserved it. This would be a hell of a place to be left. Would H. bury me? I wonder."

On April 2 there was this: "We're going over tomorrow." Everything but their tent, stove, two days' provisions and the bedding had been freighted to the top.

That night the boys and fifteen others moved their tents to a place which the old-timer, "Grizzly" Meyers, had picked out as the safest place in sight. Wisps of snow had been slithering off the mountain for several days. The weather was warm. No Indian would make the climb either that day or the day before, and most of them had gone back to Dyea. Meyers was not the only one who talked avalanche, all the way back to Sheep Camp tents were being pulled up. But nobody knew where to go. At the bottom of the pass there were at least a hundred markers, tall poles stuck into the snow, to identify each man's outfit. Should they move this gear back after all the labor of getting it there? And where would they put it? There had been talk of slides for over a week but nothing had happened, and tomorrow they'd be climbing The Chilkoot and out of the valley for good. A hundred or more took the chance.

The spot which Meyers picked for himself was not very wide, and it was all that eighteen men could do to get in there with him. Of that night Ver Mehr wrote: "We were sleeping squeezed together like sardines. Nobody saw it happen. Terrible sound. Really deafening. Worse than thunder. Then awful silence. All over before we could get to our feet."

About seventy persons were believed buried under the fall of snow. Ver Mehr said they dug out fifty bodies, among which was that of a woman. Less than ten persons were found in time. Some reports say six, others nine. The Mounted Police came down at once from the top of the pass and organized the digging crews. Ver Mehr said they dug for a week. The entry in his diary was: "I don't think we'll find half the people that were here." As the bodies were found they were carried back to Sheep Camp where a morgue had been set up. The Police forbade any approach to the pass until it was felt that the ascent was safe.

The avalanche had clasped its victims tightly. Survivors described the experience. They said they had been unable to move at all, caught in their sleeping bags and blanket rolls, imprisoned by the pressure. Those near the surface, who had not been crushed by the tremendous fall of wet snow, did not suffocate for their breath melted a small area away from their mouths and nostrils. They called out to their rescuers, whom they could plainly hear above them, but their voices did not carry through the snow, and the men above them were unaware of their cries. Those who were not discovered within a short time were anesthetized by the cold before they died. When the snow melted in June the bodies came into view.

The three boys went over on April 10. The entry for that day reads: "Easter Sunday! Stormy all week. Every kind of misery. This has been the most horrible month of my life. Left camp about 5 A.M. Clear for the first time. Made the top by 10 A.M. Slipped twice. God! Blue sky and sunshine here. Can see a lake below. Our troubles are over, thank God! Ray was wonderful. He carried the dogs over, one at a time. Good Ray! Two trips to Hawley's and my one. I'm wondering why I'm alive today. Not because I've got guts."

There was a note at the bottom of the page: "We went to sleep in the sun. Woke up with snow falling like bullets all around us. In a blinding storm and darkness we were able to give the N.W.M.P. the go-by. Why not?"

From Skagway the trail also followed a river for the first few miles and then looped upward toward the pass. The trail here was wide and gradual, twenty miles from beach to summit. The Chilkoot was sixteen. In 1887 William Ogilvie named the pass behind Skagway for Thomas White, who was then Minister of the Interior. That year the unfortunate Captain Moore, recently settled at Skag-wah, cut a trail over the pass. In 1897 George A. Brackett built a toll road over Moore's trail. It was suitable for horses, even wagons, Brackett boasted, and was photographed with a buckboard and team to prove it. Brackett's road soon had its name changed to Dead Horse Gulch for the road was impassable after June when the snow began to melt.

In the summer of 1897 nearly 2,000 pack horses were shipped to Skagway and the next summer there were twice that many for hire on the trail. Thousands of the animals died in the endless quagmire. They slipped and fell into the mud pits, packs and all, and when their owners were unable to get them out they were left to die without so much as the mercy of a bullet. The few men who carried firearms did not want to waste bullets on the doomed animals. They were soon tramped to death by the horde of men and women bringing other struggling creatures up the trail.

Thirty thousand persons crossed White Pass in 1897. They complained that the trail was "intolerable," that it was "a stinking abattoir," that they were forced to walk over thousands of bloated, wormy hides packed tight in the mud. Some tried to stop the pack trains from coming up, some turned back, some went over to Dyea and carried their own packs over Chilkoot trail, "the poor man's pass." There were pack trains there but they could make the climb only as far as Sheep Camp. The Chilkoots, now joined by Sticks, Auks, and others, were freighting for forty cents a pound but they could handle only a fraction of the gear going over. The men toiling over The Chilkoot were "the original A. P. A.," Alaska Pack Asses.

Once over the passes the two trails met either near Lake Lindeman, or farther down about Lake Bennett, and from there the men went on together to Dawson on rafts and barges, on anything that would float.

10

KEEP A SHARP LOOKOUT!

THE DESCENT from The Chilkoot was rapid. Crater Lake was just below, a steely cyclopean eye in the soft slopes of snow. Going on down, the men passed Long Lake and Deep Lake, small pools of ice. Then the snow billows closed into a tight, wooded gorge which came out at Lake Lindeman. The Klondiker was now less than ten miles from Chilkoot but he usually made camp here, where there was firewood for the first time in many days of traveling. In summer they began building their boats at Lindeman. In winter when the ice was still thick, a dog sled could cover the lake's nine miles in forty minutes, and the men worked from five in the morning until ten at night, getting their outfits ahead before the break-up.

When a dog was working on the ice little frost balls formed under his nails and between his pads. The bits of ice were painful, cutting him like glass, and soon brought him to a stop. At the first sign of a limp the driver would examine the dog's foot. The quickest way to thaw out the paw was for the man to put the dog's foot into his mouth, and when it was warm to dry it off carefully with his shirt. More than one journal-keeper has told of a dog stopping, turning around to his master and lifting up his paw. An "inside dog" knew better than to stand still on the ice. If an "outside dog" knew no better he soon found himself freezing to the trail.

The timber around the first two lakes was quickly depleted the first summer of the rush so it was an advantage to continue on down the trail to where the trees were still growing at the water's edge. When a man had to walk a mile for his timber, whipsaw it into boards far back in the forest, or "snake" the logs to the water's edge to be sawed, he lost a lot of time he could not regain. Late in the summer of 1898 there were steamers on the first lake to carry Klondikers all the way to Dawson, but until then the only way to get there was on a raft or homemade boat.

The next camp after Lindeman was thirty-mile-long Lake Bennett, reached by a short portage. Even in winter the frozen stream connecting the two lakes was too twisted and rough with boulders for practical sledding. Bennett was the boat-building center. A tent city soon sprang up, with sawmills, hotels, restaurants, and dance halls. Planks at ten cents a foot made the price of a catboat come pretty high. For a time the "old settlers" charged rent for camp sites, but the Mounted Police finally put a stop to that.

All of May the boatbuilders heard the ice breaking up with explosive cracks. The detonations echoed back and forth across the lake. As soon as the ice began to go the country was fresh with spring. Austerity vanished overnight. The sound of a thousand saws, and four times that many tapping hammers, had overtones of bird twitter. Sparrows and tom-tits arrived and the skies were crossed with clouds of ducks. Grouse with their chicks scrambled through the grass. On the hillsides wildflower patches of purple, pink and yellow came out between the snow, and above them were straight granite cliffs.

Winter was sloughed off very quickly. The men worked literally day and night. There was nothing for the dogs to do but eat and sleep, scratch themselves, keep an eye on the camp. The men scanned the lake for the last block of ice upon it, impatiently waited for the slush to move on, and at sight of the first clear water put up their sails and were on their way. Eight hundred boats set out on the thirtieth day of May, 1898.

There was no special kind of boat for the Yukon trip, every man had his own idea as to the best way to get down the rapids. Some built wherries, others rafts. There were amazing floating contraptions, with and without sails, some with steering sweeps, some with rudders. Some were big enough to carry and quarter five men, their dogs and their gear. It was common for several men to get together and build a boat large enough to take them all. A twenty-two-foot catboat with a six-foot beam would draw only two feet of water and could carry two tons of freight.

All sorts of names were given these boats—women's names like *Ida, Gussie, Pearl, Lizzie* and *Rebecca*. The names of states and of presidents were used. McKinley's was the most popular. There were names like *Four Leaf Clover, Lucky Star, Lucky Number, Golden Horseshoe*. Most of the boats had an American flag strung on somewhere. They made a weird flotilla. Some were sailed with blankets. They were often top heavy. They sank, they listed and careened, leaked, were gulped by riffles. All of them, even the soundest ones spanking down the current, were stalled on the mud bars sooner or later. Before the twentieth of June, 1898, the register at Tagish Post showed that 3,850 boats had passed that point in two months. By the end of the summer the figure was 7,080. The number of passengers was close to 28,000.

Although the boatbuilding camps were much pleasanter places than any stop the Klondikers made along the passes, there was still haste, competition, a continual pushing which kept everyone on the edge of his nerves. The experience of the pass had toughened them to accident and death. Wretchedness had made them insensitive to each other. Men died of disease in tent after tent and no one but a partner would take the time to bury them. Some fell through the ice, which softened invisibly from below in treacherous traps. When one partner died, the other usually gave up and turned back. It didn't look like country a man could tackle alone.

When an accident cost a man his outfit there was nothing to do but go back to Dyea for another one. The alternative was robbery. Crimes of violence began to appear. If a man was going to be murdered he was not shot, he was hacked with an ax. If there was an argument of any kind it drew knives.

The weaker in spirit reconsidered the whole idea of going to Dawson. They had learned about the mud bars that criss-crossed the river, grounding the boats until the gear was removed and men got into the water and pushed the boat free. And after another few hundred yards the boat stuck again. "The bars and the muddy water are so near the same color that you can't tell the difference till you've struck something. Then it's all hands out, and if you can't budge her you carry the gear to shore, and then you try. It's mighty cold water."

Resting from a bout with the whipsaw, they heard old-timers telling stories about wind. "A favorable breeze sprung up and we got going. In two hours it was a regular gale. We made for shore. That wind never let up, it knocked our tent down, blew the coffee right out of the cup. When things calmed down we shoved out into the river so as to take what advantage we could out of a good strong wind but we had hardly gone half a mile when it died down and we had to row all the rest of the way to our next camp."

Nailing the boat together, the builder wondered if it was strong enough to buck the rapids. He thought of what he had heard about the rocks in the river. "There's a rock in the Thirty-Mile called 'Casey.' A fellow hit it on the nose but he wasn't hurt himself at all. He clumb out, dripping and mad, but his money belt was still fast to him. He lost every pound of gear that he had but he went back out for more.

Well, he come back over the Chilkoot, and he built at Lindeman, come through the lakes, Miles Canyon, The Squaw and
everything else. And if he didn't wreck on it again! What he
done, he stepped in and out of one or two tents till he found
what he was after, and right then and there he blew his brains
out."

Many an amateur boatbuilder looked at the thing he had
created. The raw red lumber was spattered with pitch. The
box-sides were two feet high, the tarpaulin sail dragged de-
jectedly. He didn't even wait to see if it would hold water
or not. He left it askew in the limestone gravel and went
home.

In summer the days were long. The sunshine seemed endless to men traveling on an open boat. The blizzards had not
been pleasant but they came and went. Eventually there was
some relief from a storm, but there was no escaping the sun
and its blistering burns. The Yukon summer temperature is
surprisingly high. It quickly reaches the nineties and remains
there, scarcely cooled by thunder showers or an hour or two
of twilight out of every twenty-four.

Although the moist, warm blanket of stifling air seemed to
be moving it was not so; there were few freshening breezes.
The undulations in the air were mosquitoes, great black
blotches of them, careening, diving, singing with ecstasy. This
delicacy of tender flesh! Let the bears and the moose run up
to the snow line! (They did, for safety, at the first larval
stir.) Let the Indians sit in their thick columns of smoke! (It
was their only protection.) Here was boatload after boatload
of provender, a banquet fit for Anopheles.

No Yukon explorer failed to mention the mosquitoes. No
Klondike diary overlooked them. They were dreaded above
all other perils. Men would run the rivers' rapids with some
semblance of courage, but under an assault of proboscis
stingers they winced and covered up their eyes. Frozen toes

and snowblindness brought trouble of their own, but mosquito welts itched a man's hide until he was frenzied. Blasphemies, puffed from swollen cheeks, gave him little satisfaction.

The explorer Dall, in writing of his travels on the Yukon, said: "The mosquitoes were like smoke in the air. Through constant and enforced observation, I came to distinguish four kinds,—a large gray one, and another with white leg-joints, a very small dust-colored one which held its proboscis horizontally in advance, and another small one which carried its probe in the orthodox manner. All were distinguished from the civilized species by the reckless daring of their attack. Thousands might be killed before their eyes, yet the survivors sounded their trumpets and carried on the war. A blanket offered them no impediment; buckskin alone defied their art. At meal-times, forced to remove our nets, we sat until nearly stifled in the smoke, and, emerging for a breath of air, received no mercy. My companion's hands, between sunburn and mosquitoes, were nearly raw, and I can well conceive that a man without a net, in one of these marshes, would soon die from nervous exhaustion."

Explorer Schwatka, in writing of his experiences on the river, stated that the mosquitoes were at times so thick he could not take accurate aim with his rifle when he might have shot game for the party. He also had some experience with mosquito netting. Wrote he, "If the insects are so thick that they constantly touch each other on the mosquito-bar when crawling over it, it will be of no protection whatever if the meshes are of the usual size. They will come in so fast that comfort is out of the question. Even if there are two or three to the square inch of your bar of many square yards, it surprises you how few get through, but the minute they begin crawling over each other they seem to become furious, and make efforts to squeeze through. The doctor, in a fit of exasperation, said he believed that two of them would hold the legs and wings of another flat against its body while a third shoved it through . . . but I think they are too mean to help each other."

In this section of the Yukon's headwaters there were also gnats. Of these Schwatka writes: "These flies made it necessary to keep constantly swinging a towel in the air, and a momentary cessation of this exertion might be punished by having a piece bitten out of one that a few days later would look like an incipient boil. One of the party so bitten was completely disabled for a week, and at the moment of infliction it was hard to believe that he was not disabled for life."

Leaving the colors of Bennett, the purple dark canyons winding down to the white beaches, the red-stained mountains of hematite with their crowns of ice, the blue glaciers, the still lake reflecting it all, the boatman steered for the beetling rock at the entrance to the river-way which would take him down into the next lake. At the spill the current ran four miles an hour, but the water soon swirled into a thick roll of mud and coiled slowly into Tagish Lake over driftwood and bars. This link between lakes was Caribou Crossing, called so because the herds crossed here into the feeding grounds to the valley beyond.

Tagish spread before them, in open country again, another mirroring body of water, rimmed with wide, flat terraces that stepped up into the distant mountain ranges.

Halfway down the river between Tagish and the next lake, Marsh, were an Indian village on one side and Tagish Post on the other. Here the Mounted Police halted the boats both to register them and to see that each man showed a customs receipt for his outfit. If a boat failed to stop, a shot was fired across the water directly in front of it.

Beyond Tagish there were no mountains. The timber was gone. Lake Marsh was a bowl of mud twenty miles long, discolored by the spongy walls of silt which were its banks. Glaciers fed it sand and debris, and the miry bottom oozed under the ripples. The lake was named for Professor Othniel Charles Marsh of Yale, but the Klondikers called it "Mud Lake" from the first.

These names, Lindeman, Bennett, Marsh, as well as numerous others, were given to the geography by Schwatka, who believed he was the first white man to explore the upper Yukon country. But in 1882 Arthur Krause of the Bremen Geographical Society had crossed the Chilkoot and gone down the lakes as far as Tagish, returning by way of the headwaters of that lake. Schwatka, therefore, did not know that the German scientist had already named Lindeman, calling it Krause Lake for himself, and he gave that body of water the name of Krause's superior, Dr. Moritz Lindeman, Vice President of the Society. Bennett was named for James Gordon Bennett, the owner of the *New York Herald,* who was famous for having sent Stanley into Africa to find Livingstone.

Fifty-Mile River ran out of Lake Marsh. It was a torrent that widened and grew swifter with every mile until it was five hundred feet wide and falling with a six-mile current. After thirty miles or so the river seemed to end abruptly against a stone wall, but actually it narrowed to less than a hundred feet and shot down out of sight.

From the very beginning of the journey the boatmen had heard the warning, "Keep a sharp lookout!" and had called it over the water themselves. The trip was a first experience, the men did not know what was coming next, a barricade of fallen timber, a shallow, a boulder, or a finger-spread of streams, one of which they must quickly choose. The lake shores were curved with buttresses and coves, and the passages were blocked with sentinel rocks. The rivers were serpentine. The boat could splash around a bend into almost anything. If a hazard ahead appeared to a boatload of men they tried to warn others coming behind them. The Mounted Police advised a careful and sharp watch at all times.

When the men came to the buttes of the Fifty-Mile, they

knew they had reached the first of the three worst obstacles in the river, the channel named for the Indian fighter and ranking officer of the United States Army, General Nelson A. Miles. The channel caught the full force of the river, sucked it through a narrow gate in the canyon's basalt walls, and pulled it on in a side-sweeping roll that did not loosen until it was torn apart by the whirlpool called The Squaw. A forest of black spruce and pine on top of the palisades heightened the steepness of the gorge.

The river leapt in with thundering reverberation, falling fifty feet at the first drop, and spuming up again. In less than a mile it was grabbed by The Squaw and spun around. From there it raced on, full of wreckage and lost goods, through two miles of flat country to a chain of stubby hills that blocked its way. There the stream narrowed again, this time to a twenty-foot sluice, and the first plunge down was more abrupt and more dangerous than the plunge into Miles. Waves tossed and kicked in wildest confusion for a quarter of a mile and then fell, boiling upon boulders that filled the remaining two hundred feet of the channel. In this stretch the spray rose fifteen feet and the whole cut was a seething scene of galloping "white horses." From White Horse Rapids it was a sheer nine-foot drop, and then, churning over and over, but calmer than it had been, the river bubbled the boats on into Lake Lebarge.

Before attempting to run the rapids of Miles Canyon, the boatmen usually got out and took a look at it. They crowded on top of the palisades. They would cut a tree down and throw it into the water to see what happened. It usually disappeared. If not it went downstream buffeted like a cork, first one end up and then the other. A boat would come down the chute, sail furled, gear tied, the men hanging on for precious life. It might capsize, and from the cliff the men would hardly see where the boat and its occupants scattered, they would pass so violently. Another boat would come into the channel empty, and perhaps make it. Finally, the Klondikers would cut a slab of bark off some tree and pencil in their names and the date. Then they would go back to their boats, empty them and prepare to portage the goods ahead, cutting the boat loose to make it if it could. Or else they would hire a pilot. The Indians were getting $10 to take an empty boat all the way through Miles Canyon, The Squaw and White Horse Rapids.

In The Squaw the trick was to keep the boat out of the swirling water, to hug the palisades. If the boat was pulled in, it would spin until it broke apart or was smashed against the walls. Sometimes The Squaw, herself, cast it out unharmed into the river below. But nineteen boats were lost to her in 1897, and that first summer two hundred persons died of injuries or drowning in these three ordeals of the river. In 1898 the Mounted Police were on hand to bar all boats carrying passengers unless they were being taken through by a licensed pilot. There was loud criticism of this. The men asked each other if the action had been taken out of an interest in their welfare or to collect the pilot's license fee which was required. The charge for piloting rose to $25, and white men now competed with the Indians.

More than one Klondiker with swift-water experience got his first taste of big money here. Jack London, for one, had made $3,000 the year before by hiring himself out as a pilot. The delay made him late. The Yukon River was a flowing belt of ice blocks before he reached the mouth of the Stewart. There a blizzard halted him for the rest of the winter and he did not see the gold fields until spring.

The White Horse Rapids were extremely difficult to navigate but, on the other hand, the river had wide ledges and the men could carry the boat along here if they wanted to. In fact, it was possible to portage all the way from the top of Miles. A crude windlass had been set up to hoist the gear out of the boats and onto the top of the cliff. The trail went all the way down to the bottom of White Horse. Opposite this foot trail, on the side of the canyon, was McCauley's roadhouse and tramline. The tramline was a four-mile track of skinned pine poles on which the freight was moved at five cents a pound, in boxcars pulled along by horses. It also came out below the rocks of White Horse.

Ver Mehr recalled that their party had stopped at Cranky Creek, a thread of water this side of Miles Canyon, and had gone to the bluff to take a look. "Grizzly" Meyers was still with them and upon his advice they hired an old Indian called "Daddy" to take them through. "He sat there on the bank and smoked cigarettes while we took the gear out of the boat. Then two of us got in with him. He said he was hired to do the steering and not the rowing. You have to row out of The Squaw. Hawley and me went with him and Ray and the dogs went back up on the bluff to watch.

"Well, we shot in and out of Miles so fast we hardly knew what happened, and we had hardly caught our breath when Daddy hollered, 'Row shore! Row shore!' And we sure did. We pulled for all we were worth. And then we felt that boat crack flat on her bottom and we knew we were out of there.

"We bumped to the end of the straight-of-way and turned and slid into White Horse. There were so many boats heading in there with us that we were scared we'd get hit for sure. But Daddy brought us through all right. We landed as good as new. Daddy just leaned on the sweep and smoked his cigarette, looking out over the calm green grass like nothing had happened. We gave him two five-dollar gold pieces that he tucked into his poke. The thing was already as fat as a muskmelon.

"We were soaked to the skin and while we sat there on the bank, resting and drying off, we saw some barrels of whiskey come down. A crew of men were standing in the water below, ready to catch them. Fifty barrels had been turned into the river at the top of Miles, and, sure enough, all fifty of them came through.

"Daddy told us the Indians made their own liquor. They learned how from a soldier stationed at Wrangell a long time before, when there was an army post at Wrangell. The Hootz-noo tribe had a village there, and the soldier showed them how to make a mash out of molasses, berries, wild apples, flour, any old thing they had on hand that would rot and ferment. They put a little cayenne pepper in for flavor. Well, when this stuff fermented, they ran it through a still that they made out of two five-gallon coal-oil cans, connected with a hollow stem of seaweed. They called this Hootz-noo liquor 'hootch,' for short, and they drunk it hot off the still. You know, I forgot all about that story until Prohibition, when people in this country began making 'hootch' in their washtubs.

"Daddy sure liked to talk. He told us one story after the other. He told something real interesting about the salmon. They come up the Yukon same as they do everywhere else. Well, it's two thousand miles, about, from the Bering Sea to Lake Tagish where the last of the salmon are seen. They swim right up the White Horse and The Squaw and up and out of Miles. He said they weighed a good forty pounds apiece. The bears always hung around there after the salmon. The river was so choked up with fish that the bears just had to reach in and scoop them out. Of course, the Indians got both the salmon and the bear.

"The very next trip after ours that Daddy made, he lost the boat and was drowned with all aboard. I used to wonder if some cheechako found his first gold in Daddy's fished-out poke."

On the flats below White Horse many camped until they had brought their outfits down from Miles. In 1897, if a man had lost his boat it was a serious thing, there being no other way to continue the trip to Dawson. In 1898 he could wait for the next steamer.

The first of these upper Yukon boats were two forty-foot steamers, the *A. J. Goddard* and the *J. H. Kilbourne*. The parts were brought over the Chilkoot Pass and reassembled at Lake Bennett. The first boat to reach Dawson from up the river the second summer was the *Bellingham*, which arrived on June 14. Within the week eight steamers came in, and on June 23 the *Victoria*, in from St. Michael, continued up the river to Rink Rapids with three hundred and fifty persons who were going out over the Dalton trail on horseback. The fare for this trip was $250 from Dawson, including steamer, horse and board.

Other boats going to Bennett were the *Flora* and *Nora*, which connected with a sister ship, the *Ora*, at White Horse. The fare from Dawson to Bennett was $175, including board but not bedding. Coming downriver to Dawson the fare was only $75. Also on the Bennett run were the *Willie Irving*, the *Anglian*, and the *Clara*. There were sternwheelers on this part of the river too, among them the *Casca, Sourdough, Yukoner, Bonanza King, Australian*, and the *Gleaner*.

The sternwheelers carried only passengers, mail, and express. The freight was put onto hundred-foot barges and pushed ahead of the steamer. Each barge could carry from a hundred and twenty-five to a hundred and fifty tons, and each steamer had at least one barge in front of it, while many had two or three, manipulated by ropes and tackle. To push these barges down the river required enormous skill, but it was done every day, over the rapids and through the rocks.

The powerful engines of the sternwheelers burned a cord of wood an hour and covered the distance between White Horse and Dawson in forty hours. Coming back upstream over the same route required four days, barges empty. These were all hundred-ton boats on the upper river. Those which were on the lower river, between Dawson and St. Michael, were four-hundred-ton boats, but otherwise quite similar with their three decks, two funnels and perch for the lookout.

Work on the railroad over White Pass was begun in August, 1898; by March of the next year a roadbed had been cut through the pass; by July 6 it was completed to Lake Bennett, a distance of forty miles. In 1900 the railroad reached White Horse over a hundred and ten miles of track, saving the last Klondikers nearly three times that distance by trail.

The next, and last, lake was Lebarge. The country was wooded once more and the resinous smoke of pine fires filled the air. Many of these were campfires, purposely smoky to discourage mosquitoes. Miles of forest were also burning, set afire by the campers who often left fires for the next boatload of men that might come along. A few reindeer wandered along the shore.

Lake Lebarge has been called the most pictorial of all the lakes. Its thirty-mile length varied in width from five to ten miles, its shores thrust out into headlands that seemed to be islands. The slopes were mystery-dark forests, the water was intensely blue, and the beaches were white. Granite mountains receded to the east in a triple chain of polished domes which were fingered with the foliage of the woods. The mountains on the west were red. Several streams flowed into the lake, muddying it with yellow ribbons.

The lake was named for a French Canadian, Michael Lebarge, who had been a voyageur for the Hudson's Bay Company and who later joined the telegraph explorers and went with Kennicott into Siberia. He was with Kennicott's successor, exploring the lower Yukon, and later reached Fort Selkirk. He arrived just ahead of the news that the project had been abandoned. In the meantime he had heard of a lake of unsurpassed beauty, which had been discovered above the fort. It was the only lake known to exist in the Yukon. Lebarge had hoped to see it, had talked much about it. Because of his enthusiasm the lake was often fondly called "Lebarge's lake." His disappointment was deep at having to leave the country without having seen his lake and he planned to return, but never did. The Tagish Indians called the lake Tlootatsai, but the telegraph men always called it Lake Lebarge, and that was the name they wrote down on the maps.

Lake Lebarge emptied into the Thirty-Mile River, another rough stretch of water. The half-submerged rocks seemed to leap out of the water as the boats came skidding to them over the foam. It took two men on the sweeps, steering first to one side and then to the other, with the water convulsing the boats and spinning them like driftwood. Casey's Rock was at the end of this river. If the boat missed it, all was well for the Five Finger Rapids and Rink Rapids.

Beyond Casey's Rock, the river was called the Lewes, although every mile of water from the rivulets of snow that melted off the passes was properly the Yukon. In early days the river's complete course was not known. Some thought the Teslin was the source of the Yukon, others thought it began at its confluence with the Pelly, at Selkirk. Still others gave the name of Pelly to the Yukon all the way from Selkirk to where the Porcupine came in. The name Yukon was first used by J. Bell, on an exploration trip for the Hudson's Bay Company in 1846. In that year he reached the mouth of the Porcupine, at the Great Bend. Below this point the river was called Kwikpak by the Russians, the name being a native word for "big river." Above this point the river was known by an Indian name, Yukukakat. *Kakat* meant river, *Yuku*, big. It was also called Yukukonkakat. Bell wrote "Youcon" for both the name of the river and the fort.

Meanwhile, Robert Campbell, another Hudson's Bay factor, had explored the headwaters of the Pelly and concluded that this should be the name of the river all the way to the Great Bend. The name Yukon does not appear on Arrowsmith's map published in 1854, that of Pelly standing for the entire length of the stream as Campbell named it. In 1861 a Russian map showed the "Yuku" River to Fort Selkirk. On the United States Coast Survey map dated 1867 the river between the

Porcupine and Lewes is named Yukon for the first time, although a later map, one accompanying Raymond's official report of 1871, shows this name only on the portion of the river below Fort Yukon, giving the name Lewes to the river all the way from Fort Yukon to Lake Lebarge.

On the Lewes, as the Klondikers called the river from Lebarge to Selkirk, the Hootalinqua River poured in shortly after passing Casey's Rock. Beyond a driftwood wall, boats were stopped by the Police for another check-up, and then went on at four miles an hour, the oars scarcely touching the swift water. Big Salmon and Little Salmon came in, then the rocks appeared which marked the entrance to Five Finger Rapids. These rocks looked as if a stone bridge had fallen into the river, but once a boat slipped safely through them, and was past white water, there was nothing left to face but the Rink. In a short time this last whirlpool caught the boat and spun it around a little but it was really nothing to the hardened boatmen. They soon saw the high plateau on which old Fort Selkirk stood, and there they swerved from the Pelly's mouth and were at last on the full stream. They entered it between splendid parapets of stone which continued for a hundred miles.

Fifty, sixty, seventy-five miles a day, the little boats went down, keeping together, warping their way through hundreds of evergreen isles. Six miles an hour was a dizzying speed in a catboat. The men hung onto the gear. They stopped only to eat, never to sleep. At Selkirk and White River they had to again give account of themselves to the Police, but they flew past the Stewart and Indian and Sixty-Mile. The triumphant hour was near, the Union Jacks of Dawson were flying just around the next bend of the river.

11

THE QUEEN OF THE YUKON

IN August, 1896, when Robert Henderson reached John Ladue's store at Sixty-Mile, he told him the good news of his strike on Gold Bottom, and paid him from his gold to prove it.

When Ladue got around to taking his boat down the river to Deer Creek, to see for himself what Robbie Henderson had got up there in that moose pasture, his eyes popped as he swung around the last bend of the river. The lonely bog that he expected to see was not lonely any more. He couldn't count the tents pegged down in the mud. Nor the boats staked to the beach for half a mile. He had a difficult time finding a place to get up onto the shore. But Ladue was happy. "Robbie's hit it! He sure has, it's a stampede!"

At first Ladue could not believe that nobody had heard of Henderson and that the stampede was not to a creek called Gold Bottom but to another one which all referred to as the Bonanza.

"Where is it?"

"Right up the creek—the first gulch you come to. You won't miss it."

"What are they getting?"

"Well, I, myself, washed $10 from a pan the first of the week.

I'm scraping it right off the rim. Mister, you better get your-self a shovel."

Not John Ladue. He'd seen fourteen years of stampedes and he was still a poor man. He was sure he'd come out better in the long run if he'd stick to the sawmill. The miners all had to have lumber. Another thing, they would need pro-visions. After looking over the Bonanza, and carefully count-ing heads, he went back to Sixty-Mile to move his sawmill and what goods he had to the mouth of Deer Creek. He got in touch with Arthur Harper, who was keeping store at Fort Selkirk. He came at once.

They went up to Fort Cudahy and tried to buy the Deer Creek mud flat from the Dominion Government, but they could buy only 178 acres of it. The Crown wanted to keep the other 22 acres for its own use. The Mounted Police were moving up from Fort Cudahy and would have to build a barracks. Harper and Ladue subdivided their 178 acres into town lots. There was plenty of room, they made the streets sixty-six feet wide.

Harper was too ill to remain in the country over the winter and he went out to Arizona. Ladue built a cabin in the middle of town and opened his first barrel of whiskey. The sawmill made a reassuring drone, cutting spruce behind him at $100 a thousand feet for raw lumber and $200 for planed. The lots were going nicely at $500 apiece. The camp was called the Harper and Ladue townsite but in six months its resi-dents learned it was to be Dawson City. Ogilvie named it for his chief, George Mercer Dawson, director of Canada's Geographical Survey.

From a population of four or five hundred, that first winter of 1896, Dawson grew to 5,000 in the summer of 1897, and to 30,000 the following year. Ladue's town lots were then selling for as high as $10,000 apiece—to a successor. Harper had died in Yuma, in November, 1897, and Ladue in New York the following year, both from tuberculosis. Ladue had returned to his home town of Schuyler Falls, New York, where his girlhood sweetheart married him a few months before his death. It was said that her well-to-do father would not consent to the marriage when they were young, because of Ladue's lack of means and dubious prospects of acquiring any. She waited, and at forty-three Ladue was not only one of the Klondike "millionaires," but famous, as well, for having founded a city.

When the first scows began swarming in from the passes in 1897, Dawson became a city of tents. Those who could not afford to buy one of the lots pitched their tents on the hillside, and reached them by squirming trails. Or else they lived on their tarpaulin-rigged boats until they could find a creek to move to. The creeks were crowded too. After the first few weeks of the rush the scows were lined up three and four deep, tied one behind the other, in a wobbly two-mile clutter from the mouth of the Klondike to Moosehide Hill.

Front Street faced the Yukon River. It was the business section of Dawson. The shacks were new that summer, bare, rough-lumber boxes one-story high. Between them were tent stores and tent hotels. Some of the latter were two stories high. Three hundred log cabins were up, and several large buildings including the company stores. The warehouses were long, low structures covered with corrugated iron. The Police post consisted of a number of log houses arranged around three sides of a square. These were used for quarters and storerooms, a post office, court room and other government business. The fourth side faced the Yukon and was closed off by a fence.

There were no sidewalks in 1897. The melted snow and May rains slushed the streets six inches deep with mud. A few high trees still remained at the northern edge of town and behind them could be seen the patch of shale which the slide had torn out of the wooded hillside. The patch looked exactly like a huge moosehide stretched out to dry.

Deer Creek, now called the Klondike River, swirled around into the Yukon, dividing the mud flat into two unequal areas hemmed in by hills. To the north of the Klondike was Dawson City, on the longer stretch of beach. To the south was a shorter apron of mud and gravel. This had been the Indian camp. The chief's cabin was still there. All the Yukon Indians were a grimy, louse-stuck bunch, reeking with rancid salmon and animal-hide clothing. The atmosphere of their villages, especially that of their summer salmon camps, permeated the earth under them and the air above. The miners had reason to call the camp at Deer Creek "Lousetown," but when several thousand of them overflowed Dawson, and had to crowd onto the bank below, the name was changed euphemistically to Klondike City.

Dawson was never a "wild west" town, another Creede or Angel's Camp. The majority of its bearded, booted, buckskinned population was neither quick on the draw nor heavy of poke. Dawson had no starbright sheriff. They didn't "have a man for breakfast" there every morning.

It wasn't posse country, nor six-shooter country. The Dominion Government was spending $396,000 a year to keep law and order in the district. The Mounties had the job. In 1897 their number was increased from thirty to eighty and the next year two hundred and fifty crack Winnipeg constables were added. There never was a stick-up worth mentioning, nor a big robbery. Now and then a cabin was entered and the grub stolen, or a baking powder can full of dust was lifted, but miners weren't highjacked on the trail the way they were around Skagway. During the winter of 1897 Soapy Smith and a few friends visited Dawson, having walked in over the ice all the way from Skagway. They were met by the police who headed them back to salt water in spite of the fact that the temperature that day was forty below. Once a mule in a pack train coming down from the creeks got out of line somehow and was lost for several hours with $49,000 worth of Clarence Berry's gold on its back. But it was safely found, with the heavy pouches still strapped on.

Neither the trading companies nor Wells Fargo was ever robbed, although gold into the millions of dollars' worth was shipped out regularly. The nearest thing to a calamity of this sort was the Chinese pirate rumor that was circulated just before the *Portland* returned to Seattle for the second time in 1897. About the only excitement they had in Dawson were stampedes and fires, or watching the ice break up on the Yukon in spring, or holding protest meetings against the Canadian way of doing things.

From the beginning, the capital of the Yukon Territory had law and taxes, and census takers and visiting ministers, and a copy of *Burke's Peerage* on the governor's shelf. Queen Victoria's photograph and the Union Jack were never out of sight. There were any number of "Honorables" and "Sirs" in town. A score of world-wide correspondents were there, including one for Reuter's. Lloyds of London sent an agent to check its risks.

While the police saw to the law and order, and maintained a wood pile for offenders, moneys due the Crown from assessments, fines, and taxes were pursued by a handpicked set of officials sent from Ottawa. The first set lasted only a year. They were called on the carpet to testify for themselves on charges of corruption and mismanagement brought against them by the miners. They were exonerated but gradually replaced. By the time the second set was functioning, the gumboot miners had lost their claims and the Dominion was dealing almost entirely with companies. In Dawson the sinister character was not the saloonkeeper, with his girls and games. Even in a silken waistcoat and a handlebar mustache he was still innocuous. He was merely another businessman and pretty well liked in the community. The "villain" in Dawson, so far as Americans were concerned, was the gold commissioner. There wasn't a miner on the creeks who had a good word for the man who collected the annual royalty. There was no love lost, anyway, between the Americans and the Canadians. There were recriminations and distrust between them the whole time the Americans worked the Klondike, which wasn't long. In 1899 they were off to Nome, where there was no government at all. Americans felt the lion's paw heavily in Dawson.

In 1898 crowds of men loitered in the streets all summer. They milled about so thickly that the dogs and horses could hardly get their drays and carts through. They were a slow-moving swarm of idlers left over from the first Klondike winter, plus new arrivals spilling in from the passes and coming ashore in droves off the continually arriving steamboats. Those from the year before had neither mines nor hopes of getting any. They had stampeded in vain all winter and barely kept themselves alive on the food they had brought in. Now they were waiting for some stroke of luck to get them out of Dawson, though none could imagine what that might be. They had been sleeping in the saloons, now they lived in the streets. The first warm days felt good. The sun penetrated their rags.

Joaquin Miller was one of these men. He had been caught in Dawson when the steamers failed to arrive at the end of summer. He had no outfit, nor the means of buying one. He had come in with only a knapsack and a return ticket to San Francisco. The ticket was worthless; he could not dispose of it for a sack of flour. He had no alternative but to try to walk out of the country. But long before he neared Circle City, about two hundred and twenty miles from Dawson, early October storms whipped him back and the cold froze his cheeks and nose. He tried to go on but could not and finally had to retrace his steps. It took him thirty-five days to walk back—a death-defying experience for a fifty-six-year-old man.

He was out of food, he could not stop, except momentarily, lest he fall asleep and freeze to death. Only strength of will drove him on, though he had to crawl the last miles. In Dawson he was taken in by the Sisters of St. Anne, who nursed him back to health. Although he was severely frozen, prompt treatment saved all but an ear and a toe.

Joaquin Miller, born Cincinnatus Hiner, reported the Bonanza as a poet saw it, through lavender mists of heliotrope veiling the late summer hills. He had cupped his ear to the "twittering brotherhood of the forest" and ignored the prospectors talking bedrock, muck, and taxes. Miller was not a novice in mining camps, he had whirled many a gold pan himself, in Colorado, Idaho, and California, but for some reason he could report the Klondike only from a scenic, sentimental eye. He sent out packages of manuscript filled with cerulean impressions that were published throughout the country.

When he was gone from Dawson, Gene Allen, editor of *The Klondyke Nugget,* wrote in part: "His glowing words were eagerly devoured by millions of readers, many of whom rested neither night nor day until they traveled and saw for themselves. But what an awakening! Where, oh, where, are the gorgeous blossoms changing the complexion of the hills from base to crest like the blushes of a maiden? Where are the endless varieties of nature's jewels which gladden the eyes of our traveler, and the mighty game on every hand, and the trout in every stream, and the gold glittering in every gravel bed?"

In May, Miller was found by a friend from home, Howard V. Sutherland, the former editor of two of San Francisco's famed weeklies, *News Letter* and *Wasp,* who had resigned the latter post to try his luck in the Klondike. He had been entrusted with a letter from the poet's aged mother. When Miller saw the familiar handwriting he wept audibly. Inside the envelope was money enough to buy a steamer ticket. "But I know I'll never see her alive," Miller said. "It's too late." It was. She died while he was on the way home.

Sutherland brought Miller to his tent and while they were eating, Colonel Steele of the Mounted Police passed by and spied the poet, whose description of crossing the Chilkoot the summer before with fresh-picked violets in his hands was already famous, but Miller did not know it. Steele, like many others who knew the facts, deplored these romantic touches. He pulled back the tent flap and gave the old man a tongue lashing. "You're responsible for the death of many fine men and the ruin of thousands!" he cried at Miller, who lowered his head and held it meekly over his plate. When Sutherland felt Steele had bellowed long enough he reminded him that Miller was a guest at his table. Either the remonstrance or Sutherland's British accent, for he was born a Londoner, quenched the astonished Steele, who excused himself and backed away, with a last-shot warning to Miller about not writing any more poetry about the Yukon.

Sutherland said he had felt foolish after the Colonel left, for his "table" was one of several sacks lying on the bare ground and they were eating out of the frying pan with two tin spoons. In the heat of feeling he had forgotten where they were and wished he had chosen other words for Steele. He tried to cheer up Miller after the scene but it was impossible. Miller was gone from Dawson in a few days. "He was not liked there," Sutherland said. "No one but myself came to wish him godspeed on his journey."

Few arrived in Dawson wearing puff ties and spats. Most of the 1898 cheechakos looked, and were, no more prosperous than the disappointed men they saw crowded to the water front. First impressions of the town were of its steaming muddy streets—for it rained frequently early in the summer and the temperature was seldom under eighty; of its hundreds of British and American flags blowing as if for a holiday; of its dog-drawn funeral carts, endlessly passing by on their way uphill to the cemetery; of the enormously high prices which kept most men from buying even a square meal. A canned oyster stew was $15 a bowl. A cucumber was $5, a radish $1. Porterhouse steak was $8 at the Arcade restaurant, one of the few places where they served beefsteak. Moose was commoner. The Arcade was called a "second Delmonico's" because the waiters wore alpaca jackets and held napkins over their wrists.

Dawson was cramped for space. Rough cabins rented for $75 and $100 a month. There wasn't a yard of water pipe or sewer in the city. The cabins were unfurnished in the civilized sense of the word. The only inducement an advertisement could carry was the phrase, "no lice." To build a cabin cost about $1,500 for green lumber and labor. The price of a lot was "wild," it was worth whatever the owner could get. One corner lot on Front Street sold for $20,000.

Drinking water was scarce. It came from two springs which seeped from the hills in back of town. Some of the cheechakos went into business delivering water for twenty-five cents a gallon. Two public privies were built on the tide-flat. The Klondike eddy churned with the refuse and garbage the river brought down from the creeks and what was added to it at Dawson. It belched swill halfway across the Yukon River. Flies, mosquitoes, bacteria procreated with abandon. The odors penetrated. And there was no night and no shade. In July, Dawson was blistering. "It's the hottest Arctic Circle you ever seen," the cheechakos wrote home.

Every man wanted to get out of town but he soon discovered that the gold-bearing creeks, which were up in the hills three to thirty miles away, were completely staked. If he still wanted to hunt for gold, the rest of the Yukon valley was his to prospect. Stunned at this turn of events, crowded out of Dawson, bewildered and disappointed, hundreds of newcomers joined the aimless throngs on Front Street.

The street was hung with banners calling attention to leading saloons and theaters, extolling the local brewery, advertising pack trains, announcing the arrival and departure of steamboats. Signs, bills of fare, letters were tacked to every wall and post within reach. Many picked up their mail this way, from door jambs and random cracks. It was much simpler than waiting in line for hours for the mail to be given out. The post office was the leading crank subject of Dawson, lambasted by everyone, Canadians as well as Americans. The mail was distributed by two harassed and inexperienced police clerks, in a small cabin where not more than eight or nine people could collect at once. While the clerks delved into sacks of unalphabetized mail (it seems there was never time to stop and sort it, the clamor to get at it was so insistent), the line outside grew ever longer. Rather than wait five or six hours, many bought their way ahead in line from regular standers who sold their places for an ounce of gold. Or they hired somebody to get their mail and leave it in an agreed place. Women often did this, for a dollar a letter. It was easy for them, they had the privilege of the side door.

Theater bills, gossip, personals, bargains were placed in spots convenient to the eye. It was one way to get back to San Francisco. "Make me an offer for my outfit. Find me on the scow *Bessie*, opposite the Pioneer. H. J. Kreling." Before the newspapers came to town, items of public interest were posted in the street. "Billy Cole, the man who was stabbed last night, is coming along fine, although he may not have the same use of his back as he had." Wives sent messages to the police to post them for husbands who had failed to write or come home. Friends found each other. Business was transacted. "If B. B. Johnson will communicate with Alfred Herold he will learn something to his advantage."

Many things were for sale in Dawson, most of them stacked on boxes in the street. There weren't many shops, show windows didn't exist. Prices fluctuated with the season. The first fryers that came up from Seattle in spring were sold three for

$100. Eggs were $3 each, watermelons were $40 each, apples and oranges were $1 each. As soon as the boats began to come in Signor Gandolfo rented a five-foot space between two buildings, put a tarpaulin overhead, and opened a few boxes of fresh fruit. If his prices were high, Gandolfo didn't think of lowering them. The rent was $120 a month.

C. A. Bartholam, a Klondiker with foresight enough to bring seeds with him, was a better businessman than Gandolfo. He staked a "worthless" bank of the Klondike, a mile above town, and planted vegetables. The dampness and long hours of sunshine provided an ideal "hot house," and within a month his cabbages, cucumbers, tomatoes, turnips and carrots were ready for market, and he was ahead $1,000 on an investment of fifty cents.

Some things were scarce the winter of 1897. Salt was worth exactly its weight in gold. There wasn't a safety pin to be had; there was no window glass for sale, no chinaware, only a very few nails and these sold for $28 a pound. A small cache of cigars dwindled away. Bull Durham reached $1 a sack. The only broom was sold for $14. But by summer Dawson had these things, and other unheard-of Arctic luxuries— pineapples and bananas from the Sandwiches (which on July 7, 1898, the United States would annex and call the Hawaiian Islands), curled ostrich plumes from France, Turkish rugs, chocolates, opera glasses, tennis rackets, cribbage boards, silk hose, chewing gum. A cow and kitten arrived. The cow gave two milkings and died, but while she lasted the thin, blue-white drink cost $4 a glass. The kitten was delivered to the Yukon Mining Exchange.

Horses came in on barges from the lakes, with hay to be sold at $1,200 a ton. In August the price dropped to $800, then to $400. It was the high cost of feed that boosted the hiring charge of a horse and wagon to $150 a day, without a driver. His hire added another $15. In 1897 there were only eight horses in Dawson, and these had been killed at the end of summer and sold for dog food. It was not believed that a horse could endure the extreme cold, and if it could not work no man was paying high prices to feed an idle animal through the winter. A new horse would cost him less than feed to keep the one he had.

But in 1898 the police experimented. Their mounts had lived through the winter in Manitoba, which had a rigorous climate to be sure. Perhaps they would survive in Dawson. In September they were turned out into near-by valleys, where they made out well enough. Like reindeer and caribou, they dug through the snow to the vegetation beneath for their food. In 1899 the local red-topped grass was cut and dried, and over a thousand horses were kept at work all winter, packing to and from the mines. Reindeer, the ideal work animal for the country, were not used. Breeding grounds were not established by the Canadians and the Alaska government stations were not parting with any of their deer for Canada's use.

Dawson had a variety of services to offer. You could get your watch repaired, your front teeth filled with souvenir nuggets, you could take a "swimming bath" at the local gym for $2.50. A shave and haircut cost $1.50. You could have your photograph taken or your dandruff removed. It cost $2 to have a shirt washed, but then starch was $2.50 a box instead of a nickel at home. You could have your palm read. Mrs. Lowe combined washing clothes with palmistry and hung a sign on her tent declaring so. Lulu Craig started a school.

The three Dawson papers, *The Klondyke Nugget, Yukon Midnight Sun,* and *Dawson Miner* carried ads of auctioneers, "lady typewriters," jewelers, chemists, blacksmiths, brokers, assayers, undertakers, paperhangers, carpenters, furniture upholsterers, barbers, a masseuse, a garbage collector. Police Surgeon E. A. Willis opened a drug store. There were solicitors, dentists, physicians, mining engineers. It was necessary to have received a degree from a British or Canadian college before one could be licensed to practice medicine or law. Of the seventy doctors in Dawson, almost all of them were Americans and not allowed to open offices. However, they were all busy, Canadians and Americans alike, with or without permission. They charged $5 a visit and many of them were making $1,500 a month in sick calls. Americans in the legal profession really felt the discrimination for they could not bring a case to the Dominion court.

Dawson had a kind of "Blue Cross" in St. Mary's hospital, which sold annual memberships for three ounces of dust, entitling the holder to an all-expense service in times of sickness, however often, including nursing, board and washing, doctor's fee and operating costs. Non-subscribers paid $5 a day to the hospital and another $5 to the doctor for his daily visit. The Jesuit, Father Judge, built the hospital.

Judge had lived in the Yukon many years. He followed the stampeders from Forty-Mile and built a place of shelter where he could comfort and care for others. He knew the Yukon winter, its loneliness and disease, he knew that many would need him. Some he would feed, others he would nurse, many he would bury. In a few months his fifty beds were inadequate and pallets were put on the floor. In a chapel beside the larger "hospital" cabin, he sometimes fell asleep at his prayers. There was no one to help him that first winter, and the responsibilities and hours of work were endless. One night the chapel caught fire from a burnt-out candle at the knees of the drowsing priest. He awoke in time to save the hospital but his chapel was gone. Big Alec McDonald, "the King of the Klondike," promised to build him another one in summer, and he did, complete even to the organ.

McDonald was not of Judge's faith, but, on the other hand, Judge did not inquire into a man's religion when he came to him, or was brought on a litter. In Dawson they used to say of Judge, "He gives you the beans first and prays afterward." The summer of 1897 the sisters of the nursing order of St. Anne came to help him, and the hospital was enlarged to three stories and a wing. On January 10, 1899, "the most beloved man" in Dawson died.

There were other early churches in Dawson, of the Church of England, Episcopalian, Presbyterian and Methodist faiths, and there was a second hospital, in 1898, called The Good Samaritan. From the summer of 1897 the Salvation Army maintained a Shelter.

There were two banks. Until then the miners had entrusted their pokes to the trading companies and saloonkeepers, which was where the money went anyway. Money? There wasn't any, they used the raw dust. Currency and coin that turned up was scorned for cheechako money. To settle an account, the string was unwound from the small mooseskin sack which everyone carried (called a poke) and the dust was more or less cautiously poured out onto the saucer of a "blower." The degree of caution depended upon a man's proximity to pay dirt. The gold was weighed on the blower and any noticeable overweight was poured back into the poke.

The exchange was $16 an ounce because practically all of the town dust came from the Klondike creeks, which produced a coarse grade of gold liberally weighted with impurities. Gold from the American creeks was finer and purer and worth $17 and $18 an ounce. But the Americans didn't care, $16 an ounce was good enough, and they kept on shoveling.

In 1898 Dawson was like no other place in the world. It wasn't a mining camp, a frontier settlement, or a village. It wasn't a watch-and-chain, derby-hat, high-collar sort of town. It didn't have horse cars or gas lights. You couldn't send a penny post card from Dawson. They had the cards but they cost a dollar to send out. There wasn't a telephone, buggy or potted rubber plant in the whole Yukon. They sold mink capes and chamois-skin underwear but there wasn't paper and string to wrap them in.

When months of darkness settled on Dawson, when the

Yukon River froze as twisted and tight as a rope, and only an occasional dog team came in from the outside, it was pleasant to remember that Sweet Little Marjorie Rambeau had been there, with her mother, and that Lillian Russell was promised the following summer. When the men on the creeks were lying dead with scurvy in cabin after cabin, in Dawson they kept on jigging to "Turkey in the Straw" and drinking Tex Rickard's watered-down rye. When the beefsteak gave out they ate an Arctic delicacy, the pickled nose of moose. When fire burned out half the town, when nineteen-year-old Myrtle Brocee shot herself, when seven men froze to death on a stampede to Swede Creek, "Swiftwater" Bill Gates, the town's Lothario, bought Gussie Lamore a new hat to cheer her up. The millinery of her choice was wide and black, with jet plumes flowing around the brim. It cost him $275. Even when it was sixty below, gold had a marvelous warm color.

To live up to Dawson took disdain for minor catastrophes and an indifference to greater ones. To keep looking the queen of the Yukon straight in the eye took nerve and no end of pay dirt.

12

THE PASTURE

THE GOLD creeks began on the south bank of the Klondike River, a little more than three miles west of Dawson. The first one was Bonanza. Thirteen miles from its mouth was the spur called Eldorado, a creek fifteen miles in length. Continuing up the Klondike River above the mouth of the Bonanza, small tributaries ran in, the richest one of which was Bear. Beyond was Hunker, a heavier stream than Bonanza but not so rich. Miles on, after the Klondike swung around to the south, a few more gold-bearing creeks came in. All Gold, a Flat Creek pup, was the last. There were no claims staked on the Klondike itself. It was too turbulent and deep a stream to work. There was no navigation on the river, only a barge at Bonanza which took the miners the few yards from one bank of the Klondike to the other. There was a foot bridge between Dawson and Lousetown but the only trail to the creeks was on the Dawson side of the river.

Bonanza, Eldorado, and Hunker all rose on the Ridge, a chain of hills overlooked by a promontory called The Dome. The south side of the Ridge gave rise to Dominion, Sulphur, and Quartz creeks, tributaries of the Indian River. The creeks did not run through gorges slit down through the hills. The whole country was swampy, a pasture-rolling land of low crests which divided the wide, meandering creek beds. Stunted timber and a three- to five-foot matting of russet-colored moss had originally covered it. Then, spring came with wild flowers, butterflies, birds, the usual masses of berries that rambled so luxuriously everywhere in the southern Yukon region. Then, herds of caribou and moose spent the season grazing in the valleys. But when the miners came and sawed off the trees, pitted the hills and beds, dumped dirt and ashes by the ton, leveled and scraped and stacked, the Klondike valleys were destroyed and the land was ugly. The only green-growing things that stayed on were the niggerhead tufts that rolled like loose boulders in the trail's ooze, and the devil's club vine with thorns and spiked leaves that even penetrated leather. When one of these barbed thorns got into the flesh it had to be cut out with a knife.

The Bonanza trail was wet all summer long, the muddiest and slipperiest part of it being between the Eldorado fork and claim *Sixty Above,* which was near a place called Carmack's Fort. The wedge where the Bonanza split into Eldorado became known as Grand Forks, after the name of Belinda Mulrooney's two-story hotel there. The Eldorado trail was drier, coming out of the hills more steeply and being in a sort of woods of underbrush and saplings. The trails were not paths, they were the general direction in which a man was going, and little more. The hiker made his way around or over the continual dumps and holes. He circumvented cabins, sluices, dams, he forded back and forth across the creek beds, he avoided the bogs if he could. In winter the frozen snow made a good sledding surface, and traveling the creeks was much easier then.

In the fall of 1898 a dog freighter named Tom O'Brien said he would build a tramroad for the sleds all the way from Dawson to Grand Forks. He didn't build a road, he only leveled off some of the worst places and stationed brawny guards at the beginning of the Bonanza trail. He gave them some scales, with instructions to charge a toll according to the freight going over. He first demanded a dollar for each hundred pounds. Later he came down fifty cents, but the miners were good and mad by then. Another fight was on between the creek men and the gold commissioner, who had permitted O'Brien to levy the toll. No man wanted to pay for the use of a public trail. Gene Allen fought the issue vigorously in the *Klondyke Nugget* until O'Brien had to face the situation in court. The miners won, in February, the following year.

Within two weeks after Carmack struck the Bonanza, the creek was staked from end to end. They prepared to take the tributaries next. The largest one of these came in at Grand Forks, where twenty cabins and two hotels were already going up. The crowds congregated there, clustering in small groups, anxiously talking creeks. They had heard the rumor that the Dominion was about to do away with the custom that a man could stake on every creek in a district. Thereafter, the Dominion would limit them to a single claim on any one creek in a district.

They were all on Bonanza. That meant that they couldn't stake another creek, not unless they cut their names off where they were. It was difficult to know what to do. The old-timers had come. They shook their heads at the sight of the pasture and many of them wouldn't even cut a post to claim 500 feet of it. Yet in places men were making "wages," an ounce a day, and some occasional big pans had been washed. Five hours' work on one claim had produced $329. From a sluice running over *Fourteen, Fifteen* and *Sixteen* below *Discovery* they had cleaned up $4,000 in two days. Ladue had weighed the sum in his saloon where everybody saw it. But Bonanza was a long creek and not all the men on it were getting rich. Some hadn't seen colors yet. They weren't all working; some were building cabins and getting their firewood together. Winter wasn't far off.

They hadn't staked the tributaries yet, although they'd been looking at some. If good dirt had been seen nobody was telling where, not until they'd decided whether or not they were staying on Bonanza or striking another *Discovery*. Knut Halstead and John Erickson came down from the big tributary at the Forks telling those who asked, "It's a moose flat, there's nothing there." Louis Empkins and his partner, a Frenchman named Demars, went up the gulch and reported the same thing. Dave McKay looked over a Bonanza pup that came in about three miles above Grand Forks. "More pasture," he said.

In general the Bonanza Valley did not look like gold country. It was blanketed with reindeer moss and partly forested. In places it was a mile wide. The ground was spongy with backwater pools, sump holes and bogs. The old-timers tasted the water and crumbled the sand, and said they wouldn't be caught dead looking for gold on a creek like that.

The only prospectors who were called old-timers by other miners were the men who had been in the Yukon since the beginning of the eighties. They were greatly respected for their knowledge of creeks. Even the Forty-Mile men, who had made the rush in 1885, thought twice before disagreeing with a man who had worked the Stewart or the Little Salmon. As for the unemployed farm hands and hack drivers who lately had been coming into the country during the summer, they were greenhorns. The old-timer took one look at these city prospectors, in their toothpick shoes, with red bandannas hanging out of their pockets and half a pound of grub under one arm, and blew the plug juice from the corner of his mouth. And now, standing calf-deep in soggy moss, he wondered what had got into him to let these damn fool cheechakos run him all the way down from the Arctic Circle to stake a swamp. He cussed himself for ever starting.

More than one cheechako cut his name off his posts when he

saw the way the old-timers felt. And others, going down to Forty-Mile for the winter's provisions, discovered that the trading companies wouldn't give them the miner's customary credit. "You won't get gold there. Go on back to Miller or O'Brien and we'll give you the grub." Many had to. They had been drawn into the stampede and had missed the last boat outside. The traders wouldn't exchange a $50 sack of flour to own a claim outright on a creek with the dubious prospects of the Rabbit. They refused to call the creek Bonanza.

Those who could sell, did. They took half a case of whiskey, or a sled dog, a sack of beans, a little dust, whatever they were offered. If there were no buyers, and there were few for the claims above the Forks, the locators simply pulled out. *Seven* was at the Forks. Louis Rhodes, a cheechako who had only been in the country since April, jumped *Twenty-One Above* when its staker left. The others kidded him so much he said that for two cents he'd cut his name off, too. But he didn't.

Skookum Jim had gone up to the Siwash village for tea and dried salmon to see him through the winter. Ladue gave Carmack a job in the sawmill so that he could earn enough to stock up on grub, buy a few tools, and get to work on *Discovery*. Tagish Charlie wasn't doing a thing about his 500 feet. John Jacob Astor Dusel, on the claim above Jim, placed his posts generously, so that he could take in the dirt opposite the mouth of a gulch that came in from the south. The gulch was later called Skookum, which means "good" in Siwash dialect.

There were several men who had made a good cleanup that summer, who could afford to take a chance on Bonanza. They had plenty of provisions, the necessary outlay to build dams and sluices as soon as the ground thawed in summer, and their pokes were heavy enough to weather a loss—just in case the old-timers were right and Bonanza was a freak, a field with a few deep pockets and the rest of it barren ground.

Klondike gold was found in two places, at first in the creek beds and, months later, on the hilltops, which were called "benches." The bench gold had been deposited by ancient creeks which had curled from the glaciers eons before the present ones had found their channels. Slides had occurred frequently and almost everywhere. Gold was spread unevenly down the slopes and often rich accumulations lay barely covered over in most of the gulches. The miners thought this surface dirt was the exposed bedrock and after they had scraped it up, abandoned the claim. They rushed off to find more riches lying under the moss.

Twenty-five-cent dirt was passed over, fifty-cent dirt was dug only because it indicated that bigger pay was coming. And if the pay wasn't there the miners moved on. Over that way somebody was getting $5 to the pan. Over there somebody else was getting $12.50. A pan was two shovelsful of gravel washed at the creek side. In a few places a patient man was on barren ground digging down, desperately, doggedly, hoping to hit the paystreak with every shovel thrust. Finally Rhodes hit a "second bedrock," which, of course, was the only bedrock the creek had. At once everyone began digging for it and because of this fresh start on Bonanza many claims were re-opened which would otherwise have been deserted.

To dig for "the pay" the ground had first to be cleared of moss, rotted vegetation, mud, surface sand, all of which was called the "muck." Under this were perhaps fifteen feet of crushed rocks and water-worn debris which carried small amounts of gold. The richness of this gravel usually indicated the nearness of the paystreak. If the pans paid something going down, the paystreak was very likely to lie upon the bedrock. If the pans were empty, it was best to start digging another hole. Just before reaching bedrock there was usually a fine layer of black sand, also with pay in it, and then came the rich dirt itself. Often this yielded $50 or more a pan.

Prospect holes were sunk more or less blindly. While digging, the dip was watched for a hint as to where the bedrock might be lying. The bedrock, or the bottom of the creek, was not necessarily the valley's basal rock. When the hole reached bedrock, tunnels were forced through the gravel for fifteen or twenty feet, with the miner making test pans all the way. If the take got bigger he expected to come upon the paystreak, while pans that dribbled away warned him he was off direction.

The paystreak and the windings of the creek were far from being in the same place. The creeks scrolled through the gulches in patterns of their own, weaving around the paystreak, sometimes crossing it, oftener missing it by a hundred feet. There were no surface clues as to what lay under the moss. The only way to find the gold was to sink these prospect holes and look for it. And it was rarely near the top, although in a few cases the bedrock was only three feet down. Most of the time it was from fifteen to thirty feet underneath the gravel.

On the large rivers fine dust was sometimes caught on the sand bars when the spring freshets came rolling down with their gold-flecked foam. Rich strikes had occurred on a few bars of the Pelly, Lewes, Hootalinqua, Stewart and Birch, although more commonly bar gold was coarse and too dispersed to be worth the trouble of panning out. There were no bars on Bonanza. It was only a shallow creek.

Before 1896 mining in the Yukon was not a year-round job. If Carmack had made his strike earlier in the summer, during the cleanup on the creeks, few men would have been free to stampede for Bonanza. The creeks until then were worked only in the summer, during the months of July and August, when the hot sun thawed the ground and the gravel could be shoveled up quite easily. The creeks were running then and there was plenty of water to wash the gold. But during the rest of the year the ground was frozen as hard as concrete and could not even be picked into. Operations might begin as early as June, depending upon the creeks. When the heavy snows melted, the streams became torrents, rushing down with boulders and uprooted trees and whole chunks of the frozen bank which they ripped away as they came. In September there might be early frosts and even snowfalls, freezing the ground while the men were still at work. They could depend only upon two full months at the diggings, but since daylight was endless in summer, a great deal of work could be done. Those who stayed in the country over the winter had no work to do. After the cleanup there were only idle, monotonous months of twilight and dark ahead. Carmack's strike happened on August 16, at exactly the right time for a general stampede.

Among the cheechakos who hurried from Forty-Mile were Phiscator, Cobb, the Wordens, Clement, Lippy, Berry, William and Samuel Stanley, Picotte, Hall, Keller, Wilkerson, McNulty, all men who were later among the Klondike "millionaires." They scattered over the creek with a hundred others and were in the *Sixties Above* when the Circle City crowd arrived. In the latter bunch were Frank Densmore and Harry Spencer, two partners who had good holdings on the Birch creeks, and Bill Farrell, Charlie Meyers, Neal McArthur, Skiff Mitchell, Tom O'Brien, "Circle City" Mickey, Murph Thorp, Billy Chappell, and "Nigger Jim" Dougherty, a white man, who came to the Forty-Mile in 1885, made a fortune, lost it on the outside and had now recently returned to find another. Jack McQuesten also came down from his store at the mouth of the Stewart and staked.

By the time the "second bedrock" was discovered it was late in the season and only a few men were deep enough to see what kind of gravel they had below the "summer diggings." They were called so because gravel worked in summer was that which thawed loose with the hot sun of July and August. The "winter diggings" were in frozen gravel which had to be thawed with long-burning fires before it would yield to a pick. The skeptics, who saw no color at all in their top gravel, wanted to try some of the other creeks which were tributary to Bonanza before it was too late to wash a few prospect pans. There was the big pup at the Forks. Empkins and Demars had admitted they each staked 500 feet on it. "As long as we went up there," they said, "we figured we might as well locate. But there's nothing there. We didn't find a dime."

Then one morning Stander, Whipple, Phiscator and Clement were all found to be missing from the bunkhouse at the same time. And soon after that Keller shouldered his rifle and said he was going up the big creek to get fresh meat. "I ought to get a moose up there, don't you think?" Cobb, who was Phiscator's partner, set out with a party of Russians and Swedes for a faraway creek.

"A cowfield" . . . "A five-cent creek" . . . "Nothing there". . . . A newspaper man by the name of Johns and his partner, Bruceth, weren't convinced of the barrenness of Bonanza's big pup. They decided to prospect it themselves. After they were gone, curiosity as to the general exodus got the better of several others who were sitting around the stove. It wasn't long before they were all stringing up the gulch.

Johns and Bruceth had only gone a few hundred yards when they learned what was up. Keller, Stander, Whipple, Phiscator, and Clement were staking. "What's going on?" Johns asked. The intruders were told, by Whipple, "If you want to stake, well go ahead but keep your mouth shut." Whipple was staking a *Discovery* although everyone knew that Empkins and Demars had been there ahead of him. Confronted by Johns, Whipple said, "No post of theirs reads *Discovery*."

"You can't claim it either," Johns told him. "This is Carmack's creek. This is Bonanza's pup."

Whipple answered, "You go ahead and take care of your own business, I'm staking a *Discovery*." For his second claim he took the one below Phiscator, who had staked off his 500 feet below *Discovery* while Whipple and Johns were arguing.

Discovery was the third claim above the Forks, less than a quarter of a mile from the bunkhouse.

Clement, Keller, and Stander staked above *Discovery* in that order. Empkins' and Demars' posts were on *Seven* and *Eight*. About that time Erickson and Halstead turned up. They began staking *Nine* and *Ten*. Bruceth took *Eleven* and Johns, *Twelve*. Meanwhile, Stander got into an argument with Whipple over *Discovery*, threatening to take it. Whipple gave in momentarily and Stander offered *Six* to Erickson. While Erickson was pulling up his stakes from *Nine*, Whipple changed his mind. In disgust Erickson returned Stander's *Six*, hammered his stakes back on *Nine* and left the creek, swearing at cheechakos right and left. One of the other stakers saved *Thirteen* for a friend. The men from the Forks had arrived—Sloan, Chisholm, Ben Wall, Densmore, Harry Waugh, a dozen more.

That night they held a meeting to select a name for the big pup. Whipple wanted it named after him but he had had too many fights that day and nobody would give him the satisfaction, although he was well known in the country and had been a good prospector. Halstead, a great reader in the winter, suggested "El Dorado." It seemed to please most of the men and the next day the creek was recorded under that name, written in the book as "Eldorado."

Police Captain Constantine immediately went up to refresh the men on the new laws. Whipple had to make up his mind between *One* and his discredited "Discovery." The latter was numbered *Three*. Whipple finally took *One* and Halstead jumped *Three* just as Whipple pulled his stakes. Halstead couldn't resist doing it because Whipple had tried prematurely to jump a claim of his on American Creek the winter before. Phiscator didn't want to drop his Bonanza claim and he let Cobb record *Two*. Constantine struck off the name of the absent owner of *Thirteen* and Hollingshead jumped it.

Eldorado gold, like that on Bonanza, was first found on

rimrock, or surface gravel at the creek's edge, where it had been washed off the hills. And, again, when this gold was gone the cheechakos rushed off, concluding that Eldorado was another skim diggings like Bonanza. Phiscator and Cobb managed to get rid of half of their claim for $800. Johns got $500 for half of *Twelve*. But these claims were close to the rich dirt which Clement had found. Claims that were three and four miles away sold for very little. A sack of flour bought half of *Thirty*. *Thirty-One* sold for $100, only $80 of which could be raised in dust and the rest was welcome in beans. The stingiest claim of all was *One*. Whipple couldn't find five cents on it and he sold out to Skiff Mitchell and Billy Chappell. They were pretty sure the cheechakos hadn't got to bedrock on Eldorado. Whipple should have known it too.

From Eldorado they stampeded two smaller pups, Oro Grande and Gay Gulch. They opened Victoria, Adams, and Skookum. A Russian, Solomon Marpak, found good dirt on the nine-mile Bear. Andrew Hunker and Charles Johnson, two partners who had missed both Bonanza and Eldorado, wandered up the river to another tributary of the Klondike, where they got $3 pans and located. This was the sixth of September. They were less than two miles from Henderson's place on Gold Bottom.

It was at this time that Henderson was visited by the party of prospectors who told him about Carmack's strike on Bonanza. It was several days before he could go through the ordeal of climbing the Divide to look at the creek he had lost. Finally he went, and after disconsolately trudging the length of Bonanza valley, he went over to the little Bear to see what that creek had. There Marpak told him about Hunker and Johnson. This was almost too great a blow for Henderson for it was his creek where the men were working. He went there to challenge them, but upon seeing how much richer their *Discovery* was than his, he acknowledged their right to the creek. Also, they were on the main stream. Gold Bottom was one of its pups. Henderson staked *Three Above* on the new creek, which was called Hunker for one of its discoverers, but he never worked it. That winter he was ill and did no work at all.

During the winter of 1896 only the twenty-five-mile Bonanza and the fifteen-mile Eldorado were worked, although Hunker had opened the creek which was named for him and Marpak had found the Bear. There were claims on both these creeks but no work was done on them until the fall of 1897. In June that year a tributary of the Indian River, which was given the name of Dominion Creek, was found on the other side of the Ridge. It was bigger than Bonanza, and when all of its thirty-odd tributaries were staked there were 150 miles of fresh claims. At about that same time, Sulphur Creek was discovered, offering thirty more miles of claims, including the tributaries, and in September the thirty-five-mile Quartz and its pups were staked. Soon the Indian's other creeks were gone, Ophir, Nine-Mile, Eureka, Gold Run, Wolf, Big Creek. The Klondike's Leotta, Too Much Gold, All Gold were taken to the last inch. By the summer of 1898, when the gold hunters began to arrive by the thousands, there were few creeks left. On July 1, 1898, nearly 10,000 claims had been recorded for the coming year. The only way to get a claim in the Klondike was to buy one and they cost from $5,000 for an unproved mine to $50,000 for one which had recognizable pay on it. The mines had been "stripped" on Bonanza and Eldorado but they still sold for high prices. Charles Lamb, who bought out Demars the winter before, in July sold *Eight* Eldorado for $350,000, which the *Klondyke Nugget* reported to be the largest single sale of the summer.

In addition to the creek claims there were hundreds of bench and hillside claims staked late in the summer of 1897. Lancaster's Cheechako Hill became Gold Hill, and others were French and Skookum. Good benches were also found on Bear, Hunker, Quartz, and Dominion. These hill mines were very deep. Lancaster dug a shaft 79 feet into the hill before he hit bedrock. He rocked no less than $2,000 a day thereafter for the next eight weeks. On the claim next to him, Davidson rocked ten pounds of gold a day for three days in succession. At $17 an ounce that was good wages. A very common take was $100 a day.

French Hill was the only place Ver Mehr and his two partners could find to dig when they arrived on the creeks early in 1898. They were still staking the sides of the gulches. The three boys, Ver Mehr, Ray, and Hawley, tramped all the creeks without finding a place they could have. Everyone was so busy the boys couldn't get them to talk or give them any "pointers," as Ver Mehr expressed it. The only man who didn't seem to be in such a hurry was Arthur Biggs, an old-timer who hadn't scoffed at the Bonanza but had been unfortunate in picking a mine with only fair pay. He told the boys they had been getting nuggets as big as thumbs off the hills. The boys separated for different benches, Ver Mehr going above Adams Creek. He dug, shoveled and washed the ground in several places but couldn't get a glimmer and was about to return to Dawson to wait for his partners when a man passed on the trail inquiring for a Jack Ver Mehr. Messages were passed along the creeks that way, by the men going back and forth. He was told that Hawley had struck a mine on French Hill and he hurried there, where he found Hawley and Ray at work with a rocker. They had got almost $4,000 and Hawley estimated at least $22,000 more was underfoot. But in a few days the gold disappeared from the gravel and though they "tore the hill to pieces" they didn't find another grain of gold. Their neighbors convinced them that they had been digging a slide. They tried all summer to find some spot worth prospecting over the winter but nothing turned up. Ray went home. Hawley took a job as a clerk with the Alaska Commercial Company and Ver Mehr went to work for wages at a company mine on Dominion.

13

DIGGING FOR THE PAY

CHARLIE ANDERSON had
been working a remote creek far up near the source of the
Sixty-Mile River and had heard nothing about the Bonanza
and Eldorado strikes until he reached Forty-Mile to buy provisions for the coming winter. He was an unhappy Swede when
they told him that all the claims were gone. As the stories
grew of the treasures that he had missed, and as his disappointment increased accordingly, he was treated to liquid
consolation. He had a three-pound poke on him. It was all
he had got in his cleanup. In size the poke was small, the
dust would only have made a coin purse fat. He was ashamed
of it. A year's wages.

They told him what McKay and McGillivray had got. And
what Clement had got. They told him what happened to
Rhodes. His pay had kept doubling and tripling until he had
to hire two men to help him shovel gold. He was afraid the
mine would freeze on him before he got to bedrock. He hit
it. His first pan was $65.30. He had $7,000 on the shelf in
his cabin and he was still shoveling for the cleanup in summer.

Anderson tried to vision $50 sliding out of the pan. He
could see it glittering in his trembling, imagined hand. The
170

best he had ever washed was "bit dirt." A bit was a York shilling, worth about twelve and a half cents. The boys hated to see Anderson feel so bad about missing the Klondike. They kept the whiskey flowing, and nobody so much as thought of mentioning the empty claims. Finally, Anderson shouted a few furious words and flung his miserable poke from him onto the table. He called upon absent divinities to witness his poverty.

"You've got enough there to buy a claim," someone said.

"It looks like about seven-fifty," someone else said.

"Eight hundred," Anderson told them.

"You can have mine for eight hundred," a man said, sitting down at the table with Anderson.

Another Swede in the room left, saying he wouldn't stay there and watch an honest man buncoed.

Before falling asleep, Anderson parted with his poke and became the new owner of *Twenty-Nine* Eldorado. In the morning, when he was aware of what he had done and what he had got, he begged for his poke but he didn't get it. The deal was considered a fair and square one. After thinking it over, Anderson got some flour, beans and bacon on tick and hauled it up to his 500 feet of gravel, which was now covered with the first snowfall of the winter. He wondered if he could bunk with the fellow in the next cabin for the next few months, while he built fires in the snow like the rest and tried to melt a hole thirty feet deep.

Charlie Anderson's *Twenty-Nine* paid him $130,000 from the first hole. The rest of the dirt looked so good that he came back from his honeymoon in the fall of 1898 and made another $100,000 before he finally sold out and went home to build a castle in the village of San Rafael, across the Golden Gate from San Francisco.

"Burning" a mine was not an original idea. The Russians had been doing it for centuries in Siberia. In 1887, Fred

Hutchinson used fire for the first time in the Yukon. He was on Franklin Gulch in the Forty-Mile district and had found exceptionally deep gravel. He had just hit the paystreak when winter froze him out. However, he saw where the paystreak was headed—directly under the creek. He chopped through the ice and melted the ground under it with a smouldering fire, keeping a coffer-dam around the opening of the shaft. The operation was a curiosity on the creek but he got his gold. After that a man now and then tried burning, but it was a tedious and difficult job, and, anyway, almost all of the Forty-Mile was very shallow and bedrock was easily reached during the summer.

The deep mines of the Klondike were something else again. In the Yukon, winter or summer, the ground was always frozen below six feet and to dig a fifteen- to thirty-foot shaft required tremendous work at any time of year. The sun thawed the gravel at the rate of about two feet every twelve hours but that was too slow, it might take a man all summer to prospect his mine. The cheechakos thought of a better method. They would burn out a hole during the winter, put the pay dirt aside in a dump and wash it in the summer. Skookum Jim, the most industrious man in the Klondike, lit the first fire in September. Soon the whole valley was a smoky glade, in which the figures of men moved in an eerie twilight, which was whitened only by a glaze of snow and a reappearing moon. The fires burned ten hours at a time, then the ashes were shoveled away and the miners picked the earth loose and put the clumps into awkward wooden "buckets" to be carried over to a dump. As the hole deepened, the dumps grew higher. At cleanup time they were at least thirty feet high, with the windlasses built upon cribs.

A deep hole was difficult to burn because there was no draft, and once the fire began to blaze, hazard was added to the undertaking inasmuch as the man had to climb the ladder quickly and get out before he was caught in the suffocating smoke. Tough green birch ladders were let down into the shaft. Digging frozen gravel was slow work, they went down a few inches at a time. Sometimes the shaft struck a frozen sump or a wedge of ice where the seepage had collected in summer. The hole was usually wet. A "bitch" or miner's candle, burned in the dirt wall.

It took a month to pick through fifteen feet and weeks more to drift for the paystreak. If pay didn't appear in eighteen or twenty feet of drifting, or tunneling, it was necessary to sink another hole. About five of them were sunk on every claim. If a man was really unlucky he missed the paystreak in all the holes. "Luck!" they said. "That's what the mining game is. I've seen it more than once where a man dug all year with nothing to show for it, and the man digging only ten feet away on another claim was picking out nuggets bigger than the first fellow's calluses."

In summer washing was not done in a miner's pan but in a sluice line, which was a series of wooden boxes, each of which was fifteen feet long, a foot high and a foot wide. They were telescoped into each other and set on trestles to run at a gradual decline. Fifteen or twenty box lengths would take care of the average claim but on the larger properties a hundred or more were fanned out from the cut in the dam. Dams were built to check the creek and divert it as needed on the sluice lines. Dirt was shoveled into the box to about half its depth and then the water was turned in. The rush softened and broke up the clumps of gravel and the gold was loosened and sifted down to the cross cleats, or riffles, at the bottom of each box. The muddy water ran off into a tail race at the end of the sluice line. Several hundred pounds of dirt a day were washed.

If the gold was running heavy the box was cleaned after each operation, otherwise only once, at the end of the day. The water was turned in for a certain length of time, perhaps twenty minutes, and then cut off. When the mud and gold had settled to the bottom, a fresh spurt of water was let in. If they were cleaning up, the boxes were tipped to keep the water back and a man stepped into each one with a whisk broom, a paddle, and a gold pan, and began brushing the mud, whisking it to dislodge any nuggets, swirling and rinsing the contents of the box in his gold pan, in the same way that gold is washed beside a creek. It took about thirty minutes to wash a pan of dirt, a careful and skillful process in order not to wash away any gold. Since gold is nineteen times heavier than water, the particles sank quickly except when they were lodged in the frozen dirt.

The take was called the pan, and this was how the "thousand-dollar pans" were washed. They practically always represented the total daily take, washed from an enormous amount of dirt. They were not the gleanings from two shovelfuls of gravel. But men in Capetown, Pittsburgh, and Kentucky who joined the rush to the Klondike didn't know this. They only knew that the Klondike pans had beaten the record of the Wake-Up-Jake Company in the Cariboo which had held the world's championship with a fifty-two-ounce pan worth $936. Three- and four-thousand-dollar pans were suddenly reported from every Klondike creek the summer of 1897.

Even on the hill claims, where water was unavailable and they used rockers instead of sluice lines, the daily take was still called a pan. A rocker, a Chinese invention, was a box worked like a cradle. The top of it was a hopper made with a perforated sheet-iron bottom. Two shovelfuls of dirt were thrown in, several dippers of water were poured on and the rocker was moved back and forth until all the mud slid through onto an apron made of a double thickness of blanket. The holes in the hopper were a quarter of an inch in diameter so that any nuggets in the dirt remained behind to be gathered up. Any grains which escaped the blanket fell upon a plate containing quicksilver, which retrieved the last trace of color before the water ran off. The water was caught and used over and over. From time to time the mud was scraped from the blanket and washed in a pan. The blanket was rinsed eventually in water containing quicksilver. The gold and quicksilver formed an amalgam which was heated to reclaim the gold.

Both sluice and rocker methods were wasteful. Although the boxes were burned at the end of the season, and their ashes sifted, nevertheless gold escaped in the tailings, the residue of rocks and dirt which ran out of the sluice line. The tailings were never rewashed. Yet an estimated fourth of the Klondike gold was in them. The book sellers and peach pickers and shoe clerks were getting rich too fast to think very much about it. They dug and washed with reckless haste. Only eight weeks to get the gold out and go home. The creek might dry up early. They might get malaria and have to quit work. It was better to fill up the old tobacco cans as quickly as possible and let the run-off go.

And yet a man might have struck the richest ground in the district and still be unable to take out his gold. He would not know that he had the richest ground, he would never get very far into it. Even if he had all the dirt out on a dump how would he wash it? Everyone had come to the Klondike to dig "poor man's mines," placers that didn't require expensive machinery, the kind of diggings that Secretary of the Interior Gage described as belonging to any man with "a brave heart, sound body, nerve and courage." Unfortunately, those who made the trip with only these assets at their command, discovered that capital was a still more necessary assistant.

In 1898 few miners could depend upon scraping wages off the bedrock, yet they had to pay the hired hands, as they went along. Timber was gone and they had to buy fifty or more cords of wood to burn the holes, at $30 a cord. It cost $1,000 to build a dam, $1,500 to build a run-off ditch and $30 apiece for sluice boxes. In 1898 they were using fifteen to the average claim instead of five. These building costs were computed by figuring lumber at 40 cents a board foot and skilled labor, such as carpentry, at $2 an hour. Tools, nails, wheelbarrows, grindstones, a portable forge, a gold scales, rope, quicksilver, magnetic sand, oakum, and pitch, all kept up the operating costs. In addition to his expenses of working the mine, a man had to have a cabin, firewood, food and clothing. And it was almost impossible to get along without sled dogs, which cost $350 each, and were fed on bacon costing 40 cents a pound. After the gold was dug and washed and in the bank, a 10 per cent tax on all of it over $2,500 was due the Crown. When costs and living expenses were added up, it was a sour Klondike miner who hadn't struck it rich.

Many cheechakos were idle during the winter of 1898. When several thousand men discovered that all the creeks were staked, they awoke from their dream of becoming millionaires and sat on a packing box or sack of grub somewhere, maybe under a tent, maybe not, and tried to think out what to do next. It was a hard blow for a man to take after the trip he had come through, the money he had spent, perhaps owed. There he was in Dawson, with what was left of his flour and beans and bacon, with his leaking scow, pick and shovel and gold pan. He was broke and he didn't have a chance in the world to dig a pokeful of nuggets.

He could either sell his gear and go home or he could stay and work as a mucker on a mine, earning $15 a day, or he could try to get a job in town. Men were needed to cut wood, haul water, dig graves. He could get a job as a cook if he could open cans. They hired men in the sawmills and warehouses and breweries. They needed night watchmen, porters, men to drive the dogs or take the pack trains back and forth. The wages were good but there weren't town jobs for all. If a man wanted to earn money over the winter the one job always open to him was day labor in the mines. Not many worked outlays anymore. It was too risky putting in a year's work on a claim that had already been cleaned up and none of the new dirt was as rich as Bonanza and her big pup. Better to work for those who had the money to pay wages, or for the companies.

There was always the stampede, the poor man's hope. Perhaps a creek would turn up somewhere with nickel or two-bit dirt on it. (The 1898 cheechakos weren't so choosy as the men of 1896.) They didn't have to wait long for a stampede to start. Almost every day there was one to some part of the Valley. They seldom amounted to anything. A man on a string of water somewhere would wash bright quartz, blaze his name on a tree and come running to town to record. At the recorder's office he would be surrounded by a mob, all eager and ready to follow him back to wherever he came from. Many kept a pack of blankets and food made up for just such trips. The excited staker might think he had slipped into town unnoticed but somehow, through somebody, the news would get out and the single word, "Stampede!" would instantaneously spread through the streets, cabins, saloons, dance halls, like a shout of "Fire!" and men would start running from all directions at once. In fact, one could hardly break into a fast walk without being asked the question, "Stampeding?"

On these runs they set out seldom knowing their destination. Each man followed the man ahead. They sometimes rushed over the trails for three or four days, coming back a roundabout way to where they started from, having got lost or been put off. At such times they accused the bunk house owners of starting stampedes to bring in business. In summer the steamboat companies were accused of the same charge, after the men had jumped aboard a specially chartered boat to hurry up or down the Yukon to a creek with nothing buried in it but mammal bones. But not even faked stampedes could disillusion a cheechako with a brand new shovel. He was ready when the next red-eyed man ran into town waving a poke of gritty dust from some false bonanza. There was always a chance that he might have found a good creek.

They ran everywhere, to the creeks of the Indian and Stewart, to streams emptying into the Yukon from the west. They ran to Reindeer, Montana, Dion, Bryant, Baker, Ensley, Calder, Moosehide, and Rosebud. The only creeks that had $1,000,000 on them were Hunker, Bear, Sulphur, and Dominion. The Dominion stampede occurred early in July, 1898. A thousand or so men had started for the creek when the gold commissioner found that two *Discovery* claims had been recorded. While the commissioner decided what to do the police cleared the creek and held it. Finally, since the claims were five miles apart, both men were permitted a *Discovery* and on July 9 the creek was officially re-opened. However, it was soon learned that the commissioner's office had favored some individuals with a head start of two days, further reason to intensify the bitter feelings which already existed between the miners and government officials.

The most nonsensical stampede of all was one to the near-by islands in the Yukon, after two Swedes, chopping wood on one of them, said they had panned $8. Somebody immediately, and irrelevantly, named the place "The Isle of Monte Cristo," and the rush was on. The stampeders actually dug themselves under water before they gave up, wondering how you could tell whether or not a Swede was joking.

14

LAW AND ORDER

RESENTMENT against the Canadians started early, as soon as the Americans paid a 35 per cent import duty on the shirts and underdrawers which they had on when they were crossing The Chilkoot. From then on, every tax, restriction, and law which the Dominion called attention to rankled them the more. If it wasn't the toll road, it was the heavy annual royalty levied upon the gross output of the mines. If it wasn't the $100 annual renewal fee on the miner's lease, it was shortening the creek claims from five hundred feet to one hundred feet. If it wasn't the debatable method with which this hundred feet was determined, it was corruption in the recorder's office. If it wasn't graft, it was favoritism. The Americans agreed among themselves that the only way to get any business done with the officers of the Dominion was to bribe them, and, after they had paid their way around the delays which paralyzed Dawson's administration, they grieved to Ottawa. The committee of three which they sent out to have a talk with Sifton in regard to reducing or abolishing the annual royalty, complained also of defects and deficiencies at Dawson, protested the new mining laws the Dominion had given them (which contradicted the old way of doing things), and voiced their personal dislike of the men in charge of Dawson's affairs.

It never occurred to the Americans to leave if they didn't like it. The Yukon was so remote from civilization that appointed officers and posted laws were merely absurd to them. For nearly twenty years they had governed themselves satisfactorily by means of Miners' Meetings which all attended. Decisions were made with the consent of the majority and punishment was direct, quickly carried out, and always respected. Problems and disputes were brought before these meetings for settlement. The miners agreed upon lengths of claims for the different creeks, governing their decisions by relative richnesses. They banished troublemakers and men of undesirable stamp. They worked out a system of water rights. It never occurred to them that they needed a man in a white wig to tell them how to mind their business.

The Dominion saw the stampede as a mob of greatly varied individuals whose aims and conduct might not always be for the common good. This was no small community of persons known to each other, who were joined in the common pursuit of prospecting, whose isolation threw them upon mutual strength and ingenuity. There were relatively few old-time prospectors in the Klondike during the rush. The men, and women, who went up were not prospectors, they were gold diggers. They didn't even expect to hunt for gold, it had already been discovered. They went up to pluck out nuggets like holiday plums from a very plump pudding, or to get them away from those who did.

It was easier for 300 men on a score of creeks to get along together than it was for 5,000 to do so on two. When the first horde of Klondikers arrived in 1897, Bonanza and Eldorado had been staked from one end to the other. When 25,000 more persons came the next year the shovels were scraping on every gulch. Some system of claiming had to be worked out, and if the Canadians were disposed to serving themselves from the pot of gold while giving away 300 miles of creeks, it did not seem unjust to them. A sudden gust of outsiders had descended, announcing themselves to be fortune hunters, saying frankly that they were taking everything they could lay hands on and leaving. Understandably, the Canadians wanted to be around.

The Klondike had an area of 800 square miles. The Canadians intended to survey it themselves and therefore barred all other surveyors from the region. A district the size and complexity of the Klondike could not be left to run itself. Sifton chose the best men he could find to do the job. Haste had been necessary and lack of experience was inevitable. What government servant had been a prospector? Who among them was an explorer, familiar with the remote regions of the country? The Klondike's administrators were also cheechakos.

When the miners' representatives presented their grievances before Sifton he said that while he did not intend to ignore the charges that had been made, neither did he intend to presuppose that men who had been honorable in their former responsibilities had suddenly turned into scoundrels. Major Walsh had arrived in Dawson to take over his delayed duties as administrator of the region. Thomas Fawcett, the gold commissioner and temporary head, returned to Ottawa. Walsh had started for Dawson in the fall of 1897 but his late arrival at White Pass, and illness, prevented him from continuing the journey. He remained at Lake Bennett until the last of the ice went out, and was in Dawson on May 21, 1898. Because of his ill health, he felt unable to remain in the country another winter, and left at the end of July.

Some Americans felt that if Walsh had been there at the beginning, and had been able to stay on, much of the unpleasantness would have been avoided. He had the reputation of a leader, trustworthy and able. His frontier exploits in the police corps had made him a popular figure. Fawcett had been asked to take over until Walsh arrived, in order to relieve Captain Constantine, who, as head of the police in the district and the Dominion's only authority there, had been exercising the duties of judge, administrator, and mine recorder. Before the rush it had been easy enough for one person to perform all of these duties, with time to spare, but not in 1897.

Fawcett was waiting on Walsh, and Walsh was thinking of his own successor, for he had agreed to come only for a year. It was understood that a more permanent form of government for the Klondike was being worked out. In the beginning everything was temporary and undecided, and subject to delay and change. No man wanted to embarrass his successor by instigating a program which might not have that man's sympathy and which he would not wish to continue.

While Walsh felt that Dawson needed to be "purged" (of her immorality, not her officers), he did nothing either to end or condone her imperfections. He took on no duties the two months he was there. Disappointed in his meaningless visit, the Americans hoped for the best from William Ogilvie who was then named first governor of the Yukon Territory. Formerly "the Yukon" was only a geographical distinction within the North-West Territory, but on May 28, 1898, it was created as a separate division with an administration of its own.

Ogilvie was, of course, familiar with the Yukon and well known there, having been the Dominion's surveyor for the past ten years. Although he had no administrative experience, Sifton felt that for these reasons he was the logical man for the appointment. He arrived in Dawson in September, 1898. In the meantime, since the latter part of July, the district had had no official administration although the summer months were ones of great activity on the creeks, for they were washing the gold then, and consequently the government offices in town were at their peak of work. The recorder's office, the tax office, the brokers, moneylenders and police were all churning through the summer's accelerated business. Under the circumstances complaints were inevitable. The Miners'

Meeting was revived and at its first session a petition was drawn up demanding a parliamentary investigation of affairs in the Klondike.

The new governor arrived and dived into his tasks, hoping to clarify and organize them. He was notified to begin an investigation of the miners' charges against the former administration, for which a Royal Commission was being sent to assist him. The inquiry was a fiasco. The report which Ogilvie sent to Sifton reduced the complaints to trivialities and assured him the stories had proved to be without adequate foundation. The miners were unable to prove anything, since their case was limited to the charges made in the petition, in turn based on events which had happened in the past. Many of their witnesses had left the country, having seen enough of the Klondike the first year without remaining for a second. Fawcett, their chief accused, was gone. And, finally, the miners could employ only Canadian counsel. Fawcett's administration was exonerated. Three decades later a Dominion chronicler, John W. Dafoe, remarked: "Taking into account the remote location of these gold fields; the difficulties attending their administration; the complexity of the problems which boiled up day by day for the puzzlement of the officials; the pressure upon the facilities of transportation, provisionment and government for a vast mob of nondescript fortune hunters from all over the universe, the results in the Klondike must establish it as one of the most successful achievements of its kind in history."

But the miners knew that Fawcett kept the registry of claims secret, an unheard-of procedure in mining country, and that information about them was sold in his office. Carelessness, ignorance, and partiality caused many a mix-up in the mine recorder's office. The names and numbers of claims were recorded inaccurately, so that a legal record was not forthcoming when necessary. Claims were recorded more than once; they were listed under the wrong creeks; records were lost. The surveyors had bungled their jobs. Some measured the creek claims along the banks of the stream, others measured them in straight lines in the direction of the stream. It made a considerable difference in the size and length of the claim. It was possible to measure a man off the creek altogether, by cutting him out with straight lines.

There were also hillside and bench claims which were measured 250 feet up the slope in the first case and 100 feet square in the second. However, it was assumed that the claim owner had acquired the rights through to bedrock, wherever that might turn up. The owners of creek, hillside, and bench claims were continually applying to the gold commissioner for adjustment. The man on the bench, at the top of the slope, was, in certain circumstances, entitled to the gold in the creek bed far below him. The men on the hillsides demanded the yield of all slides which, in ages past perhaps, had pushed the gold off the slopes down into the creek.

As for the mining laws themselves, no American had confidence in the Canadian's interpretation of them. The laws were vague and often left a contradictory choice as to their meaning. Some of the provisions were based upon conditions in other gold-mining sections of the Dominion and were not practicable in the Yukon, which had methods and seasons peculiar to itself.

Before the Canadians brought in their mining laws, there were no fees in the Yukon, no certificates, restrictions, or forfeits. A miner picked out his place, hammered down four posts to mark off his claim and went to work. If he liked the place, he eventually recorded it with the Police. If he changed his mind, he simply cut his name off the staking post and went somewhere else where he thought the dirt was better. The claim he left was then open and could be "jumped," or taken, by any man who came along. It was the custom to allow a man only one claim to a creek, so that everyone would have a chance to make a strike. The Canadians restricted the miner to one claim in an entire district, which meant he could stake on only one of the many Klondike creeks. If he wanted other mines he had to buy them. Or, if he wanted to try another creek he had to give up the mine he already had.

The creek claims had always been 500 feet in length, from rimrock to rimrock in width. Sometimes they were narrow and sometimes half a mile across, depending upon the formation of the valley. The Canadians reduced the length to 100 feet, but such fury was raised that they gave up another 150 feet. The claims were still just half the customary size, except in the case of a *Discovery*, which was permitted to be 500 feet in length. Every alternate block of ten claims was reserved for the Crown. (At first they had thought of keeping every alternate claim.) These conditions applied only to the new creeks which were opened. Those who had 500-foot claims staked before copies of the laws reached the district were allowed to keep them.

Hillside claims were something new in the Yukon. Before 1897 nobody would have thought of looking for gold on the side of a hill. It was believed to exist only in creek beds. But in July that year, Albert Lancaster, a cheechako who arrived late, could find no place left to dig. He went up and down the creeks looking for a mine of any sort but he located nothing. He was the kind of person others liked to make the butt of a joke. When the prospectors saw a really green cheechako they were unmerciful. Sometimes they would advise him to dig a hole in the Klondike River. They told Lancaster to "go up there on the hill and dig." He did not know it was a joke and he actually sunk a hole. He dug in it all month, going down quicker than a gopher. His neighbors enjoyed it. And then one day he struck a pocket. Then another. He was taking a fortune out of "Cheechako Hill." Before the end of summer men by the score were staking the other hillsides. The explanation was that, in some places, a more ancient creek bed existed than the one which was visible, and that geological history had deflected and hid it during periods of upheaval, leaving no clue on the surface.

The Canadians couldn't believe in the hill claims at first. They permitted the men to have one of them, in addition to a creek claim because they thought them unequal in value to the latter, so that actually a man could have two Klondike claims if one of them was on a hill. At first these "dry" mines were not even acknowledged by law. Not until "Caribou" Billy got rich on the hill where the Little Skookum joined Bonanza. When, across the gulch from him, two partners named Petersen and Kresge washed out $6,375 in ten days, the stampede started to the hills. But those who dug and found nothing believed that the pay holes must have been salted.

Salting was a familiar trick resorted to in order to sell worthless claims. A small amount of gold dust was mixed with an ordinary charge of powder and scattered into the gravel with a shotgun. By shooting into a number of places the mine would be well salted for an unwary buyer. Since everyone knew the fickleness of paystreaks the seller could not openly be accused of chicanery.

The price of a mine was set according to the kind of pay dirt that lay on either side of it. The price was high if an adjoining claim had proved good, even if the mine to be sold had not been prospected. Proximity was an irresistible lure.

To take up a claim the prospector located his ground, staked his posts in the proper way, giving the name or number of the claim, the length of it, his name, and the date. If it was a new creek, one not previously prospected, his ground was called *Discovery* and he was entitled to stake one 500-foot claim, not two, as the custom was in former years.

After staking, he then recorded in Dawson, for a fee now, of $15. However, he could neither stake nor record, nor turn a shovelful of dirt in the Klondike unless he possessed a Free Miner's Certificate. Most Klondikers bought one in Victoria,

B. C., en route to Skagway or Dyea. Otherwise they acquired one in Dawson at a cost of $10.

While the Free Miner's Certificate entitled the holder to game, fish and timber, as well as to any gold he might locate, in 1898 less and less of everything was to be had. Remaining stands of timber had been sold to mining companies. Water, too, was finally denied the gumboot miner by giving dredging permits to companies in five-mile sections.

Absentee owners bought the Klondike placers as members of companies, although it was illegal for one miner to stake for another. If he did so his own property, as well as that of the person for whom he staked "fictitiously," was forfeited to the Crown. The discrimination made the miners bristle.

The Canadians expected action from the miners. They had ten days to record after staking, unless they lived more than ten miles away from the mine recorder's office. If so, a day was added for each ten miles the man had to go. Once the claim was on the books, a three-months' assessment period began. During this time work had to be done on the claim every day of the week except Sunday. The usual day's work was ten hours long. Any kind of work could be done, such as building the cabin, setting the dams, cutting timber, sinking a shaft. Or a man could simply start digging. As long as someone was living on the claim and work went on continually during this initial period the law was fulfilled, but if the claim was idle for three consecutive days, not counting Sunday, it reverted to the Crown. The only acceptable excuse was severe illness.

After the assessment period was worked out the miner could dig or dawdle as he chose, the government wouldn't interfere until clean-up time when the taxes were due. The ministers in Ottawa had given but fleeting thought to a daily royalty. Their first imposed tax was 20 per cent of the gross output of claims producing over $500 a day, and 10 per cent on claims yielding under that amount. Subsequent receipts of Yukon gold made public by the United States mints, and the observations of bankers and others competent to judge, disclosed the fact that the tax returns were too small. It was hoped that a lighter burden would be more agreeably borne and the tax was amended to a 10 per cent levy on production over $2,500. In March, 1899, the exemption was increased to $5,000. When the returns were added for 1898 and 1899 the Canadians knew they were still $5,000,000 short.

The laws were stiff for those who trifled with them. The forfeit was the claim. A man lost his mine if he molested the staking posts once he had recorded. He lost his mine if he was in default of payment of the royalty. The penalty for making fraudulent statements of production was also listed as cause for cancellation of the claim, but if a miner cleaned up and got out, making a token payment as he fled, how was the government able to detect the fraud? The sluices were not policed. The gold commissioner accepted the miners' affidavits.

The severest penalty of all was reserved for the man caught on a claim belonging to the Crown. He was promptly deprived of any claims he might have, whether or not they had been acquired by staking or purchase. He was forbidden to ever again mine in the Yukon territory, and to make certain that he would not try to, the police escorted him to the border.

At the end of the season, if the miner wanted to stay on, he notified the recorder and paid him another $15. (In 1897 the claim renewal fee had been $100.) He also renewed his Free Miner's Certificate for the coming year, but $10 now. Then he got together fifty cords of firewood, and laid by $1,000 worth of grub. He checked the candles and the liniment. There were eight months of icebound solitude, hard labor, and darkness ahead of him, and more than likely, a siege of scurvy.

15

HIGH LIFE

IN SPITE of the fact that Dawson was disciplined by the Dominion, which always kept a strict, if puzzled, eye upon her moods and manners, she was wholeheartedly American in spirit. The Americans outnumbered the Canadians fifty to one and what they were, Dawson became. The Klondikers had rushed in by the thousands, in a celebrating frame of mind, all of them certain of immediate wealth. They were brash about it. And Dawson became bold, demonstrative, a little too rough at times. In general, her attitude was that the devil could take the hindmost.

When a man was broke, and 10,000 of them were the winter of 1898, they took what menial jobs there were and lived it out, expecting nothing. They got nothing. In Dawson there was no sentimentality for a penniless man. The city liked a good spender, that was why she was there, and she did the most she could to keep on glittering to the last. In particular she liked a man like "Swiftwater" Bill Gates.

Swiftwater came down from *Thirteen* Eldorado in November, 1896, with two hundred pounds of gold dust. He passed a washpan full of nuggets around to the girls and announced that he was going to set up the toniest saloon and dance hall in town. He had to wait until summer to get a mahogany bar and all the fixings into Dawson on one of the riverboats. Besides, he wanted fresh talent. Meanwhile he stocked Chief Isaac's cabin with whiskey and rum and called it the Bonanza saloon. He ordered a pleated shirt, a cutaway suit, and a stovepipe hat from Seattle. By the time they reached him, in summer, he had gone into business with Jack Smith, one of his partners on *Thirteen.* The new place was across the river's mouth, in Dawson, and it was called the Monte Carlo. The bartender was Alexander Pantages.

In June, Swiftwater put on his new hat and went out to Seattle to buy the best of everything. In that city he roomed at the Butler, the swank hotel of the day, and proceeded to make himself known by giving nuggets to the bell boys to point him out as the "King of the Klondike." He continued to San Francisco, where he lived like a rajah. He was a visitor the coast was not likely to forget. Five feet and a scant five inches in height, with the blackest of whiskers and a very long and wavy beard, dressed always in opera clothes, reciting amazing stories of his own wealth and of the riches of the Klondike, gathering a crowd wherever he went, he attracted not only the "most beautiful girls in the world" but also an investor. He got $20,000 from a Dr. Wolf, whose money he promised to double in ninety days.

Although Swiftwater's poke was heavy when he started out, the princely life he was leading quickly lightened it. The truth of the matter was that he was broke. He sorely needed $20,000. He had to pay for a hundred barrels of whiskey and get the girls up to Dawson. He cut expenses by taking them in over the pass but he arrived in great fashion, on a barge, with the girls sitting all dressed up on top of the barrels. Glum Dr. Wolf met him as he stepped ashore.

Wolf had beat Swiftwater to Dawson in order to make a few inquiries, none of which proved satisfactory. He did not expect to see his $20,000 nest egg again. Everybody in Dawson had an ear-popping story to tell him about Swiftwater. For one thing, he was far from being a mining expert. He had come into the country just before the rush, with other prospectors looking for wages on the Yukon creeks. He hadn't made any. He became a handyman and bullcook in Circle City, and the winter before had only by chance overheard a bunk house conversation about a new bonanza on a creek above Forty-Mile. At that time the news of Carmack's strike was not generally believed up there. The men who were discussing it hadn't seen the creek and didn't put much stock in the story. But Swiftwater took a chance. Within the hour he was poling up the Yukon and in a few days he was working a lay on *Thirteen*. The claim belonged to J. B. Hollingshead, who had jumped it. He let the mine out on a lay to Swiftwater and five others. Almost immediately one of the men struck pay dirt, but it was decided to keep the matter secret until they could make a deal with Hollingshead. He was glad to get rid of the mine for $45,000. Immediately afterward the gold began to fly out of the ground. The first clean-up paid each of the partners $155,000. Swiftwater bought into other mines but none of them were ever any good.

In one way or another Swiftwater had spent his gold. Before he left Dawson he sold out his share in *Thirteen* and, with none of the other mines paying, he was now actually in debt around town. It was customary to settle up at the end of summer when the gold had all been washed from the winter dump. Wolf was the first to know that Swiftwater's dumps on Quartz Creek were worthless.

Aside from bad luck and no mining judgment, Swiftwater had an amorous nature, which cost money in Dawson. He always said that any woman was worth her weight in gold, but Gussie Lamore made him prove it. This was in the days when he could, when he still owned a part of *Thirteen*. He lost his heart at first sight of the petite, plump Gussie, with her ruffled skirts swinging a daring inch above the tops of her boots as she waltzed around the dance floor in the arms of one of its patrons. Gussie and a sister, May, had just arrived from an establishment in Juneau. Before the evening was half over, Swiftwater had promised Gussie her weight in Eldorado gold if she would marry him in the morning. She weighed a hundred and thirty-four pounds. Gussie took the money and stalled for time. When Wolf was in Dawson she had not yet married the thirty-six-year-old Lothario. The year that Swiftwater knew Gussie was punctured by spats and battles.

Wolf soon learned the story of the fried eggs. It seemed that early that spring two crates of eggs were brought in by dog sled, especially for the restaurant where Swiftwater and Gussie took their meals. Soon after the eggs arrived another quarrel started between the two and the following morning they were seen to go separately to breakfast. Swiftwater got there first. When Gussie arrived the waiter served Swiftwater a platter of eggs. Gussie ordered hers, but there wasn't an egg to be had. In a few moments Swiftwater received another platterful. Then another. But he didn't eat any of these. He went to the door and whistled for the dogs that were always lying about in the streets. There was soon a leaping crowd at his feet. Daintily, one by one, he threw fried eggs out the door, not once turning around to look into Gussie's furious eyes. When the waiter had brought out every egg in the house, each one fried crisp and tempting, and all the dogs in sight had enjoyed them, Swiftwater wiped his hands on the waiter's napkin and strolled out. The scene cost him $2,280, the sum he paid the proprietor of the restaurant the night before in order to own every egg in Dawson.

Wolf was a sober man. He sat in Mrs. Healy's boarding-house and waited for Swiftwater to show up. He even doubted that he would do so. When the barge was reported coming down the river, Wolf went to the beach. Before Swiftwater had time to raise his hat to the welcoming crowd he heard a few private words from Wolf, who gave him the usual twenty-four hours. No one was more astonished than Wolf when Swiftwater handed him $40,000 the next afternoon. Who gave Swiftwater the money was never known, although most believed that Jack Smith did. It was not long before Swiftwater dropped out of the Monte Carlo, "bought out" by Smith.

For a while Swiftwater tried in vain to find pay dirt on his new mines. He induced the Dominion to grant him a large concession on Quartz Creek and he even went to London in 1899 to interest investors and to buy the world's largest hydraulicking machine. But it was no use, he never hit it again. He gave his last two coffee cans full of gold to Gussie, to go to San Francisco and bank it. She promised to marry him whenever he arrived, but when he caught up to her he found himself jilted. A consolation marriage to a younger sister, Grace, ended in three weeks. Other marriages, other mines, engaged Swiftwater. He tried Nome. He went to Peru. He was never a rich man again. But when he had it, the sky was the limit. That was the way he ran the Monte Carlo. The usual limit was an ounce, but in Swiftwater's place he always said, "The sky's the limit, boys! Tear the roof off!"

All the big saloons had a separate room for gambling. Even if a man didn't have stakes he could go in and watch the play. The appearance of a man was never against him. You couldn't tell the millionaires from the muckers, they were all rough-dressed and dirty. So long as a man had a mine he was welcome anywhere. The way Dawson looked at it, he might hit bedrock any day, he might be a millionaire the next time he came to town.

The gambling rooms were always crowded. Ver Mehr said, "We were all beggars for luck up there. Bedrock, cards, pill balls, it was all the same thing." The games were faro, rouge et noir, roulette, poker, blackjack, dice. To play, a man threw his poke to the dealer, who hefted it, called its worth to the dime and slid it into a drawer. When the player left the table, if he was ahead, his poke was returned to him together with his winnings, the latter in chips. These he cashed in at the cage. Lookouts were hired to sit on a perch above the level of the tables. They watched games and players to see that the house lost no money through carelessness. Arguments were infrequent, and not many tried to slip the dealer a poke with a bag of shot concealed in it. Between the lookouts' rifles and the police, who regularly made the rounds of every establishment, night and day, the games went on with little interruption.

Big winners would always "order up the house." Big losers often did the same. In Dawson they took things easy. The money didn't grow on trees but there was plenty of it underfoot. In the big places there was nothing unusual about $1,000 throws at dice or a $5,000 pot of poker. Sam Bonnifield and Harry Woolrich always played a heavy game. In Dawson every day some man lost a fortune on a number or the turn of a card. Perhaps then it took nerve to call for drinks for the house, light up a $1.50 cigar, and grin. Maybe not.

The saloons were open twenty-four hours a day, except Sunday. All places of business were required to close for the Sabbath. Dawson had its blue laws. You couldn't buy a loaf of bread or get your shirt washed, you couldn't go fishing on Sunday, whether for food or pleasure, you couldn't shoot crows. Those who broke the law paid a $2 fine, which was no hardship, and those out of funds went to the wood pile. Yet, the Dominion was understanding, it didn't shut down the entertainment. A most sensitive interpretation of the law found that selling whiskey was a business but that gambling was not, nor dancing, nor attending the theater. It was legal to go to Big Sal's cabin. (Most of the girls were in Paradise Alley, or over in Lousetown, but Big Sal was independent and lived close in.) Wherever the red curtained cabins were they were always open.

Every third door was a place to buy a drink. Whiskey was

fifty cents a shot no matter where you bought it. At the Combination, Mascot, Pavilion, Monte Carlo, wherever they had a show in connection, the price of a drink entitled the patron to go and watch. After the performance there was dancing, and to participate in this cost a drink a dance, consumed at the finish of each number. At the bar the girl received a chip a customer and at the end of the evening cashed them in. Drinking in the theaters and dance halls was not saloon drinking. On Sunday the law saw a distinction.

Each bar token was worth twenty-five cents to the girl, and if she was both ambitious and good-looking she would certainly be "in the chips." This brought her a nightly bonus of around $25, in addition to her salary, since at least a hundred dances made up a night's work. Quadrilles and waltzes were the most popular. Until three in the morning there was a continual rush for partners to dance the "cowtillion." As long as the fiddles cried on, the dancers would follow the leader to sashay, promenade and change, big hats, gumboots, galluses and all.

The girls' salaries were never less than $50 a week, often more, and they also gathered a fair-sized poke of nuggets on the side. Flush and happy patrons usually liked to make a personal contribution. The girls sewed the biggest nuggets onto belts and jealously tried to outdo each other. There were some heavy belts in Dawson but the boa that Anna Kane acquired went around her two and a half times. When she walked out onto the stage to sing she sagged a little with the weight of it.

Show business was good in Dawson. Saloon entertainment included vaudeville and variety. The opera houses offered wrestling matches and dramas. "Camille" one night, "Uncle Tom's Cabin" the next. Eliza crossed the ice on sheets of newspaper and the bloodhounds were Malemutes. The concert halls billed the celebrities.

The Oatley sisters, Polly and Lottie, arrived on the *Leah*

late one June afternoon and immediately began singing and clogging on a piece of boardwalk in front of the Pioneer saloon. They were an instant hit, and every night for the next two weeks continued to dance on the street, picking up the pokes and nuggets that were thrown to them until they were able to buy a hall. They didn't take in less than $5,000 a week thereafter for the rest of the summer.

Dancing was one thing a miner would crowd to the door to watch. Cake walks, jigs, the buck and wing danced by two pretty girls was Dawson's best show for the money. Two other sister acts arrived. They were Florence and Myrtle Brocee, and a team called "Jacqueline and Rosaline."

There were more than enough sopranos. Anna Kane was the best. They called her "The Nightingale of the North." She had competition in Nellie La Marr, Blanche La Mont, Josie La Vore and Minnie La Tour. They all made $150 a week, in wages. There was one tenor in town, Irish Freddy Breen. He sang about mother. Show girls and dance hall girls "lived private" and were not in quite the same class with the ladies of Paradise.

Rodeos, circus freaks, acrobats, all kinds of specialty acts came to Dawson—Lady Godiva, Little Egypt, tableaux of Famous Heroines, a man who mounted a scaffold to be hung every night, and live. The minstrels came, and Edison's moving pictures. Fare like this brought in nearly $1,000 a day. There was no night in summer. The big places like the Monte Carlo, Tex Rickard's Northern, Harry Ash's Dominion, and the Pioneer which was owned by three former prospectors, Densmore, Spencer, and McPhee, took in thousands of dollars every twenty-four hours. Once Jimmy McMahon spent $28,000 in a single evening at the Northern.

These places not only sold liquor, they also provided entertainment, gambling, and dancing. The Monte Carlo had a saloon up front and a small bar in back. In the theaters the patrons who could afford it sat in curtained boxes, where only champagne, at $40 a quart, was served. In these establishments even the porters got rich, not alone on tips, but by scooping the sawdust off the floor to pan it for spilled dust. A porter in the Pioneer boasted that he made twice his wages every day just out of the spittoons in the place.

It has been said that there were more musicians in Dawson than dealers, and the number of the latter was not small. Street bands were made up of disappointed miners, who went from corner to corner, passing the hat as they performed on flutes and fiddles, cornets, mandolins, any instrument they were pitiless enough to tackle. About eight o'clock in the evening the most proficient went to their ounce-a-night jobs at the dance halls and shows. There, a fiddle or two and a horn were accepted as an orchestra. (In 1898 pianos came in, and the man who played one was called a professor, for no reason at all.)

Ver Mehr remembered Ikey Sutro's band. Ikey, who opened the first pawnshop in Dawson, came by several musical instruments which he assigned, from time to time, to friends out of funds. The group went about town attempting to play "The Beautiful Blue Danube" and later shared the hat with Ikey. He, himself, played the hand organ and when the lay effort was too nerve-splitting he went along to supply a kind of redeeming accompaniment.

Most of the summer of 1898 there were four "regulars" from the pawnshop. Ver Mehr described the fiddler as a man "about dead from consumption, down at the heel and out at the toe." The fiddler's brother, long-winded enough to try the cornet, "would have been hung for it anywhere else." A Dutchman on a trombone won every tune by a couple of notes. "And the drummer must have been a blacksmith." None of them played by note but the Dutchman was the only one proud of it.

Popular songs of the day included "Put Your Arms Around Me, Honey," "After the Ball," "Doris, My Doris," "Two Little

Girls in Blue," "The Bird in a Gilded Cage," "Comrades, Comrades," and "Just as the Sun Went Down," as well as the ageless "Genevieve." Many of Stephen Foster's ballads were sung, also. Other tunes heard during the nineties, made popular by New York and London shows, were "Ta-Ra-Ra-Boom-Der-E," "There'll Be a Hot Time in the Old Town Tonight," "You Don't Have to Marry the Girl," "That Up-to-Date Girl of Mine," "She Got It Where McDooley Got the Brick," "Put Me Off at Buffalo," "Down Went McGinty," "I'm the Man Who Broke the Bank at Monte Carlo," "I Got Mine," "Across the Bridge He Goes," "The Gold Miner's Dream," and "The Old Stage Door." Many lyrics of the period still survive, such as "Only One Girl in the World for Me," "The Sunshine of Paradise Alley," and "Somebody Loves Me."

16

STARVATION WINTER

WITH THE rush the trading companies had, businesslike, increased their stores, sending in extra provisions with every steamer, but neither company had believed that 5,000 people would remain in Dawson over the winter of 1897–98. A great many of these had come in light, expecting to buy their supplies from the traders all winter. Others had lost their outfits on the trail, and not a few had abandoned them as winter closed in and haste was necessary if they were to reach Dawson alive.

The custom in these mining camps was for the miners to give their orders to the companies when the boats went out in the summer. When the goods arrived they were kept in the warehouse until the miner picked them up. He usually waited for the first good snowfall before he sledded his winter supplies up to his claim. The order was paid for at the end of summer, at cleanup time. The companies always kept a backlog of supplies for emergency's sake, including luxuries the miners might not have ordered before the cleanup. The lucky ones with extra dust could indulge themselves accordingly.

The stampede changed this. The companies attempted to fill their warehouses over and above what the miners had ordered. Extra boats were put on the river to carry supplies in from St. Michael. Every boat was scheduled to make at least one extra trip above the usual number. The *Bella* and *Portus B. Weare* were to make four, the *Alice* three, the *John J. Healy* two, the *Margaret* and the *C. H. Hamilton* one each. The last-named was the North American Transportation and Trading Company's newest boat, and she was making her maiden voyage.

It was getting near the end of September and the river was rapidly falling. The North American Transportation and Trading Company still had four hundred paid orders unfilled, and the Alaska Commercial Company had received only a third of its paid orders. Between them the companies had on hand less than a thousand pounds of food. Still the *Alice, Bella, John J. Healy* and *C. H. Hamilton* had not arrived. Captain J. E. Hansen, in charge of the Alaska Commercial Company's store, boarded the *Margaret* when she went out. The company had a large warehouse at Fort Yukon where Hansen hoped to secure supplies. There he learned that all the boats had got stuck on the bars below the ramparts. The river had suddenly lowered and there was no way to get the boats off.

When Hansen returned to Dawson by canoe with the news, the town was thrown into a panic. The miners came down from the creeks and demanded their orders. John Healy had long since left Dyea, and was now manager of the North American Transportation and Trading Company at Dawson. He permitted only a two weeks' supply of food to be given out from his stores. Both Hansen and Healy begged the men to be patient. "There's time yet. The river can rise again. One or two of the boats will get through." But the miners were frantic. Every man wanted to get his supplies, regardless of the next man, because work on the claims had to continue or else they were in danger of being forfeited. Mining law stated that a claim left idle for more than seventy-two hours could be jumped (taken by another who would work it), while

if abandoned altogether the location reverted to the Crown.
Without provisions, work on the mines would have to stop.

The company managers realized that hardship could be
avoided if the stores on hand were distributed equally among
the miners. Although the rations would be meager no one
would go hungry. The miners who had paid for their orders
and whose goods were piled up in the warehouses protested
against this measure and demanded what was theirs at once.
The companies refused to give it up. The next move on the
part of the angry miners was to try seizing the warehouses.
But the police intervened and stood guard over the stores
from then on.

The miners held a meeting. "Send the gamblers and the
other sports back to salt water!" They called on the police to
send all non-producers out of the country at once. "The bar-
tenders and the dealers have no call to stay!" A few hundred
people started down the river to Forty-Mile and Fort Yukon
where they hoped to find food.

A great many people were waiting for the boats to take
them out of the country. They had made their cleanup, sold
out, and were waiting for transportation. These people had
neither homes nor food of any kind. The restaurants refused
to serve meals. Some started back to Dyea by dog sled. The
fare was $1,000 and the "passenger" walked behind the dogs
all the way. The sleds were for food, fuel, blankets and camping necessities on the thirty-day trip.

And then on the twenty-eighth of September the chuggy
little *Portus B. Weare* came around Moosehide Hill. And
two days later the *Bella* was in, without her barge. They
brought only a small amount of food, having been held up
at Circle City.

All summer long the steamers had been passing Fort Yukon,
Circle City and Forty-Mile in order to get as many supplies
to Dawson as possible. There were not many miners left at
these camps, but there were enough of them to get together

for an armed holdup by the time the *Portus B. Weare* approached Circle City, creeping along in the shallow water, with everyone aboard watching the river for the dreaded bars. It was easy enough to board her and demand that the captain give up a part of the cargo. There were only twelve miners in the holdup but each hungry man had a rifle. When the captain refused to give up any of the food, which he was under bond to deliver to Dawson, the rifles were leveled on the crew and passengers until sufficient food was removed to see the miners through the winter. The captain was paid for the food at "Dawson prices" and permitted to proceed. The same thing happened when the *Bella* came along, other stranded miners having heard of the *Portus B. Weare* episode.

Captain Constantine, the Mounted Police Inspector, was on the *Bella,* but he could do nothing about the holdup since it occurred in United States territory. When Constantine reached headquarters at Dawson he immediately issued the following warning:

> The undersigned, officials of the Canadian Government, having carefully looked over the present distressing situation in regard to the supply of food for the winter, find that the stock on hand is not sufficient to meet the wants of the people now in the district, and can see but one way out of the difficulty, and that is an immediate move down-river of all those who are now unsupplied to Fort Yukon, where there is a large stock of provisions. In a few days the river will be closed, and the move must be made now, if at all. It is absolutely hazardous to build hopes upon the arrival of other boats. It is almost beyond a possibility that any more food will come into this district. For those who have not laid in a winter's supply to remain here longer is to court death from starvation, or at least a certainty of sickness from scurvy and other troubles. Starvation now stares everyone in the face who is hoping and waiting for outside relief. Little effort and trivial cost will place them in comfort and safety within

a few days at Fort Yukon, or at other points below where
there are now large stocks of food.

C. CONSTANTINE,
Inspector Northwestern Mounted Police

D. W. DAVIS
Collector of Customs

THOMAS FAWCETT
Gold Commissioner

September 30, 1897

A mass meeting was called by Constantine and the notice
was read. Captain Hansen went to every cabin in the district
to warn the men of the seriousness of the situation. "Flee for
your lives!" he told them. Healy, sitting in the offices of the
North American Transportation and Trading Company, was
angry. He called Hansen an hysterical cheechako. Hansen was
younger than Healy and a newcomer to the country. "There's
nothing at Fort Yukon," Healy told the people. "If you're
leaving you better get out of the country altogether. And to
do that you better wait until the river freezes so you can get
out with a dog team."

The miners would not leave Dawson. They said they were
sure the whole thing was just a trick to boost prices, and,
moreover, they reported having seen enough flour and sugar
and beans to feed the whole camp, "if the companies want to."
They grumbled that Healy didn't look scared. "If he eats,
so will we."

It was October 15. The cheechako boats were still arriving
from the passes. Eight of them, loaded with supplies, were
pulled past Dawson by the mush ice. It was twenty above.
The *Portus B. Weare* made a desperate try for St. Michael,
to take out as many passengers as could cling to her. The fare
was reduced to $50 in the emergency. On the twenty-second
of the month the *Bella* followed the *Portus B. Weare* with
a hundred and sixty persons aboard. There was no charge on

the *Bella,* the Dominion Government having arranged with Captain Hansen to take all persons out free who were not provided with food for the winter, on condition that they would not hold the *Bella*'s officers responsible for any delays or possible non-arrival at destination, and that they would cut wood and aid the steamer's voyage in any way the captain saw fit. Moreover, every passenger signing on agreed to leave the steamer upon request if the ice should run so thick as to endanger the steamer's progress.

After the *Portus B. Weare* and *Bella* were gone, a rickety tug, the *Kiukuk,* set out and broke down three times before she had gone thirty-five miles. The third time she was locked fast in the ice. The *Portus B. Weare* and *Bella* got as far as Circle City where the ice pushed them onto the shore. Discovering there was no food to spare at Circle City, many tried to go on to Fort Yukon in small boats. In three days the river closed and the marooned travelers were forced to walk the remaining eighty miles to Fort Yukon in a continuous blizzard. Some died. All were badly frozen.

By December, nine hundred people had left Dawson to walk out over the trail to Dyea. Each was given a three months' ration pack, paid for by the Dominion Government. The Americans sent E. H. Wells, one of the miners at Dawson, to Washington to plea for relief. Congress voted $200,000 in behalf of the starving people of the camp and placed the project in the hands of Secretary of War Alger. It was decided to send a reindeer relief train and the Reverend Sheldon Jackson, general agent of education in Alaska, was commissioned to get it there. Jackson was a Presbyterian missionary. Since the only children in Alaska were Indians, and these had the attention of various missions, the program of the Department of Education was quite naturally administered through them.

Among the various activities of the missions was the reindeer project. In 1891 the revenue cutter *Bear,* returning from the Arctic where it had gone to the aid of the ice-locked whalers, was hailed and stopped by a band of starving and half-naked natives of the King Islands. The plight of these people was brought to the government's notice and $25,000 was raised to buy a herd of Siberian reindeer for them, the idea being that the animals would be not only a source of food, but of clothing as well. The plan was successful and in ten years the herds numbered 1,280 head and were distributed to the missions at Cape Prince of Wales, Port Clarence, Cape Nome and Unalaklik on Norton Sound.

However, when Jackson reached Washington to take charge of the relief expedition, it was found that all the deer were on the way to Point Barrow, again bringing aid to the whaling fleet. There was but one thing to do and that was to go to Norway for more deer. Jackson set out and, after long weeks of delays and not a little confusion, was able to buy 530 deer and to secure the services of 57 drivers who, with their families, whom they wanted to bring with them, brought the number in the party to over 100. A ship was chartered but when the deer, the Laplanders and Finns, the sleds, special harnesses and other freight, were all aboard there was not enough room left for the necessary moss with which to feed the deer. On Jackson's order, five hundred tons were stowed on and the rest was left behind.

From New York the reindeer party was hurried to Seattle by fast train, but at Seattle there was a wait of nine days on account of missing the boat to Dyea. While they were in Seattle several of the Laplanders caught the measles. The deer were out of moss and had been put to pasture in one of the city's parks. In a week four of the animals had died. The rest were sick and eight more were lost on the trip up the canal.

At Dyea the marine officer whom the party expected to meet, to take over the expedition, was not there. Jackson, meanwhile, had been called away to other duties, and at Seattle had left the group in the temporary charge of an assistant. The officer at Dyea had not received orders regarding the expedition, due to mail irregularities at Skagway. The *Seminole,* which had brought the party and the relief stores up from Seattle, took them on to Haines Mission, near Pyramid Harbor, where the overland trip was scheduled to start. Half of the deer were dead from feeding on dry alfalfa. Reindeer moss was less than fifty miles away on the Dalton trail.

When at last the officer appeared at Haines with proper authority to begin the expedition, the snow had melted and the sleds were of no use whatever. There were 144 deer left out of the original 530. A wire from the war department directed Jackson's assistant to have them taken to one of the reindeer stations, to book passage home for the drivers and their families, to sell the relief stores, if he could, and ship back any that remained. And then buy himself a ticket for Seattle.

In the meantime, beans in Dawson went up to $1.50 a pound. Food was scarce but nobody starved. In fact, Mrs. Healy said that the situation had been greatly exaggerated in the papers, that no possibility of famine had ever existed.

Before the late boats had got stuck on the bars a number of disappointed cheechakos had started for home. They hoped to earn their passage money by cutting wood for the steamers at the various fueling stations along the river. Many of them were at Fort Yukon when the word came that the boats were stuck two hundred miles below. Knowing they would have to remain in Fort Yukon the rest of the winter, the miners asked the companies there to advance them provisions enough to prospect the local creeks. The company agents refused to do this since these were not men of the country, whose credit was good. Moreover, they did not have provisions enough to distribute more than the barest necessities for the time being. The miners conspired to seize the stores at Fort Yukon, and would have had not the *Bella* arrived with Captain Ray and

Lieutenant Richardson aboard. These were the two officers sent by President McKinley to locate a suitable site near the boundary line where a company of infantry might be stationed later in the year.

The company agents immediately asked the army officers to guard the warehouses. Richardson stayed at the Alaska Commercial Company's store and Ray went two miles down the shore to the North American Transportation and Trading Company's building. Major General A. W. Greeley, later describing the situation in a book, wrote as follows: "Ray and Richardson were alone, without a single soldier, but they acted with daring promptness. Ray hoisted the American flag over the two depots of provisions, announcing that he was taking possession of them in the name of the United States, and stated that they would be held for the benefit of all destitute persons. An organization for the resolute defense of the stores was formed, and the battle was won. Awed by the firm attitude of the officers and by this display of Federal authority, the lawless element abandoned their plans, and the winter passed quietly."

When Ray and Richardson took possession of the two warehouses the miners demanded of them if they were officers representing the government "which would care for its people in need," or were they representing the companies.

The miners next waylaid Ray as he was coming back from his watch at the warehouse. After the interview, Ray went back and "gathered a posse," according to an eye-witness account, and returned with the men walking behind him. The miners ordered them to halt at a line which they had drawn in the snow.

A Canadian from Victoria, named Todd, stepped around from in back of Ray and walked across the miners' line. The miners drew their guns, raised their rifles, and got ready to use whatever weapons they had. Todd stepped back. The posse had first been ordered to arm themselves but later the order was rescinded. There was no alternative now but to accept the miners' terms.

A committee of seven was elected to pass upon the claims of the destitute but their methods proved too lax, and Ray took over. He raised the American Flag. Then he issued seven months' outfits to the men, taking their notes in return, while he guaranteed the companies that the United States Government would make good any notes that remained unpaid at the end of a year. The "desperate men of the North, ready for any enterprise," as Greeley called them, went prospecting on the barren creeks.

In Dawson, mining went on throughout the winter as usual. Occasionally caribou were killed by hunters and brought to town. Captain Healy discovered he had enough of everything to just go around, except flour, and Captain Hansen found that he had some flour. A fifty-pound barrel of "Price's Best" cost $100.

As soon as the ice went out on the Yukon the miners came to town to wait for the first steamboat to bring them in supplies. As each early cheechako scow touched the beach it was surrounded by men eager to buy a little sugar, or tinned fruit, a can of milk, anything the newcomers would part with. Nuggets were exchanged for trifles of food. One miner filled a cheechako's palm with gold dust to get his two-pound tin of butter.

On June 8, at four o'clock in the morning, the first cry of "STEAMBOAT" rang out shrilly and was passed along from one person to another, bringing the whole town down to the beach. The dogs were yelping, the sawmill was tooting.

"Is it the *Merwin?*"

"It looks more like the *Alice.*"

"Come on, *Alice!*"

"River, let the dear little *Alice* in!"

The small boat bucked the eddy inch by inch. She came in so slowly that she seemed hardly to move in the sight of the hungry and impatient people crowded to her dock. At last they could read her name. "Why, it's the *May West!*"

When she docked, the captain came down to the beach and told Fawcett, the gold commissioner and temporary administrator of Dawson's affairs, that the *Portus B. Weare* and *Bella* were still on the banks at Circle City. The *May West* had been stranded at the mouth of the Tanana when the river dropped. She wasn't from the outside at all, but she brought Dawson a few supplies.

After the *May West* came in, the *C. H. Hamilton, Portus B. Weare, Bella, Seattle No. 1, W. K. Merwin, Alice, John J. Healy* and *Margaret* arrived in quick succession. None of the boats had been lost. They had all been stuck in the ice. Five of them were there to deliver what passengers they had left and the others had come back to see what happened to Dawson.

On the twenty-first the Columbia Navigation Company's new and palatial sternwheeler *Monarch* arrived. She was the first boat to come in from salt water, and she had beat the *John Cudahy*'s standing record of eleven and a half days. The *Monarch* made it in ten. The journey from St. Michael usually took thirteen or fourteen days, although running time was only about eight days. The rest of the trip the boats were either on the sand bars, discharging freight or fueling up.

The newspapers which the *Monarch* brought in were snatched up at once, for a dollar or more a copy. People wanted to know if New York City was in ashes. The news of the sinking of the *Maine* had just reached them from a cheechako who had arrived by way of the pass and had brought a Seattle newspaper with him. He parted with the paper for $160. The fellow who bought it rented a tent and sold tickets at a dollar each to hear the story read. He made $1,000 before a dog team came in with 1,600 copies of a later edition. These early reports gave credence to the rumor that Cervera's armored cruisers, a full half of the Spanish fleet, were then steaming toward New York harbor to take that city. The papers which the *John J. Healy* and *Monarch* brought in had the news of all that had happened since the *Maine*'s explosion on February 15. The papers were read aloud from boxes on the street corners, with prolonged cheers interrupting the readers as they described the fall of Manila and the early battles in Cuba.

17

"YOU JUST CAN'T TELL
LIES ABOUT KLONDIKE!"

WHEN PEOPLE first heard that the Klondike nuggets were as big as potatoes and the paystreak was up to a 100 feet wide, some thought it was a lot of wild talk, especially those who had dug for gold at one time or another. However, the boats kept bringing down millions of dollars' worth of negotiable grit all summer, along with the men who had done the shoveling. The lucky miners, who were themselves as astonished as anyone, were only too glad to oblige the public with descriptions of the country where they had found the treasure, to supply details of weight, value, texture, color, shape, to rattle off figures and estimates, and not forget to add that there was plenty of gold left for anybody who wanted to go after it.

The reports were startling. A ledge twenty feet by four had paid two partners $40,000 in less than a month. A man by the name of Alexander McDonald had got to be worth $7,000,000 in six months' time. Somebody by the name of Fred Bruceth washed $61,000 worth of gold in one day. The nuggets were scattered over the ground. You simply reached down and picked them up. There were creek placers on top of the hills. "You might as well believe what you hear," the men carrying heavy pokes off the steamers told all within earshot, "because you just can't tell lies about Klondike. It's all true. It's the greatest strike in history. Three or four million will come out this year, and Eldorado alone has got at least five million more in sight. This year many of the claims weren't even touched. There were only a couple hundred of us there last winter. Thousands are up there now, they'll get $50,000,000 in '98. They're at work on a dozen new creeks."

All summer long the dog and horse trains brought the gold down from the mines for shipment out from Dawson. Every dog train had fifteen or twenty dogs to it, each animal carrying from twenty to thirty pounds of gold. A train of fifteen dogs carrying thirty-pound packs would be bringing down $122,400. A horse carried five times as much as a dog. The trains were on the trails twenty-four hours a day, six days of the week, for two and a half months.

The pack trains made good money for their owners. The charge was forty-five cents a pound to carry gold. General freight was packed for less but a horse could carry twice as much of that, and the rate for it was only twenty-five cents a pound to anywhere on Bonanza, thirty-five cents the length of Eldorado, and fifty cents to Hunker Creek. In winter the rates went down to ten and fifteen cents a pound, by dog sled. Sam Bartlett, an old-time packer known on every Yukon creek, became one of Dawson's richest men. He was one of those who wouldn't stake Bonanza when he could. It was his opinion that Ladue had started the stampede to get men up to his new townsite. He was one of the first to squint at Bonanza and turn it down. Later, when the old-timers came back and had to buy onto the creeks, he still didn't want any of the shoveling. He came back with eleven dogs and in summer unloaded a scow of mules. He had more animals working for him in a few weeks than McDonald, Lippy, and Berry together had men dumping dirt for them. And Sam had the most money "in hand."

The first summer the gold was taken to the company warehouses, but in 1898 two banks opened for business, the Bank of British North America and the Canadian Bank of Commerce. The first conducted its business in a tent and the second in a cabin so small the customers had to stand outside. The "vaults" in the cabin were two tin-lined wooden boxes four feet long, three feet high and three feet wide, with a lockable lid. When both of the boxes were full they held approximately $1,000,000. On a table pushed to the open door the bank drafts and bills were bundled in stacks a foot high. Not a weapon or guard was ever in sight. The notes and currency were exchanged for the gold, weighed at the other end of the table on a large scales. There were also assaying offices in Dawson which bought gold, and a smelter which turned out small ingots if the miners wanted to take the metal out that way.

At the end of summer the Bank of British North America had put up an "elegant and imposing" two-story building of planed logs, with a flagpole out in front, and the Canadian Bank of Commerce was also in better quarters.

The first bedrock struck on Eldorado was on Sloan's and Wilkerson's *Fourteen,* and they hit it in December. While they were digging for it they took out $10,000 in nuggets, worth an average $10 apiece. At eighteen feet they struck black sand and the test pans began washing at $12, $14, $50, $85. They found from $5 to $500 a pan until the pay stopped. In May, before they washed the dump, they sold out for $100,000.

By Christmas they were all on bedrock with the pans paying from $3 to $5 on the average. Big pans turned up continually. Clement on *Four* got $57, McLanie on *Fifteen* got $112, Lippy on *Sixteen* got $212. The men knew then they would have a tremendous cleanup as soon as they had the water. The dumps grew bigger and bigger. Those getting poor pay on Bonanza came over and bargained for lay work, labor payable on bedrock or in the cleanup on a percentage basis. Men were needed to get the dirt out and onto the dumps before the creek started running in May. The only way to get the men to work was to offer them shares. They brought their own grub and moved into the owner's cabin with him.

On *Five* Berry washed a pan worth $300 on March 20. On April 13 he got a $495 pan and within the next two days got $1,200 more. He put twenty-five men to work. Keller, working the other half of the claim, was still in $5 dirt. Berry had the paystreak. On April 20 McDonald's foreman on *Thirty-Six* got an $800 pan. A few weeks later he showed McDonald a $1,700 pan but admitted he had picked it, that is, he had put the best dirt he could find into the pan before he washed it, picking the dirt here and there out of "pure" pockets. After that he went back to "shoveling square" at anything from $15 to $150 a pan. *Thirty-Six* had the richest dirt on Eldorado. McDonald beat Berry's $10,000 box length by $7,000 one afternoon.

It was true that Bruceth had got $61,000 in one twenty-hour work day. He had a dozen or so men working for him on ten-hour shifts, and one day in July they collected the above sum from a sluice line of five boxes. In the same way, Densmore and Spencer washed ninety pounds of gold, $24,480, in a single day. They used the money to build a saloon, taking as a partner a third Eldorado king named McPhee. All the men on Eldorado got rich. Red McConnell and Jim Tweed shared $200,000 in the cleanup. *Twenty-Five* and *Twenty-Six*, belonging to the Stanleys and Wordens, paid out $112,000 from a seventy-five-foot strip. *Five* and *Six* paid Berry a probable $250,000 before summer. He bought out Stander before they were on bedrock. What he paid for Stander's half of *Six* is not known. But he paid $22,000 in wages, took home $130,000 in dust, $84,000 in nuggets (not counting Mrs. Berry's) and left between $15,000 and $20,000 for operating expenses at the mines during his absence in the coming year.

As for Clement and Keller, half of whose claims Berry owned, Clement had made $50,000 washing the dump for a month, and Keller had got out $35,000. They were glad enough to sell their remaining halves to Berry and go home. Again, what Berry paid for them is a guess, but since they were "worked out" he very likely got them for the proverbial song.

Not only were the pans bigger on Eldorado, the nuggets were also larger. Chunks of gold weighing half a pound or more were picked up rather generally. The biggest nugget came from McDonald's *Thirty-Six*. It's value was $585. Bert Hudson, working for Berry on *Six,* picked up a piece of gold worth $257. Many of the larger nuggets were chunks of quartz embedded with gold, not pieces of pure gold in themselves. The small nuggets were usually pure metal. These were the kind that Mrs. Berry, and also Mrs. Lippy, liked to find. The ladies each had several thousands of dollars' worth to take out with them when they went home in June.

The first summer, the Eldorado laymen made good "wages" for their six months of digging. In June, when they began to collect, there wasn't a man among them who didn't make $10,000, and many made that five and six times over. The men who had the lay on *Seventeen,* which belonged to Picotte and Hall, were offered $50,000 for their dump but they refused to sell. Even Picotte and Hall tried to buy them off the patch sixty by forty feet which was the area of their lay. The cleanup was close to three times that much, and it turned out the paystreak on *Seventeen* was exactly there and no place else.

Hollingshead owned several mines. He tried to get men on *Thirteen,* but nobody would take it because it was an unlucky number and the surface dirt was pretty bare. This was the claim that made Swiftwater Bill a rich man. Hollingshead sold out before he realized what his four laymen had got. They had found enormously rich dirt in the first hole and had covered it up as a ruse, pretending they had found nothing. They dug six more holes, all of which they said were "fair." By that time the costs of claims on the creek were going up fast and the four men paid Hollingshead's price, payable on bedrock. The first hole was re-opened to pay him and from then on it was no secret that *Thirteen* was as good, or even better, than any of them.

On Eldorado there wasn't a blank to *Thirty-Nine,* where the pay began to pinch out. As early as March no man on Eldorado would sell for less than $500 a foot and the price soon went to twice that. *Thirty-One,* which originally sold for $100, was resold around the first of the year for $31,000 to McDonald. He refused $150,000 for it within two months.

Bonanza, however, was a spotty creek. There were good claims but the dirt did not run evenly. There were many blanks between the claims which had pay on them. Below *Discovery,* as far down as *Sixty,* the average pan in the cleanup was around $1.25. Above *Discovery* it was slightly better, $2 to $3.50, sometimes $5.

In spite of huge nuggets and heavy pans the richest slice of ground in the Klondike was not on Eldorado but on Bonanza. When Dick Lowe, a surveyor, put the tape to Dusel's claim he found that it was 78 feet too long so the posts were moved back. There were many fraction claims on both creeks that year because of a lack of uniformity in measuring the ground. The claims on Bonanza were, more ordinarily, too short (which the Crown did not feel obliged to make up) and those on Eldorado were almost without exception too long. They were too long by 100 or more feet. *Thirty-Seven* was 420 feet too long. What was left over was sold by the Dominion as a "fraction." These were quickly bought up on Eldorado but those on Bonanza, what few there were, usually went begging.

Dusel didn't want to buy the 78 feet. So far he hadn't seen anything on *Two Above* to make an investment attractive, at least not one of $900, which was the asking price. Lowe didn't have a mine so he took it. This was long before the Dominion rather tardily got around to forbidding any person employed by it to stake or own mines in the Yukon Territory. That order in council was not passed until March 29, 1899. Lowe didn't want to work the mine and, like others, tried to let it out. Nobody would bother with such a small strip on Bonanza. Finally he got a shovel, pick, and a few cords of wood and went to work on it himself. He soon found "gold by the cupful." The first four pans were worth just under $700 apiece. He hired a foreman and six laborers to make up for lost time, and when they washed the first dump they had $60,000. For the next three weeks they shoveled off the surface and made $75,000 more. The fourth week paid them $68,000 and then the summer was over. Meanwhile, McDonald had bought Dusel's mine and put a crew to work. They were hauling out the gold but Lowe had the most. The paystreaks of both Bonanza and Eldorado crossed his ground, and, in addition, he had the wash from Skookum Gulch.

On Bonanza, Rhodes was the first man on bedrock. He got there late in November and washed $65.30 in the first pan, cause for enough excitement at the time. His cleanup was around $40,000.

Alexander McDonald didn't stake either Bonanza or Eldorado, arriving too late to find an empty space on either creek. He had come into the Yukon in 1895, as a representative of the Alaska Commercial Company, and was known as a mining expert, with a Colorado reputation to his credit. Among other duties, he acquired mining property for the trading company. He was a tall and heavy man whose rather stiff carriage gave others the mistaken impression of haughtiness. He was self-effacing, very slow to talk, and then expressing himself mostly in monosyllables, the most frequent of which was "no." He was a non-drinker and non-smoker and therefore not too convivial. He was a Scot, exemplifying the expected characteristics of canniness, plus caution with a poke string.

McDonald bought up mines and turned them over to others to work. No wages were paid but a share of the mine was guaranteed. If the mine was a blank those who worked for shares lost their whole year's labor. For that reason laymen left everything but five-dollar dirt. The bedrock on *Three* Eldorado was so deep that half a dozen partners had given it up before the last two reached good gravel. That was in March, 1897. On most claims the gravel was worth something for at least ten feet above the paystreak, but not on *Three*. When they did hit it the pay was as good as it was anywhere else on Eldorado. For some reason the bed took a deep curve at that point.

It was McDonald who bought half of *Thirty* for a sack of flour, then let it out. (The laymen made $40,000 for themselves that summer.) He kept on buying mines and letting them out. More than two partners could take a mine. They could take any section of it that they thought looked good. Often four or six men were working sections of a single claim. In July McDonald astonished everybody by turning out to be the owner of twenty-eight mines, all of them good, located on every creek in the Klondike Valley. Many a time it took an entire pack train to carry his gold to Dawson. One rich train he sent down was worth $162,000.

At the end of the summer he had forty claims, although he did not own them all himself but was a quarter or half owner in many. They said he was worth between $5,000,000 and $7,-000,000, depending upon the speaker's estimate of the gold that was still in McDonald's ground. People began to call him Big Alec. Only Big Alec could say, "I can dig $150,000 out of my dirt any time I want to." He could. He could actually see most of it on the surface of the cut.

18

UNDER THE SPELL

THE SPELL of the Yukon was not, as one might think, a phrase invented by storytellers. Everyone who had spent the winter inside the country knew what "the spell" was, although, later, when he tried to put it into words, he usually failed. His listeners had never lived without daylight, nor been shut away from civilization. Descriptions of black days, of intense cold that burned flesh and choked breath from the lungs, of sombre memories revolving about hunger, sickness, loneliness, months of waiting for the reappearance of the sun, evoked sympathetic sighs but hardly understanding.

The returned Klondikers told about an "unearthly silence" which unnerved them, finally, after months of it. It was something more than the usual silence of winter. In the Yukon, winter was accompanied by darkness. Some months a midday twilight broke through the storms for as long as four hours, but even moonlight was brighter. The snowfall was not always heavy. For the most part it was nearly invisible, but it never seemed to stop. It piled up cushions underfoot and swirled the landscape with half-transparent veils that deceived men with sounds that were fey and muted. At times all out-of-door activities seemed to take place in shadowy tableaux. Men emerged in and out of visions. Dogs leapt like phantoms and yet the jingling of their harness bells was sharp. The sound most distinctly recalled to mind afterward was that of distant, delicate bells which approached without warning and flew past upon apparitions. Occasionally the dogs and wolves howled echoingly from the hills. There were startling shrieks whenever the trees split the length of their frozen sap. Green logs in cabins also burst with the same shrill tears, making the occupants jump. The sound of it was like rifle shot.

The long, long winter with its eerie quietness, which only unfamiliar sounds interrupted, the never-ending gloom, the flickering of candle or lamp light for months on end—these affected dispositions and hushed Dawson. The roaring establishments died down to clicking, feltboard thrums of gamblers. Men drank in silence at the bar, warmed themselves at the red-hot stove and hardly turned to inquire how the latest creek had turned out. The sopranos sang "Home, Sweet Home," the words of which exactly fit the cheechakos' frame of mind. Once in a while a man in the saloon, who had come down from the creeks because he couldn't stand being alone any longer, would throw his poke on the bar, order up the house, and holler, "For Christ's sake, let's get the gloom out of here!"

Melancholy and helplessness came over the people the day the last steamer puffed off from Dawson's dock. "There's no hittin' for home now, come hell or high water," they all agreed and pretended to joke. It was seventeen hundred miles to Seattle, by dog sled, and not even the threat of starvation could send many of them out on it. That night the piano players and fiddlers put all they had into the new ragtime music and everybody sang "Ta-Ra-Ra-Boom-Der-E" as they never had before.

Ver Mehr had already moved into a cabin, thirty miles away on Dominion. He said, "When me and Hawley couldn't make out Ray leaning against the rail there any longer,

Hawley, he went back to work and me and my dog, Chief, took the trail for the cabin. My God, I was blue! Even the dog knew it. You know, up there a man's dog got to be just like another human to him. They lived together, shared the same grub, the same bed. Why, I would have froze to death that winter if it hadn't been for Chief. He took up most of the bunk but he kept me warm. When I cooked a meal I dished it out the same for him as for me. Well, when we got to the cabin I sat outside for a while on some wood I had piled up there by the door, and I put my arm around Chief's neck and the two of us just sat there, wondering about what was coming. It was a drizzling day. Every once in a while I'd look up and watch the birds flying home. The sky was full of them.

"Pretty soon we went inside. That cabin was the most miserable place you ever saw. Nothing but a kennel, not a bit better, and just the right size for two. I was as shaggy as my dog. I didn't smell a bit better either. We were both lousy. Everybody was. Scratching, that was the 'secret sign' of the Klondike.

"I just stood there and looked at that place. Two bunks on the wall, my dirty clothes on a nail, my sox hanging from a string over the stove. The stove was out, as usual. I had trouble with it the whole winter. There was a slab of bacon hanging from another string, where the mice couldn't get at it. Chief, he could have stood up and grabbed that bacon any time he wanted to but my dog would never have done a trick like that. He knew how things were with us. He could see we were short on grub. There wasn't a thing hidden in that cabin. It was full of picks and shovels and gold pans. Some half empty sacks of flour and beans and rice sat on the floor. They were full of mice dirt but that didn't bother us any more. We had a few tins left on the shelf. That miserable place had everything in it but gold and smoking tobacco. I wanted some of both the worst way but it didn't look like I was likely to get any of either very soon."

Miners' cabins were small and built of logs with a foot-thick thatch of mud and moss on top of the roof. The walls were chinked with mud and moss and, generally, there was a wooden floor. The scows in which the men came down the river were broken up to make the floor and furniture. What they had in the way of the latter was very crude—wall bunks, a table, shelves, seats if they hadn't picked up packing boxes somewhere. Every cabin had a stove with the pipe thrust up through an oil drum on the roof. Mud was packed between the pipe and drum for insulation. If the cabin had a window it was made of bottles and mud. The occupants couldn't see through it but in summer it let in a little light.

Daylight began to vanish in October. The trees had already lost their autumn colors, the red creeper that had run so splendidly over the stones had disappeared, and only tufts of moss remained. Frosts became thicker each night, and there were frequent snowfalls. The smallest creeks were frozen to their banks. At 15 below mush ice clotted the Klondike River and glassy sheets floated on the Yukon. The shores caught the waves, now crunchy with ice. The Klondike hardened black, then covered over with fleece until a deep bed of it lay ready for the sleds. On the big river the floating ice, which looked like enormous pond lily petals, collided, melted, drifted away, again froze together and separated, repeating this a number of times before the cold held all the pieces fast. Meanwhile, the floes had grown deep and massive and wherever they struck a bar or island they piled up. After several of these had crashed, one on top of the other, there were crags of all sizes the whole length of the river. Between them the remaining water twisted ever more slowly until the last dark drop stood still. The Yukon was tight to the shore and daylight was gone.

Waterholes had to be cut through the ice then, to the water which was five and six feet under it. When the hole hit the bottom the water would bubble up to the surface. Every day the top of the hole would refreeze for a few inches down and have to be chopped open again for use. Eventually the hole froze from the bottom and another one had to be cut. The water was always warmer than the air above so that "steam" appeared to rise from the holes. These vapors, which drifted wraithlike through the town, added a phantasmagoria of their own. Enormous ravens stalked the streets or sat like gargoyles on the ice.

The men on the creeks lived in a still more sinister scene. It was one of tree stumps and clawed-back earth, of ashes, of heaps of fresh dirt lying in gravelike mounds between shrouds of smoke. An occasional live flame shot out of a pit, lighting the snow, but for the most part the gulches were choked with a cheerless haze and appeared to be, as some imagined, the corridors of hell. The men were underground, scraping, crawling on all fours, mesmerized, straining their eyes for infinitesimal bits of gloss. The quest was noiseless.

There was still another sight to bedevil the wits of grocers and cowboys turned into miners for a season. This was the aurora borealis, "the lights" which waved across the sky from time to time. They were less spectacular in pattern and of less brilliance than those of other regions, but they were enough for men already rasped with winter's provocations. Milky arcs were sometimes substituted with curtains hung across the sky. The filminess seemed to be drawn from a star in the north, spun out like spiders' spittle, spreading out and falling, apparently all the way down to the snow fields, then rolling up again until only the star was left, and soon that would disappear. The lights returned sometimes for nights in a row and then would not be seen for weeks. They and the recurring moon marked the passing of time.

When they couldn't stand the labor and the loneliness any longer the men took the trail for Dawson. In one of the saloons an act that was the talk of the creeks in 1898 was being put on. A man mounted a realistic-looking scaffold, permitted his arms to be tied and a noose placed around his neck. The platform was then pulled from under him and he dropped into space to dangle until his face turned purple. At that point the curtain was drawn. A different man was recruited every night so that the customers could not be sure whether or not the hanged man lived through the ordeal. It added to the horror of it for them to remain in doubt. The show was free. It went along with the price of a drink or of a cup of coffee and a doughnut. "Coffee and" was $1.25, whiskey was 50 cents.

The girls were still in Dawson. They were working hard in the dance halls and doing their turns at the Tivoli and Pavilion. The Saratoga, Bon Ton, Lucky Cigar Store and other cabins also had their full share of lonely miners. A few of the girls had gone to the creeks to accommodate the busiest of them, a well-paid gesture judging by the length of the lines outside the cabin doors. It was cold waiting turn. The doorman gave each entrant a brisk boost with a paddle to warm him up and once inside he could buy a drink or two. This brief recreation, not including the liquor, cost him one ounce of gold.

They were digging that much daily, if they were on the pay. Otherwise they would sink another hole to find it. In fact, the minimum take had to be more than an ounce a day, figuring $10 a man, two men to the shaft. It wasn't much use working for less, they would be out money if they did. They wouldn't have anything to wash in summer unless they hauled up a hundred buckets of dime dirt a day throughout the winter. Each bucket would wash about five pans. But not every pan would have colors in it. If the average pan was worth a dime, the men were making wages but not overhead.

The five thousand men digging gravel the winter of 1898 were digging sparer creeks than Bonanza and Eldorado. The total take that year was $10,000,000 and, if every man had received an equal share of it, or $2,000 apiece, there would have been little profit for anyone. If they had all made fortunes, the Klondike would have had to be far richer than it was. They would not have needed shovels, they could have swept up the gold with brooms. The way it turned out some men did make fortunes, but, necessarily, the majority got nothing for their trouble.

Lucky or not it was a hard life looking for gold. Ten hours a day of backbreaking labor was not the worst of it, nor cold weather, nor the inexperience for such a life. Although the monotony was difficult to bear, it was no worse than the endless night. What was so distressing and what broke, even killed, some of the men was the accumulated effect of all of these things, plus hunger. Besides facing the winter with an insufficient amount of food, the little they did have lacked the essentials of a good diet. They were living on boiled beans, pancakes and coffee. These were easiest to prepare yet the men were too fatigued to cook even such a meal very carefully. They usually boiled their beans ahead and from meal to meal re-heated the frozen pellets in bacon grease. Although yeast dough would have been better for bread, they made the easier baking powder variety. They had few canned tomatoes or lime tablets, and no citric acid. Few had canned vegetables left, or dried fruits. They ate the same diet three times a day and relieved it with a little taste of spirits, particularly when they were feeling poorly.

Exhaustion was the first symptom of approaching scurvy, but every man was tired. They didn't think about scurvy. Not until their teeth began to drop out of swollen gums and the pains in their legs were excruciating. Before long they would be too weak to get out of bed and, if they were living alone, they would lie there until they rotted and died.

They were found on all the creeks, bloated and black, long dead in their blankets. One man, discovered after thirty days on his back, was taken to St. Mary's hospital by sled and cured. He said he had kept alive by mixing sugar and flour in a tin cup and making a paste with ice that he picked off the wall and melted against his body. He was rigid to the hips when they discovered him, and his gums had puffed out through his lips but recovery was fast once he was properly nourished. Scurvy was the cheechako's disease. The old-timer kept well on sourdough bread and spruce needle tea.

The cold was difficult to get used to. At 25 below a blizzard was a terrifying experience. At 50 below, when there was never any wind at all, the motionless air seemed to sear the skin. Everyone took care to breathe very slowly out-of-doors when the thermometer was low. To inhale quickly was like taking in fire. Mercury froze at 40 below, and when the vial of it carried on every dog sled would not shake in the driver's hand he unharnessed the dogs and let them bury themselves in the snow for protection. He himself sought the nearest shelter, if it was only under the fur robes. No team was ever deliberately taken out to work in low temperatures. A good team was worth $1,000 or more. The Alaska Commercial Company had the prize set, five huskies bought from an Indian chief and valued at $1,700. With dogs like these no chances were taken with their lives.

All the miners, however, did not possess the necessary alcohol thermometers. They read the temperature by looking at the pain killer. St. Jacob's oil would hold up until 75 below. The best Hudson's Bay Company rum would do the same. But it was rarely cold enough to put these products to the test. The miner had all the cold he wanted when boiling water, striking the air, folded into a ribbon between the kettle spout and the gold pan. He cursed the Yukon just as roundly if the water hissed when it fell through the chilly air.

Very often the temperature inside the cabin was practically the same as that outside. As soon as the fire burned down, everything in the cabin would freeze. Jeremiah Lynch wrote of attempting a bath in two inches of melted ice water which he heated in a portable tub and set upon the floor. In a flash he had stripped, made a vain yank at the soap frozen to its dish, and stepped into the tub—only to skid on the newly frozen two inches of ice which had replaced the water.

On contact with metal of any kind the skin would stick to it and burn. A tin cup, tin plate, the utensils handled in eating had to be kept warm enough to touch. This was not easy when the very nails on the walls were covered with frost and "glaciers" formed in the corners of the cabin. The latter were created by steam from the cooking, which turned into ice wherever the stove did not heat the twelve-by-fourteen room. Most of the drinking and cooking water was picked off from these convenient icicles. In order to split the kindling the ax had to be kept under the oven. A frozen ax was a dull one and, if used, would crack anyway. Cold kerosene, used to start the fire, felt like boiling water if it happened to splash the skin.

Men awoke with icicles around the top of their blankets or sleeping bags, which might even be frozen fast to their faces if they wore beards. Moist hair around the mouth or nostrils was always a hazard because it could freeze over and suffocate the sleeper. Many suffered from frozen feet, fingers, and ears when working outside and, if the proper precautions were not taken while thawing out these parts, gangrene would set in. When gangrene got out of control the next step was amputation, a job for a man's partner to accomplish as best he could. The kindling ax was the only implement on hand and this was heated red-hot for the operation. It was hoped by both victim and wielder that one stroke would do the job but experience as well as fortitude was necessary, and not many cheechakos had either one. Whiskey helped, but they didn't always have it either.

"Many kicked the bucket," Ver Mehr said. "If it wasn't the bellyache in the summer, it was the gangrene in the winter, and scurvy and homesickness claimed their share as well."

Ver Mehr himself had difficulties. He was working alone in a hole when his pick slipped and slashed through his moccasined foot. It was several hours before they found him, during which time his foot swelled up as big as a ham and he was nearly unconscious from cold and pain. They pulled him up on the windlass and carried him to the cabin for treatment. There wasn't much to choose from in remedies. He said they poured kerosene all over his foot and lit it, a sure cure for infection. He admitted that he fainted "dead away."

There was a graveyard in Dawson, although few graves were dug in the winter. Any digging was made in the direction of the paystreak. Bodies were wrapped and put on top of the cabin roofs to wait for the thaw. The burial ground was set aside in 1897 when the frozen body of William Stickney was brought down from Lake Lebarge by his partner, who arrived in Dawson after numerous harrowing experiences. Stickney had died from exposure on the shores of the lake.

In 1898 the death which shocked Dawson was that of teenaged dancer, Myrtle Brocee, who shot herself. Her funeral sled was followed by every man in Dawson, all of whom had applauded her sister and her so many times. The coffin was banked with artificial flowers which the women of Dawson had snipped from their costumes. Two newspaper correspondents composed poetry for the occasion. Included in the stanzas, which Howard V. Sutherland wrote in "The Light-o'-Love," are the lines:

> *Kisses she gave and kisses she took,*
> *Sinned for her daily bread;*
> *But all we knew as we eyed the box*
> *Was: She is dead . . .*
> *. . . Under the white, white flakes the rose,*
> *Crumpled, tawdry and red;*
> *Hinting the pity which all men need*
> *When they are dead.*

For memories of "fair Myrtle," the men burned and picked out six feet of frozen clay in the middle of winter and carefully buried her body.

Distress increased for the men on the creeks who were not

even on five-cent dirt. Their rations were almost gone and they had no dust to buy more. Tension increased with each added day of hunger and fatigue. Disappointment, bitterness, minor vexations, thundered into quarrels which, in some cases, could be appeased only by bloodshed. Two partners on Hunker slashed each other to death. Five men and two dogs got into a fight outside a roadhouse on lower Bonanza and one of the men was killed by the other man's animals. Two other men looked on. On Milliman Gulch a man named Crofton hung himself. Suicides were reported from several creeks. Others swore they would kill themselves if they could wash enough gold to buy the rope.

A man who had turned his cabin on lower Bonanza into a bunk house was filling his old prospect holes with the bodies of men who died in the bunks. He always removed their boots to sell them to future patrons. Many of the travelers had died of pneumonia. Others had been in the final ravages of "consumption" when they reached the innkeeper's door. Severe illness was to be expected among men living mostly on flour and water. Addie Mizner, later to become Florida's famous architect, found a man on *Forty-Three Above* Bonanza stewing pieces of moccasin which he was preparing to eat. Mizner came to the rescue with a hand-out, but other men were not so lucky to have a neighbor with provisions to spare. John Gamble said it took about two hours to boil the leather to a stage soft enough to swallow. A number of men ate candles, being out of oils and fats which they craved, and were morbidly satisfied with tallow and wax. Harry Fisk sold his dog for its weight in moose. He was starving but he couldn't bring himself to eat the dog. Luckily a party of professional hunters, passing the cabin with a sled full of fresh meat, saw his chimney smoke and stopped to warm themselves.

Food was never begged. Few had it to give. But a fire was always ready for the traveler to whom warmth was sometimes more necessary even than food. Whether or not a man was at home, his cabin remained open and anyone could enter and use it. The unforgivable act was to leave without replacing the shavings and scraps of kindling which were always prepared and ready for an instant blaze. In Dawson, fire was another thing. Every Front Street building had its huge wood-burning stove, which very quickly dried out the walls and floors, making interiors extremely inflammable. The fires were never extinguished, month on end, and even the chimneys wore through before spring. Water was lacking in all practical amounts in case of an alarm. Caution was the only protection Dawson had from a holocaust, but the constant use of lamps and candles threatened destruction at almost any time. On the morning of October 14, 1898, it came.

Shortly before five o'clock in the morning a customer at the M and M saw a flash of fire leap from one of the muslin-covered windows on the second floor of The Green Tree, which was across the street. Before he reached the door of the saloon to call out an alarm, the roused occupants and visitors of the Tree were already streaming forth. The women had gathered their spangled and beribboned dresses under their arms and both hands were clutched over their pokes. Pursuing flames licked the heels of the last man out.

The Worden Hotel next door was rapidly emptying. The post office shack on the other side of the Tree crackled and its smoke was soon belching at the sky. Anxious police spread the alarm and people crowded into the streets. In half an hour both of the hotels and the post office were in ashes. And still the wind kept pulling the flames along from building to building until sixteen of them were ablaze.

The men had already run for the two fire engines, bought that summer, only to learn that the bill had not yet been paid in full and the North American Transportation and Trading Company, which was holding them, had not uncrated any of the boxes. All hands fell to. Each part had been packed in tallow and this, now frozen, had to be removed. Fortunately, a former fire chief of Seattle was there to direct the assembling.

Meanwhile, the flames continued to glide in and out of the waterfront buildings. The sawmill and hospital, which were out a ways from the center of town, were in no danger, but Front Street, Second Avenue and all the cross streets were burning crisply. The cabins in Paradise Alley were ruddier than they had ever been with red muslin in the windows.

News of the fire sped out to the creeks and in a short time the men began to arrive from as far away as Hunker. Although the fire was out of control from the beginning, no one was in danger. The saloons were cleared of sleepers and heavy drinkers, there was no one trapped in any of the buildings. The warehouses were at a safe distance but the Bank of British North America was not and $1,000 was offered to anyone who could save the building. They dynamited the larger places, and the cabins were roped and pulled out of the way, but the wind leapt the space and the fire zigzagged on. Finally the bank building was on fire. Gold coins and dust burst from the safes and had to be reclaimed later by washing the cinders in gold pans.

The whiskey was safe. Tom Chisholm, who owned the Aurora saloon, was the first to pass it out to the fire-fighters. He filled a bucket and Pimply Pete took it around. The men were trying to quench the fire with handfuls of snow but the fall had been light so far that year and the ground was merely a sheet of powdered ice. A supply of water was being handed along in bucket brigades lined up from the water holes to the flames. Pete offered every man in the line a drink, and also some who were not in the line. Porters from other saloons began running with buckets. It was observed that it was no longer possible to tell the fire-water from the water. They were in a hurry with both and in the excitement the men threw both upon the flames. It was the first big celebration Dawson had.

Wherever there were embers everybody backed up to warm

themselves and half of them were singing "It'll Be a Hot Time in the Old Town Tonight." At least forty buildings were burning. It was nearly seven o'clock. The snow-covered hills glowed a morning pink but not from the sun. The men thought it was a beautiful sight and they kept on drinking free whiskey, greatly cheered, caring not a bit if Dawson burned to the ground. In the warehouse they had finally got one engine together and they had pushed it to the water hole. In a little while now the water began to arrive at the surface of the ice. The chill stream seeped a few yards through the hose and stopped—a solidly frozen core. The next thing, the expansion burst the hose. But downtown Dawson was already a crumbling design of hot charred wood.

The following day a board of fire commissioners was appointed and a department of volunteer firemen was formed. A hundred signed up, and a chief, assistant, and three captains were named. A fund committee set about raising $12,000 to finish paying for the fire engines. Although the wind had made a calamity out of a small fire, the members of the committee were reminded that it had begun in the rowdy Tree and that also, only a few weeks before, a fire had broken out in Belle Mitchell's Welcome. The earlier fire had been confined to the cabin, which was Belle's loss, not Dawson's, and would have been forgotten if the length of Front Street had not been destroyed in the second misfortune. The committee thought the girls were getting careless and decided to discipline them by asking for a "voluntary" contribution of $50 each. They collected $4,350 from sixty-nine girls and, as gentlemen, let it go at that. The miners and saloonkeepers made up the deficit.

A man or two was sent to the woodpile for sifting the ashes in the Alley before the new cabins were finished. A guard was kept over the ashes of the bank and the saloons until a reasonable amount of the lost gold was recovered. But Dawson was soon rebuilt. The sawmills worked around the clock and every man was put to work except the dealers, who could not afford to roughen their hands. In two weeks Dawson was just about the same. Alexander Pantages quit the Monte Carlo, now owned by one of Clarence Berry's brothers, and built himself a theater on the site of the burned-down Tivoli.

Dawson had other fires. In December, 1897, the town had been more difficult to rebuild because Ladue's sawmill had been caught in the flames and there were only a few pounds of nails on hand. They had had to go to the hills for timber, saw and plane it by hand, salvage nails from the fire and dig the steely ground for buried moss to chink with. On April 26, 1899, Dawson burned again. This time it started in the rooms over the Monte Carlo and destroyed $2,000,000 worth of property. The fire would not lag until the three largest buildings in town, Alexander McDonald's three-story office building, the Aurora, and the Temenos, were blown up. The fire engines had been stationed beside waterholes on the river and were supposed to be attended constantly by a man from a crew paid to keep up the fires in the boilers. Dawson was determined not to be caught napping. However, the men's salaries were in arrears and they had abandoned their posts a few days before. Volunteers came to the rescue but, again, the hose burst with its frozen contents before a drop of water reached the fire. The next day nothing on the river front remained but great blocks of ice which had been cut and stored for summer use. They had been insulated with sawdust and wood, both of which burned away without melting the ice. The temperature was 45 below.

Lacking other noteworthy events, sociability waned and winter resumed its monotones and silences. Only one other event broke into it, the fight between Gentleman Jim Corbett and Tom Sharkey which took place at the Lenox Athletic club in New York City on November 11, 1898. Dawson found out about it in January and when it was learned that Corbett, the favorite, had lost the fight, on a foul, Gene

Allen had to print 5,000 extra copies of the *Klondyke Nugget*
to satisfy the clamor for details.

Everything printed was read, handbills, government notices,
newspapers new and old. Printing was what the cheechako
missed more than anything else from the civilized world. He
would read anything, he even saved the labels from cans and
read them over and over. No magazine or paper was too old
to be passed on. *Leslie's, Munsey's, McClure's, Ainslie's,* the
Cosmopolitan and *Century* were read even in tatters. Papers
reached the Klondike from every city in the world, cherished
by their possessors above all but gold. Papers from Capetown,
Singapore, London and Ottawa were found in cabins with
no more surprise than the volumes of Gibbon which Andrew
Hunker kept on the shelf with a winter's supply of Scotch.
Belinda Mulrooney, owner of mines and hotels, possessed the
treasure of the creeks, a well-worn copy of the popular *Quo
Vadis.* The partners, Grizzly Meyers and Dick Butler, received a bundle of Seattle papers from a friend on the last
boat of the summer of 1898, the reading of which brought
so much enjoyment to grateful miners that they fed over $400
in dust to a "kitty" which Meyers and Butler shipped out
to the sender of the papers on the first boat that left Dawson
in 1899.

Dismal days lasted until March, when men climbed the
gulches daily to wait for the sun's brief hovering on the hori-
zon. The men were then in rags, feet bound in sacking and
blanket strips, hair hanging to their shoulders. The dogs
waited with them, all eyes on the edge of snow where the
red ball would bounce up momentarily into the cool gray
sky. At the sight men threw their arms out to her and the
dogs barked. Most noted in their diaries the day on which
they saw the "dear sun" once again. Ver Mehr said, "We took
heart with the new daylight. It was the blackness that we
couldn't stand up there. Not even the men who got the gold
could like the country. Everybody wanted to get out. We were

just waiting for the ice to break up so we could. I heard men say they were going if they had to crawl all the way, and from the shape that some of them were in it looked liked they might have to."

Even with the sun in the sky there was no warmth until May. The light seemed green. Men gazed at the shimmering sun dogs as at one last grimace from the Yukon, from whose grasp they would soon be freed forever. They listened with relief to the first sound of water gurgling under the creek ice. The rivers loosened slowly and moved out in chunks. Torrents swelled over the banks and soon a maelstrom of rocks and debris began to pound past their cabins. Last year's trestles, whole trees, boxes of excrement, dead bodies washed from shallow graves, clots of frozen gravel that not even a flood could dissolve, all swept out of the Klondike valleys with heartening speed. The winter was over at last.

Almost overnight wild heliotrope, starwort, fireweed, wild roses and innumerable other flowers, ferns, and grasses colored any unmolested hills. Birches, alders, cottonwoods, beeches, willows appeared where only snow-laden firs had been before. The latter bristled with new needles and silvery cones. It was a magical transformation, complete with butterflies and birds. Men lay upon the Persian-rug colors of the moss, which spread out like springy beds, three and four feet high, and wondered if they were out of their minds and dreaming. They were soon assured of reality for, with warmth, not only a lush growth responded to the sun, but billions of mosquito larvae. About the time the temperature reached the eighties the mosquitoes were buzzing louder than band saws and St. Mary's was again filled with malaria patients.

The rush to the "poor man's mines" was over in 1899. Tons of machinery were coming in by steamer that summer and the next year would be carried by railway as far as White Horse and there transferred to barges, cutting delivery time by two weeks. Steam points had been developed for thawing the gravel. They were using steam-driven shovels to dredge, and steam engines now dumped the dirt into the sluice, pumped, drove the water nozzles that washed down the banks, and did the work of crews of men. There was regular stage service to the creeks and they were planning an electric road, once the power plant could be thoroughly depended upon. Dawson expected to have street and house illumination that winter. The telegraph line had reached them from Skagway.

Dawson had changed. "Inexhaustible riches" had made her self-conscious. She straightened and paved her streets, put in sidewalks, built brick houses, hung plate glass windows in her shops, made the girls remove all placards and names from their cabins. The old Bon Ton and the rest looked like any other dwelling. There was talk of putting this entertainment over in Lousetown. The wives were arriving.

Dawson had refinements in 1899, zinc bath tubs and pianos, billiard tables, Brussels carpets in the hotel dining rooms, menus printed in French, invitational balls. A council of ladies, esteemed for virtue, presided over the social activities. Admission to euchre parties and balls that winter had to run the gamut of their remorseless standards. For themselves they made dog driving a popular outdoor sport and crocheting a parlor industry. There was enough fancy work by Christmas to raise $12,000 at a charity bazaar held for the benefit of St. Mary's hospital. The Governor-General of Canada and his wife, Lord and Lady Minto, decided to visit Dawson in 1900.

The new life was not for prospectors. They scattered into the wildest country they could find, or went out to Alaska where one of the beaches was discovered to have sands of gold. Passengers on the *W. K. Merwin*, the first boat to arrive in Dawson the summer of 1899, told about the stampede, but it was too fantastic to be believed and was laughed at until the Seattle papers came in. After reading them every disappointed miner grabbed his gear. On one creek after another, notes pinned to the cabin doors read, "Gone to Gnome." Eight thousand men left town the first week. There was hardly standing room on the boats going downriver to St. Michael.

19

GREENER PASTURES

AS EARLY as 1895 gold was found inland on the Seward Peninsula by a miner named Johansen but the quantity was insignificant. In 1897 an Eskimo half-breed, Tom Guarick, washed half an ounce of gold from the sand in the region of the present city of Nome. During the winter of 1898 a party of San Franciscans, who had arrived in St. Michael too late to continue the trip to Dawson, crossed Norton Sound to Golovin Bay to do a little local prospecting. In the hills they found good creeks and washed several hundred dollars' worth of gold. The men were W. F. Melsing, H. L. Blake, and A. P. Mordaunt, and they were working a stream located about thirty miles from the mouth of the Fish River.

An old man, D. B. Libby, once a member of the telegraph expedition, joined Mordaunt and they went prospecting on Ophir, Dutch, and Sweetcake creeks. They were soon getting as high as $2 to the pan on Ophir, a little less on the others. Later, Blake and three others, Christopher Kimber, Frank Porter, and Reverend J. C. Hultberg, minister of the Swedish Evangelical Mission Church at Golovin, discovered a creek which they called Anvil, a tributary of the Snake River. They were getting $4 pans and wanted to keep it a secret, but after a few weeks Hultberg could no longer resist telling a fellow missionary named Anderson. With that, four hundred men rushed to Cape Nome in spite of the fact that it was January and there was no sign of a habitation or protection of any kind from the appalling storms which struck the beach. Before they ever got to Anvil Creek, gold was seen in the sand and thirteen miles of it were immediately staked out. Digging through ice, suffering intense hardships, the men kept on, continuously gouging out gold from this most incredible of placers. The Fish, Snake, and Anvil diggings were temporarily forgotten.

A city took its ragged, nondescript form along the water. At first it was called Anvil City and later Nome. The beach diggers, in the meantime, encountered a second secret party of three who had been hurriedly filling their pokes since the autumn before. They were Yon Brynteson, a Swede and old-timer, Eric Lindbloom, a Norwegian who had deserted a whaling ship, and Jafeth Lindeberg, one of the Laplanders whom Sheldon Jackson brought in to drive the reindeer relief train.

Those who reached Nome in the first wave of the stampede were joined by thousands more in the summer. Seven thousand persons were there in August, 1899, and 12,488 had settled on the strip of beach before the 1900 summer waned. This was a titanic surge of fortune hunters for so desolate a coast. Comparatively few of them had mining experience, it was a collection of city riffraff, sports, and highbinders of many callings. They made Nome one of the tawdriest, toughest mining camps on earth. Not even the United States infantry, which was called in, had any noticeable effect on the turbulent affairs. Fearful storms which periodically all but destroyed the flimsy city could not restrain it. A smallpox epidemic killed off some but did not sober the others. Nome was raw and proud of it. It was also Alaska's richest gold field. It took only two years of digging there to put $8,000,000 into the

United States mints, more than the purchase price of the Territory.

There were three beaches at Nome. Two of them were ancient rims of the continent, embankments of golden silt. The creeks that crowded behind them were Anvil, Ophir, Bering, Bluestone, Gold Run, Dahl on the Kougarok, Inmachuk, and Candle on the Kiwalik. On Big Hurrah Creek they were in quartz and 200 feet below the surface of the ground, hauling up seventy tons of ore a day.

They were finding gold now all over "Seward's Icebox." Stampedes to Little and Big Minook, Alaskan tributaries of the Yukon, and to Idaho Bar between them, had populated Rampart City. The first settlers on these creeks were stranded passengers from the *C. H. Hamilton,* one of the boats that got stuck on the river the autumn of 1897. The Minook creeks were named for the Russian Indian who first discovered gold on one of them back in 1892. The boatload of Americans were the first white people to hear of the creeks whose gold was the finest and purest found anywhere in Alaska or the Yukon, being worth $20 an ounce, while Bonanza's and Eldorado's gold was a variable $15 to $16 an ounce. Other Klondike creeks were worth up to $17 an ounce, with the exception of Bear which had $19 gold.

Cheechakos were working Columbo and Ruby creeks on the Yukon toward the west. They had staked Koyukuk on Nolan, Emma, Smith, and Myrtle creeks, and twenty steamboats were paddling up the river to a town called Peavy. There were seven dredges on the Koyukuk in 1898. The prospectors were finding good placers on the tributaries of the Innoko, Iditarod, and Kuskokwim. In 1904 there was a rush to Pedro Placer, discovered by Felix Pedro two years before in Chena Slough on the Tanana. In this region they also found Cleary, Ester, Goldstream, Fairbanks, Fox, Dome, Vault, and many more. Gold was pouring out of the Tanana Valley. Kentishna, Bonnefield, Tenderfoot, Hot Springs, all attracted hard-working miners whose efforts and belief in the country opened the lonesomest valleys and the most forbidding rivers. While seeking gold, Alaska's copper, silver, coal, and tin were revealed as well. It was a great country and people said they were glad that Sumner had got his way after all about naming the territory. He had chosen the Aleut word, *Al-ak-ska,* meaning "great country." There had been some who would have called it "Walrussia" or "American Siberia," or perhaps "The Zero Islands" or "Polario."

While Alaska's gold production was increasing by millions of dollars, that of the Yukon was slowly dwindling. From $17,000,000 in 1901, the Klondike yield went down to $14,-500,000 in 1902, to $12,250,000 in 1903, to $9,413,074 in 1904, to $7,162,438 in 1905. In 1913 it paid the companies scarcely $5,000,000, in 1929 only $654,000. The royalty had long since dropped from 10 to 5 per cent, then to half of that, and was finally replaced altogether by an export tax. The Yukon's thousands of miles of other creeks had attracted no one. Too late, the Canadians discovered that the prospectors had been legislated and administered out of the country, and all knew that without the prodding pick of the wanderer, whose only lure was Lady Luck, the wilderness would remain as it was.

The Klondike's production figures are not staggering, they seem rather small as the world's great gold fields go. In forty years the yield was $200,000,000, during which time the mines of Alaska produced $327,785,553. It took California only five years, from 1849 through 1852, to produce $208,902,699. Fifty years later, at the height of the Klondike rush, California was producing 50 per cent more gold than her young challenger. What made the Klondike unique in all the world was not the total production, it was the richness of the fields that made men hurry with shovels. The billions taken out of the Rand in South Africa have averaged a return of less than half an ounce of gold to a ton of gravel. The great Treadwell returned less than $2 from every ton of ore it milled.

California's placers paid thirty-five and forty cents to the pan and made many people very rich. The Eldorado paid fifteen times that much, one pan after the other.

Among the last to leave the country with big pokes were Charlie Anderson, Tom Lippy, Frank Phiscator, members of the Berry family, N. J. Picotte, Peter Wybird, Bill Leggett, George Wilson, John Nash, all of whom had from $30,000 to $120,000 apiece. The Alaska Commercial Company's new steamer, *St. Paul,* arrived in San Francisco on July 18, 1898, with $3,000,000 in gold, of which $1,500,000 belonged to 150 Klondike miners and $600,000 to the company. The remainder was the property of men from Alaska's Yukon creeks. This was the year's largest single cargo of gold out of a total of $13,000,000 that came down on the ships of a dozen companies and on countless gold rush craft that year, meeting the miners at Skagway, Dyea, St. Michael, and Nome. In 1900 the same boats were going mostly only to and from Nome.

While Klondike gold founded family fortunes, many of which later grew significant through good management or because of a rise in property values, the greater part of the wealth was lost almost as suddenly as it was gained. For some it was "easy come, easy go." Lack of experience in handling money, enthusiasm for the sure-thing investment, the glamorous but expensive experience of being a millionaire to all one's friends, were some of the roads to the poorhouse which many took. The Pioneer's Home in Sitka had a roll call of former bonanza kings and so did the King Country Poor Farm which was supported by Seattle charity.

At first Carmack, Charlie, and Jim had worked together on *Discovery, One Above,* and *One* and *Two Below.* That is, Charlie was supposed to be helping, but actually Jim did most of the work. They had got a cabin built and Kate with Carmack's two children were there with them.

In March, 1897, Carmack let out *Discovery* on a lay and

in April Charlie sold half of *Two Below*. He received $500 down and the rest was due on July 1, by which time the new owner had dug more than that out of Charlie's ground and paid him. It happened all too often that those who sold out early were paid with gold from their own ground and the new owners washed up the fortune. Sometimes the original owner ended by taking a lay on the ground he had staked. The man who took the lay on *Discovery* paid Carmack $7,000 before July, which was half of what he had dug.

Meanwhile, Carmack, Charlie, and Jim put up a sluice over the remaining ground which was theirs and washed gold when they were in the mood. They had to carry the dirt to the sluice in the same clumsy boxes in which they had hauled up the dirt from the shaft. They never had $25 ahead to buy a wheelbarrow. Carmack was discouraged. The sluice was no good, it fell apart, it leaked, they didn't have the money to hire a carpenter or buy ready-made boxes, they didn't have any oakum, the creek was held back on them just when they wanted to work (everyone had to wait for water, sometimes for as long as a week), they didn't have copper to line the tail race, nor mercury to put in it, their tools were all dull, and they didn't care for mining anyway.

In spite of setbacks they washed about $1,200 a week for a short time. In the middle of summer Carmack and Charlie gave up entirely. The man who had been working on *Discovery* hadn't put in much time, the dirt was poor compared to Skookum, where he had two claims that were much better. When he gave Carmack half of what he had got Carmack took it and all the dust he had, put his mines up for sale, and he and Kate and Charlie took a trip to Seattle and San Francisco. At the Rainier-Grand Hotel in Seattle they threw gold coins out of the window to amuse themselves watching the traffic jams when the people scrambled around under wagon wheels and horses' hooves to pick up the money. The Palace Hotel in San Francisco had too many floors and stairways for Kate. She nicked a trail in the mahogany, with a skinning knife she had a fondness for carrying, so that she could find her way to and from the bridal suite where they were quartered.

They were gone a year, returning when they learned that the new railroad over the pass had been completed from Skagway to Lake Bennett. The first passengers made the excursion trip in little more than flat cars provided with benches. The inaugural run took place May 28, 1898, but Carmack, Kate, and Charlie didn't make the trip until June. Their holiday ended in tragedy, for Charlie fell off the train as they were crossing the bridge at Carcross, and drowned less than a mile from where he was born.

Jim stayed on *Two Above* for six years, washing his gravel industriously, long after many another Klondiker had left the diggings with a greater fortune and lost it. In 1902 one of the companies paid Jim $60,000 for his mine.

Carmack ultimately deserted Kate and his children, went to New York, and died a penniless man.

"The richest man in the Dominion," Alexander McDonald, went to London after the cleanup in 1900 to organize a syndicate and to buy machinery. The venture broke him, for the mines upon which he depended the most turned out to be both skim and scant. He barely liquidated his debts. Dick Lowe was a pauper in five years and would have become dependent upon San Francisco charity had it not been for a Dawson girl who remembered him from better times. Like many of the girls, she left Dawson with a heavy poke. She brought out $25,000, which she had already doubled through good buys in San Francisco property, and was on her way to becoming one of the city's shrewdest business women. Lowe's benefactress took good care of him but excessive drinking had destroyed his health and in 1907 he was dead.

Tom Lippy left the Klondike with $1,500,000, and lost it

in real-estate investments in and around Seattle. "Swiftwater" Bill Gates somewhat recuperated his losses on Alaska's Cleary Creek but creditors, three wives and a mother-in-law pounced too quickly and Swiftwater fled. He was later reported in Peru where he was mining silver but without noticeable success.

The Swedes finally got rich. Swan Peterson, an old-timer who repented his hasty judgment of the Bonanza, bought in on Eldorado and cleaned up $150,000. Peter Olafson and Charlie Erickson took twice that from *Twenty-Four* Eldorado. Charlie Anderson, of course, made one of the biggest cleanups in the Klondike. Olaf Finsted, Ben Wall, Bill Carlson, Hank Peterson, two partners named Olson and Johnson, all got rich on Eldorado's pay.

Alexander Pantages, who had not dug an ounce of his Klondike gold, owned twenty-two vaudeville houses in 1913 and held the controlling interests in twenty-eight others. He opened his first theater in Dawson, on borrowed money, used his subsequent profits, and more borrowed money, to go into business in Seattle. From success there, he spread his Pantages Theaters across the nation. Tex Rickard, whose Northern saloon took in more gold even than Pantages' Tivoli, lost his money in Nome and turned to fight promoting, an occupation which, however, he had no cause to regret.

Whimsical to the last, the Klondike reserved the real bonanza for another man who didn't dig, Robert W. Service, a handsome English-born clerk who was transferred to the Dawson branch of the Canadian Bank of Commerce in 1906 and spent a year there. Fifty years later, his name is still synonymous with the Klondike. And after the buffeting she gave to Joaquin Miller, she brought him extra fame and a little money after all. In the spring and summer of 1899, he went on the road in vaudeville. For his act he came out onto the stage dressed in winter garb, fur parka, mukluks and mittens, and talked informally about his experiences on the creeks. It was a version prepared for popular taste and was well received. He was encouraged to write a book of poems about the Klondike. Curwood and London also hit the paystreak without turning a shovelful on any dump.

It is said that 100,000 persons passed through Dawson in three years' time. All were greedy for gold and each man had his own reason for wanting it, but perhaps St. John Atherton's need was the most unique. He was an ex-slave. He worked on Bonanza the winter of 1898. He had no partner and his search for the paystreak teased him through the barest gravel imaginable. But he persisted and by summer had a good dump to wash. When he was ready to take the trail home he had $30,000, and confided to a school teacher from Philadelphia that he had made the trip in the hope of getting money enough to take care of the aged and impoverished daughter of the man who once had owned him.

In 1899 the companies were buying up the creeks in blocks and paying prices which overflowed the already brimming pans of those who happened to be on the right spots at the right time. The Klondike tailings were still worth a fortune. Phiscator sold for $750,000, after he had taken out nearly that much in the two years he had worked the property. Hunker sold for $1,500,000. The Berrys sold out for $2,000,000. After Clarence's luck on Eldorado, his father, William Jackson Berry, and his two brothers, Frederick ("Fred") and Hugh Franklin ("Frank"), visited the Klondike. They cleaned up what they could—$2,000,000 from the mines and an undisclosed amount from the Monte Carlo, and returned to Fresno, California. They invested the money in oil, forming a company of their own, which they called the "C. J. Oil Company" for Clarence, and began drilling in the highly productive Kern County fields near home.

This was a far-sighted step. Most people of that day would rather have invested in gold than in oil, and mining companies had no reason to discourage them. Electric dredges were moving 1,500 cubic yards of gravel a day, at a cost of less than $100, working two-cent dirt and making more for the shareholders than the same dirt had paid the original stakers. There were dumps on every creek with dirt worth more than two cents to the pan. The profits were enormous. The gumboot miner had worked all day to move one cubic yard of gravel—206 shovelfuls. This gave him 103 pans to wash. They had to be worth more on the average than two cents.

In 1905 the hoses were washing down the hills, which experts agreed would yield $800,000,000 more before the Klondike was worked out. This figure did not include a further creek yield of $100,000,000 which was expected. It was believed that the reworked Indian and Stewart districts would give them an additional $400,000,000. Those who planned to put floating dredges on the Klondike River now would put no limit upon their expectations.

Mining engineers were doing the same kind of blithe arithmetic that the Klondike-bound streetcar conductors, fruit peddlers and country doctors had engaged in when they heard about $1,000 pans and made a rush for them. Men well used to the sight of gold, experienced in the capricious ways of minerals, practical men who mined impersonally by sample ores, machinery, and graphs were being swayed off balance by the Klondike's overpowering lure. The experts were not saying that all you had to do was shove the moss over with your boot toe and pick up the nuggets. They were saying they had to get the muck out of the way because they had struck the mother lode of the Western Hemisphere.